MAKING IT! IN HOCKEY

MAKING IT!
WHAT YOU SHOULD KNOW,

MARK MOORE
IN HOCKEY
FROM THE EXPERTS + PROS

Fenn Publishing Company Ltd.
BOLTON, ONTARIO

Fenn Publishing Company Ltd.

A Fenn Publishing Book / First Published in 2009

Fenn Publishing Company Ltd.
Bolton, Ontario, Canada
www.hbfenn.com

The publisher gratefully acknowledges the support of the Canada Council for the Arts and the Ontario Arts Council for its publishing program. We acknowledge the support of the Government of Ontario through the Ontario Media Development Corporation's Ontario Book Initiative.

We acknowledge the financial support of the Government of Canada through the Book Publishing Industry Development Program (BPIDP) for our publishing activities. Care has been taken to trace ownership of copyright material in this book and to secure permissions. The publishers will gladly receive any information that will enable them to rectify errors or omissions.

Text design: Sonya V. Thursby
Printed and bound in Canada

Library and Archives Canada Cataloguing in Publication

Moore, Mark, 1977-
Making it in hockey: what you should know, from the experts
    and pros / Mark Moore.

ISBN 978-1-55168-354-6

1. National Hockey League. 2. Hockey players—Vocational
guidance. I. Title.

GV847.M655 2009   796.962'64   C2009-902101-3

Printed and bound in Canada
09 10 11 12 13 5 4 3 2 1

To Jack Moore,
my father.

The most amazing,
all-around athlete I ever saw.

The most complete expert on excellence
in sport one could ever learn from.

table of contents

preface

FOR NEARLY FORTY YEARS, I HAVE BEEN INVOLVED IN YOUTH SPORTS AND EDUCATION.

As a school teacher, I have come to see the distinct attitudes different students take not only to school but to life. As a competitive hockey coach, I have come to see the distinct approaches different young athletes take not only to the game but to their careers. I have come to appreciate that as much influence as teachers and coaches can have, families have the most influence of all.

If you follow hockey, you may have already heard the story of the Moore family. It has been well chronicled in media across Canada and the United States—from local news channels to *Sports Illustrated*. An astounding feat: a family of three brothers who all made it to Division 1 college hockey at Harvard, **and who all went on to make it to the ranks of professional players.**

The eldest brother, Mark, was drafted by the Pittsburgh Penguins. Upon graduating from Harvard, Mark signed an NHL contract and began playing professionally until his promising career was cut short by a serious concussion.

The middle brother, Steve, was during his time at Harvard a nominee for the Hobey Baker Award as U.S. College Hockey's top player. He attracted keen interest from NHL scouts for his offensive prowess and hard-nosed-but-clean style of play. Drafted by the Colorado Avalanche, he succeeded in cracking the Avs' star-studded lineup. Sadly, it was Steve who, in one of pro hockey's most high-profile incidents, was followed and then assaulted from behind during a game by opponent Todd Bertuzzi. He suffered a broken neck and other injuries that left him unable to resume his career.

Dominic, the youngest and last Moore brother, began his NHL career with Jaromir Jagr and the New York Rangers. The following year he joined Sidney Crosby's Pittsburgh Penguins. This past season, Dominic was one of the top players and an associate captain for his hometown Toronto Maple Leafs.

This is the public story of the Moore brothers, but having known the family since the time the boys were born, their personal story is just as compelling.

The Moores, in many ways, were an average hockey family. They had no famous family footsteps in which to follow, no silver spoon, no special power or influence. Whether it came to coaches picking teams or admissions officers selecting students, nothing was handed to the Moore boys. They earned it the old-fashioned way. In what is now a humorous story to recall, I can attest to that first-hand: Back when Mark was a tiny, underage high school freshman, I myself cut him from the Junior Varsity team. Mark's mother called me, as a family friend, not to ask me to put him on the team, only to give him one more chance in the final tryout. There was no harm in that, so I agreed, and in that tryout, Mark was the best player on the ice. Afterward, in telling him that he made the team, I said to him, "Why didn't you play that way before!" Mark replied, "I didn't know I could, but now I know I have to." Sure enough, he went on to become our most reliable player and leader in ice time that season.

As the Moore brothers were growing up, much of the family circumstances had been quite ordinary, but if one thing was extraordinary, it had to be the adversity they faced. When Mark was twelve years old, his mother was diagnosed with a brain tumour. She underwent life-threatening surgery, during which she suffered a life-altering stroke. She survived, but the toll was devastating. She had to re-learn how to talk and how to walk. She spent a year in hospital, and many more years grappling with all of the profound effects. The Moores' father, meanwhile, was busy working overtime at a series of jobs in order to maintain the family's financial footing, as the lone remaining wage-earner for a family of three hockey-playing boys. The resultant void forced Mark to have to assume a huge amount of responsibility in the raising of himself and his brothers. For he and his brothers to remain on the path they had committed to, he had to become a resolute "parent" before he and they could ever become renowned hockey stars.

A dozen years later, adversity struck again, in the form of the injury that put an end to Mark's young professional career. Faced with that incredible personal frustration, Mark did not turn his back on the game, but rather turned his eyes to its innermost workings. One result was the publication of his book *Saving the Game: Pro Hockey's Quest to Raise Its Game from Crisis to New Heights*. It was a work wide-ranging, profound, and visionary, and it earned critical acclaim. Behind the scenes, what was equally impressive was the fact that it was written solely by Mark, without the aid of a ghostwriter, as some might have expected. Since I was his English teacher in the ninth, tenth and twelfth grades, Mark likes to say I taught him how to write. The truth is, I didn't have a choice! Out of a high school transcript littered with A+'s and only a handful of A's, Mark's sole B was in my ninth grade English class. True to his character, Mark went to the principal the following year (and again in the twelfth grade) and requested a transfer back into my class from the "easier grading" teacher to which the school's computerized schedule-generator had assigned him. When he got to Harvard, however, Mark was the only player among his varsity hockey team classmates whose tested writing performance exempted him from having to take the freshman entry-level writing course. I like to think a student of his calibre would have learned how to write with or without my aid.

Following the publication of *Saving the Game*, the depth of Mark's insights and his communication ability led to invitations to provide guest lectures on sports at Harvard Law School and McGill University among others, as well as expert guest columns for leading publications such as the *Globe and Mail*, *Toronto Star*, *National Post*, and the *Hockey News*. He is often invited to appear on sports media shows and to make presentations at conferences discussing a range of issues related to hockey.

Hoping to pass on to a new generation the store of hockey knowledge accumulated by him and his brothers, Mark also founded and directs a renowned hockey school for young players, which I have participated in as part of the staff. Through camps, clinics, lessons, and other programs, Mark—and at times his brothers and other pros and related experts—provide tips to youth ranging from utter beginners to active Junior and College players. Over and over, I have seen the profound influence they have had not only from their expertise but also from their example as positive role models. I have seen the immense gratitude of the children as well as the parents of players who pass through the school. Often, this has led to the desire on the part of young athletes, parents, and coaches for more comprehensive aid from Mark and his colleagues. They want not only authoritative hockey development, but also more general guidance on how to go about pursuing their careers and lives in the sport. It is toward shedding light on these questions that Mark has written *Making It.* It is the helping hand-*book* so wished-for by young athletes and their parents and coaches, on a quest to realize their hockey dream.

The book begins with that special dream. It covers the comprehensive influence of character. It details the complete range of necessary skills, from physical on-ice feats to social skills and safety. It describes the hard work of training. It explains how to deal with the circumstances families face in hockey at the various levels from mini-mites to the pros. It prescribes methods to become successful, and to remain grounded even while reaching for the stars. It is a guide for striving to reach one's potential, not just in hockey, but in life. It includes input from other top players and role models, and related experts including managers, trainers, and physicians.

Making It is a book written by a player who has made it to a high level, who has helped guide two younger siblings to do the same, and who, faced with an untimely end to the pursuit and experience of his own dreams, has sought to help others with theirs. From Mark's top-calibre hockey expertise, to his profound understanding of the game, to his proven ability to articulate poignant insights concerning it, this is a book written by a man uniquely qualified for the task.

For the thousands of young athletes I meet in my roles as a teacher, coach, sports photographer, and Junior hockey volunteer, I can think of no better source of insight and information into their journey in pursuit of their dreams than this man I have known over his own journey from childhood, to Toronto Star All-Star at St. Michael's, to graduating from Harvard, to signing an NHL contract, to mentor for young players.

Dan Nicholson
Teacher and Hockey Coach,
St. Michael's College

introduction: the smart way to strive to thrive in sports

OF THE MILLIONS OF BOYS AND GIRLS CHASING HOCKEY DREAMS, WHAT DETERMINES WHO REACHES THEIR DREAMS AND WHO DOESN'T?

Why do some athletes with seemingly "all the tools" fail to make it, while others with far less talent achieve athletic feats beyond all expectation? How do certain players master the skills the game requires, while others remain unable to do so? What is the reason some players are consistent "practice stars" but can't seem to make use of their proficient skills in real competition? How do excellent players end up on the outside looking in? On the path to realizing their ambitions, why do some promising young players suddenly crumble in the face of a single obstacle, while others plow through years of challenge and adversity to reach the top?

All of these puzzling questions have answers. Making it is not magic. Secrets to success do exist. And once discovered, they can be applied by virtually anyone. But how do you discover these secrets?

Sadly, many of those aspiring to make it never truly give themselves a chance. Some wrongly assume that they already know all that it takes, so they make no effort to learn. Others realize they don't have the answers they need, but have no idea where to find such help. Indeed, today's sports world is highly complex and competitive. Making it is neither simple nor easy. In the following pages, however, its secrets will be explained. By picking up this book and reading it, you can take a big step toward realizing your hockey ambitions.

As a child, I was part of a family where sports were very important. My mother was a teacher who coached her school swim team. She believed strongly in the value of sports for keeping kids healthy and out of trouble, as well as teaching them important life lessons that couldn't be taught in a classroom. My father was an avid and accomplished athlete in several sports. And he was an expert on athletic excellence who spent a lifetime studying and practicing what it takes to succeed.

Among sports, my mother enjoyed triathlon and my father's sports were mainly football, basketball, and tennis, but the sport I loved from the beginning—far above all others—was hockey. For almost thirty years, hockey has been a focus of my life. Over that time, I have had the opportunity to learn many things through successive phases of my career—first as an aspiring young player, later as a collegian and a pro, and afterward, as an author, expert commentator and advisor, as well as a coach and mentor to aspiring young players of a new generation.

I learned from the successes of my playing days: making it out of the fiercely competitive hockey crucible of Toronto, earning a scholarship to Harvard University, being drafted in the National Hockey League, and signing an NHL contract with the Pittsburgh Penguins to realize my dream of becoming a professional hockey player. And through all that time, I learned just as much or more from my many mistakes, struggles, and failures as I did from my successes.

Harvard: My brothers Dominic (17), Steve (5), and me (6) in the starting lineup, helmets removed for the playing of the national anthems.

Although my professional playing career was overcast and then cut short by injury, I had a bonus opportunity in being able to experience at close-hand the playing careers of my younger brothers Steve and Dominic. Both succeeded in following me first to Harvard and then to the NHL, and I was able to continue learning through developments in their careers.

From the beginning there were a number of other people I learned from as well. Just as my brothers gained many valuable lessons about making it from watching my successes and failures, I might never have made it to the college and professional ranks without the experience and expert knowledge imparted to me by elder mentors. Over the course of my career, I absorbed valuable lessons not only from my family but also from older established players and former players, as well as coaches, scouts, and teachers. I had an opportunity not just to meet Hall-of-Famers, but to skate with them, play for them, observe them up close, and benefit from hearing their tips and advice. Last but not least, in having a chance to play with players

The NHL draft: Dominic (New York Rangers), Steve (Colorado Avalanche), and me (Pittsburgh Penguins).

from different backgrounds here in North America and all over the hockey world, I was able to identify important commonalities and differences in the various paths different players took.

But when I was forced to retire from injury at only twenty-five, the question for me became: What would I do with this wealth of hockey knowledge I'd accumulated?

For one thing, I decided to put to use the skills of inquiry, research, and analysis I had honed at Harvard to complete an in-depth study of professional hockey. Combining that with my inside knowledge of the sport, I wrote the book *Saving the Game*, published for those seeking to better understand the professional game and its issues.

But what about all the other levels of hockey? For young players, an entire separate set of issues exist at their levels. These issues challenge them as they strive to learn and enjoy the game, become more successful players, advance through the levels of hockey, and put themselves in position for a shot at the pros.

Having confronted many of these issues as a young player, I came face to face with them again as the Director of Development at our family hockey schools. On one side, there was my brother Dominic, an active NHLer, one of the top players and associate captains of the Toronto Maple Leafs. On the other side, in our various programs, were players ranging from five-year-old beginners to Junior and College prospects—each hoping to make it to the place where Dominic was. No longer able to play myself, I wanted to help these young players to reach their goals. Using the intimate knowledge I had of Dominic's game, my brother Steve's, my own, and that of our many friends and one-time teammates playing elite-level hockey, I sought to identify necessary qualities for aspiring players. I also studied many of the world's top pros, searching for secrets to what set them apart, to expand the insights I could share with young players. With this accumulated mass of knowledge, I experimented in various hockey school programs and other initiatives, searching for the teaching angles that worked best.

This book contains as much of that knowledge, insight, and experience as could fit, and conform to a written format.

The reason I wrote *Making It* is quite simple: There are only so many students one can fit in a hockey school program. And there is only so much one can teach in a hockey school program. At presentations I've given for youth sports or school audiences, at our family's hockey schools, and elsewhere, people always ask, "How did all three of you achieve what you've achieved?" Children plead, "How do I become a pro hockey player?" Parents implore, "Tell us what to do to allow our kids to reach the Ivy League, to reach pro hockey!" I admired their passion and appreciated their genuine desire to learn, and I very much wanted to help, but it was simply impossible to provide answers to all of those questions in a short program or a few minutes of chatting. Over time, as I realized just how many young athletes, parents, coaches, and others shared this longing for guidance, I committed to write a book that would properly answer their questions.

Making It is that book. For younger players, older prospects, parents, coaches, and anyone else interested in hockey, this book contains a comprehensive account of how you can make it.

But this book is about more than that. As I discovered over the course of my time as a player and after, making it is not the only thing that matters. The way you pursue things matters as much as where you end up. Having my career end early and suddenly from injury, before I could reach my full potential, taught me a great deal: I realized how important it is to enjoy each chance to play and each success you have along the way. I found out how crucial it is to make the very most out of the time and opportunities you get. And I came to more fully appreciate the value of certain things I had done alongside pursuing hockey, as well as a few things I had not done.

Another experience taught me more lessons about what else matters. It came as I watched my younger brother Steve. Steve was realizing his dream, playing for the Colorado Avalanche, the first-place team in the NHL at the time. He was often playing on a line with future Hall-of-Famers Joe Sakic and Paul Kariya. He even scored a goal which set an NHL record![1] But later in that same game something terrible happened. Steve was attacked from behind by an opposing player, and suffered a broken neck and a severe head injury. Fortu-

> **"To educate a person in mind and not in morals is to educate a menace to society."**
>
> PRESIDENT THEODORE ROOSEVELT

nately, Steve survived and did not end up paralyzed. Unfortunately, however, he was never able to resume his hockey career. From all my years in hockey, and those of my parents and grandparents who had followed the game since its earliest days, we never expected to see an incident like this in hockey. Yet in the public uproar that ensued, many people clearly felt that the larger issue of violence and proper conduct in hockey needed to be addressed. As star goaltender and Olympian Roberto Luongo said, "It's a dark day for hockey. We're trying so hard… and the whole country has to see this terrible exhibition of sportsmanship."[2] We needed to make sure that people had the right attitudes at all levels and players could experience safe enjoyment of the game. I committed to doing what I could to see that the messages young players took to heart were ones of respect, fair play, and personal character.

Will you make a deal with me? I pledge to teach you what secrets I know about how to succeed in sports. And in return, I ask you—whether you are a player, a parent, a coach, or have some other role in sports—to pledge to yourself, to your family and friends, to all those you will encounter in the world of sports, and to everyone who sees your success, that you will be a model of outstanding sportsmanship.

I, Mark Moore, pledge to teach you what I know about how to succeed in sports. SIGNED: *Mark Moore*	I, _____ pledge to myself, my family and friends, people I will encounter in the world of sports, and to those who see my successes, that I will be a model of outstanding sportsmanship. SIGNED:

From the time I first started playing, I have gotten to know many people through hockey. And in my adult life, first as a professional hockey player and then as an ex-player, I have met many others who, upon hearing that I was involved in hockey, described to me their own hockey experiences. From this "database" of hockey experiences, it is clear that while many people have had terrific experiences, others have needlessly had negative ones; and that even includes players who made it. The different facts behind such experiences are not always able to be controlled. But I firmly believe that if you pursue your dream in the right way, you can minimize the chance of your career leaving a bitter taste in your mouth, and maximize the chance of your career being a great experience. And that applies *whether you make it or not.* **In life, we can't always control whether we achieve our desired outcome. And not every outcome we achieve turns out to be what we desired. But the process by which we pursue our ambition is entirely within our control.** So this book is not just about how to make it, but about how to pursue making it in the right way—so that you can enjoy a very positive experience in hockey.

Making it in hockey is a hope shared by millions of children and their parents from coast to coast within Canada and the United States, as well as overseas. Many youngsters—from the moment they first pull a hockey sweater over their head, learn to skate, or sit with their parents to watch a professional game—dream of someday becoming a hockey star.

It is a wonderful dream, but achieving it is not just a simple matter of chasing it. Maybe there was once a time when the parent of a talented child with athletic ambitions could truthfully say, "Just put your head down, work hard, and you will make it." But in our current age, that is not much more than a nostalgic myth. Today's sports world is complicated, sophisticated, and competitive. And sports have become big business. Today, prestigious college scholarship opportunities, multimillion-dollar pro salaries, and life-changing Olympic experiences are all available through sports. Media coverage is tremendous. Along with movie stars and rock stars, sports stars are society's biggest celebrities. The effects of these facts trickle down to lower levels; perhaps even to before a child's very first game. At its heart, sport is still about youngsters having fun and chasing their dreams. But around that, there is much to contend with: The ambitions that parents have for their children; the aspirations some coaches have for themselves; sports organizations and sports-related entities trying to make money; competition among individuals for awards, bragging rights, or even just a position on a team. You need a shrewd game plan for getting through it all and realizing the results you want. That includes being clear on what you'll need to do before you set off chasing your dream. A mere shot in the dark is not the kind of game plan you want, nor one that will likely work.

Just two generations ago, things were so different that my father's father turned down an invitation to play for the Boston Bruins because, in order to help support his siblings and parents during the Great Depression, he was able to make more money working as a long-distance truck driver than playing in the NHL. And from 1943–46, though my mother's father was a professional football player, he had a separate full-time job as an academic course instructor at the University of Toronto.

That is where this book can help. You can be sure that the many vying to make it are committed to gaining every possible advantage. Yet no amount of expense, effort, or political maneuvering can make up for a lack of expert guidance. In the pages that follow, you will find that expert guidance, along with priceless secrets and expert tips to help you make it. You will discover precise details of the physical, mental, and other skills you'll need. You shall learn about the training that transforms athletes with potential into seasoned, master performers. You can avail yourself of a smart strategic approach to pursuing your ambitions, and see the sweeping advantages it gives you over those always too busy playing and practicing to ever think and plan. You will discover the importance of proper preparation for those key moments that can make or break a career. In addition to everything you find in this book, as an owner of this book, you will also get special, free access to valuable bonus material, multimedia, and interactive tools designed to help you improve your experience of hockey and your prospects of making it, on my website: **www.sportsmaster.tv.***

Pursuing hockey in the right way also means learning things that enrich the rest of your life, rather than deplete it. This book will help guide you to preserve your enjoyment of the game, even as you strive to reach your dearest ambitions. You will discover how to develop your personal character and potential. You will come to appreciate the wisdom of simultaneously working on a potential fallback career. You can master important life skills such as goal-setting and time-management. And you will find secrets to success you can apply in any field, and techniques you can put to use in the service of any good purpose.

★ Use passwords from this book to access additional free material on my website at www.sportsmaster.tv, including some great multimedia features and interactive tools that can't be put in a book. Here are just a few examples of what I have spent years developing to help support your sports experience and career:

· Expert visual demonstrations of techniques used in hockey, and specialized drills and exercises for mastering on-ice skills and off-ice training

· Online personal notebook for you to record things you want to remember from this book and add your thoughts, available in a searchable form

· Interactive tools to help you track your competition, training, and personal progress

· Regularly added bonus material providing extra depth on areas of interest from this book, and covering new topics

· Ask-the-Expert feature, where you can read the experts' answers to your questions
And much more . . .

Though all of this means there is much material to cover, reading *Making It* should, in the end, prove a tremendous time-and-effort saver. I certainly wish a guide like this was available when I was young. I had to discover things in what was a much longer way, and, in many cases, the hardest way: by failing before I could learn, or getting lost before I could find my way. Had I known then what I know now, the greater would have been my successes, and the easier would have been the process. Instead, that opportunity is yours. With the aid of this book, you can discover truths in advance and get things right from the beginning. From there, the sky is the limit.

I invite you to discover in the pages that follow the smart way to strive to thrive in sports. There are many secrets to be learned, if you aspire to someday make it in hockey.

getting started: reader's guide to using this book

Making It is divided into nine sections. Within each section are chapters covering more specific subjects. Scattered throughout are boxes, sidebars, and special text highlighting different kinds of information, as follows:

1. **SCOUTS' PREVIEW:** A quick snapshot of what's about to be covered.

2. **EXPERTS' RECAP:** The bottom line to keep in mind from each chapter.

3. **THE INSIDE STORY:** Extras from the author's inside knowledge, expertise, or personal experience.

4. **ASK THE AUTHOR-ITY:** Like an FAQ, these answer and clarify questions you may have.

5. **PRO-FILE:** Bios of pros and other experts related to the discussion.

6. **TEXT HIGHLIGHT:** Key passages from the text.

7. **HEADS UP!:** If a principle has a proviso, you'll find it here, along with other issues to stay aware of or exercise caution with.

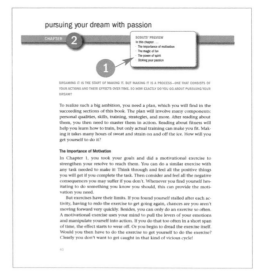

At the back of the book is a glossary of hockey terms for convenient reference.

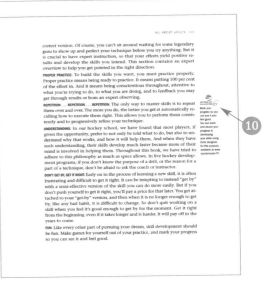

What to Expect from this Book and from Your Quest

This book is designed for an audience that includes players, parents, coaches, teachers, hockey officials, and others. Since this book is about making it, the phrasing throughout is generally addressed to the athlete. Indeed, other types of readers *should* consider the book content from an athlete's perspective, as well as their own. In some cases, due to an athlete's young age and maturity level or limited resources, a particular point will have to be taken and applied by an adult on their behalf. For this reason, if you are a young player, I strongly encourage you to have your primary support person read this book alongside you or once you are finished. Alternatively, you could make note of which matters from the book you need their assistance in applying, and talk to them specifically about these.

Players also range in age, stage of development, abilities, ambitions within hockey, and other life circumstances. This book covers a wide span of material, designed to make it as useful and practical as it can be for every player. The athlete must use their knowledge of themselves, and their support person must use common sense and good judgment, to together decide what content from the book is appropriate for them to apply in their current situation. In the case of younger athletes, more advanced portions can provide a preview of what will need to be worked on later when the athlete is better able to understand and apply these elements. In the case of older or more advanced athletes, certain items may have been taken care of already, thus allowing them to focus more attention on the other items in this book that can help them.

The following pages contain as many ideas as we could stuff in this book to help you develop and advance toward making it—from crucial overarching principles to little expert tips. We don't expect anyone to be able to absorb and apply every word. Instead, think of every chapter, page, lesson, and tip as a potential bonus or advantage you might give yourself in your quest to make it. Learn and apply whatever you can at this moment, and don't worry about what you can't.

As you read, try to appreciate the book's suggestions and their potential benefits for you, based on our experience and expertise *in hockey*. At the same time, never lose sight of the fact that you are the #1 expert on *you*. Consider our recommendations only in conjunction with the knowledge you have of yourself and how you as a unique individual best learn, understand, and develop. There may well be an approach that we have found was helpful to others in dealing with some issue, but is not practical, possible, or preferable for you. So do not feel obligated to abide by every piece of advice, or think that our way is the only way to make it in hockey. Players made it before this book was written, and players will in the future make it who haven't read this book. This book simply is meant to give you an advantage, and make progress easier, smoother and faster.

Remember too that there is a limit to what a book can do. The principles, explanations, and techniques offered here can give you a base of knowledge. The plans in this book can point you in the right direction. But making it requires more. You will still need a certain amount of talent. You will still need lots of support from people who care about you. You will still need coaches, teachers, and instructors who can observe you first-hand and are willing and able to assist. You will still need guidance from experts and loved ones. Yet, just as this book can't make it for you, neither can any of those people. You are the only one who can make it for you, and that means you need to be able to rely on yourself to do what it takes. Making it in sports requires a deep love of the game and a relentless willingness to commit vast energy and resources to achieving your goal. This book is designed for helping athletes achieve such aspirations. And while we have taken a broad view of what it can mean to make it, and a smart and balanced approach to how to pursue it, the quest to make it in sports isn't for everyone.

Assuming it *is* for you, appreciate that you may also face unexpected challenges. What kind of injuries, opportunities, and luck you have may all be beyond your control. As a result, having all it takes and doing all the right things still can't *guarantee* you will make it, just as you could have no such guarantees in any other field or endeavour. As the wise Ben Franklin once said, "In this world, nothing can be said to be certain except death and taxes."

Does all this mean making it is so hard it's not worth pursuing? Definitely not!

People *do* make it. There are hundreds of players in the NHL at any given time, and thousands of men and women enjoying hockey careers at other high levels of play. You have probably seen many of them and even met one or two. Many are realizing their personal dream, living with passion, and experiencing great fulfillment. When they were young, a lot of them were probably not much different than you. You can be one of them too. And you have a tremendous advantage through the guidance you will receive from this book.

If making it in hockey is your dream, and you have a chance to pursue it, do it! Some people never have that chance. For others, it just isn't feasible or reasonable, given their personal circumstances. But if you have the chance, **few things can provide your life with the joy, fulfillment, and meaning of pursuing a dream—***even if you never reach it***.** If, on the other hand, you never try, you risk living a life short on passion and long on** regret. To succeed in sports is the dream of millions, and for good reason. Aside from the obvious perks, sports can be a worthwhile pursuit from many dif-

Mark Moore delivering a presentation to hockey officials at the Hockey Hall of Fame.

How to Read and Use This Book

To get the full value out of this book, read the whole book from start to finish. The chapters are ordered logically, and later sections of the book often refer back to earlier sections.

The best way to read a book like this is to transform it into your personal handbook. Assuming this is your own copy, make notes in the margins to help you make sense of the material in your own words. Highlight important passages you want to remember. Better yet, make searchable self-notes in reference to the text, and create a set of digital "bookmarks," as part of the personal online notebook available and waiting for you on our website www. sportsmaster.tv.

Lastly, for anyone committed to making it, this isn't the kind of book to read once and then discard. This book is designed to be a permanent resource for players, parents, coaches, and others involved in the quest to make it in hockey. Read sections more than once to deepen your understanding and apply more lessons in that area of your game. When challenges arise on your path, return to this book to search for answers. This is a guidebook to bring with you on your journey to making it. Let's get started!

ferent perspectives: They teach you about life; they test you as a person; they challenge you physically, mentally and emotionally; they force you to strive to be your best, to overcome obstacles, and to stretch your potential; they are an experience you can share with others including family, friends, and teammates. And all of this is true whether you someday make it or not.

Dreams are made to be pursued. Let the following pages be your guide to help you pursue them in the best and smartest way possible.

1

DREAM IT!
channelling your passion for the game

A dream come true . . . Steve Yzerman holding hockey's most fabled trophy, the Stanley Cup.

THIS SECTION TEACHES YOU HOW TO TAP INTO DREAMS AS A MAGICAL SOURCE OF SO MUCH OF WHAT YOU WILL NEED TO MAKE IT IN HOCKEY.

Chapter 1: it starts with a dream

Chapter 2: pursuing your dream with passion

"**The future belongs to those who believe in the beauty of their dreams.**"

ELEANOR ROOSEVELT, CIVIL RIGHTS PIONEER

it starts with a dream

SCOUTS' PREVIEW
In this chapter . . .
· The benefits of having a dream
· The secret to powerful dreams
· Setting goals and objectives
· Believing in what is possible

THE GREATEST JOURNEYS BEGIN WITH A DREAM—A DREAM OF WHERE YOU'D SOMEDAY LIKE TO BE.

The journey to making it in hockey begins with dreaming it.

It might surprise you that the quest to make it in a sport doesn't begin with playing it! Let me tell you a story to illustrate why.

When I was a kid, my parents enrolled me in many different activities, including lots of different sports: soccer, baseball, swimming, running, tennis, skiing, hockey, and more. But only hockey captured my imagination and implanted a longing inside me to make it to the top. I dreamt of playing in the NHL. I pictured myself flying around the ice, the cold air blowing against my face. I would be weaving around and through defenders, and scoring goals. I aspired to achieve the honour of wearing the red-blue-and-white sweater of the Montreal Canadiens, and to hoist the Stanley Cup triumphantly over my head, just like my childhood hero, Guy Lafleur. Those feelings and ideas set me on a path of trying to make it in hockey, whereas I never sought to make it in any of those other sports.

The Benefits of Having a Dream

Some people love the experience of an activity, and that gives rise to a dream about it. Others may not at first have the skills to enjoy an activity, and yet they still dream of it. And there are even people who have not yet had a chance to try an activity, but they already have dreams of it. Just the *idea* of the activity captures their heart and mind, and that is enough to give birth to their dream. Whatever your case may be, from the moment that dream takes shape in your mind and takes root in your heart, you have taken a step toward making it.

Of course, when we talk of dreams in the sense of making it, we are talking about a different dream than random night-dreams, daydreams, or passing fantasies. The dream that matters is the one where you consciously picture yourself reaching a treasured place in a treasured activity, and you return to that same dream continually over time. *This* is the kind of dream that starts you on a path toward making it. To the person who has a dream, the future they imagine is something exceptional and special. The feelings they get from thinking about and pursuing it are unlike anything else. These are what set dreams apart from other "ordinary" aspirations.

There are many reasons why dreams are important for making it *and* for life.

A dream is like a distant beacon that keeps you on track, out of trouble, and away from distractions. Life can be confusing as it presents so many choices. Not knowing what to do can make life frustrating. But when you have a dream, you have a *sense of purpose* that guides your actions, making life simpler. When you are younger, options can frequently be evaluated with one straightforward question: Will that option take me toward my dream, or not? As you get a bit older, there might be a few questions instead of just one (as you will learn in Chapter 29). In either case, the answers are often obvious, and the result is an easier time making decisions, free from second-guessing. Your dream provides you with clear and decisive *direction*.

Dreams also give life extra zest. When you have a dream, you don't grudgingly drag yourself out of bed in the morning. Rather, you spring from bed motivated to chase your dream. Much like our bodies need nutrients to stay healthy and functioning well, the person inside each of us craves *hope*. Dreams provide us with a hope, and to live with that hope is a great way to live.

Dreams are a great source of energy and emotional power for tackling necessary tasks and avoiding complacency. In addition, on the path to making it, athletes will often encounter unfamiliar obstacles. In those cases, the *inspiration* of a dream can conjure new ideas and solutions seemingly out of nowhere. Creative powers you never knew you had can find new—and perhaps even better—ways to move you forward. The famous inventor Thomas Edison once said, "Genius is 1 per cent inspiration and 99 per cent perspiration." Why even note what is only 1 per cent? Because that 1 per cent is indispensable. Without it, the other 99 per cent leads nowhere. And with it, the other 99 per cent is much less of a chore. Like any other kind of genius, hockey stardom requires inspiration. And that inspiration comes from your dream.

I won't say it's impossible to do so, but I wonder: How *could* somebody make it without the direction and purpose, the hope and inspiration, the resilience and creativity, the emotional power and motivation provided by dreams?

So if you know you have a hockey dream, let this chapter give you every reason to embrace it! If someone tells you that dream is impossible, don't believe them. People *do* make it. And if you want to make it, it helps if you dream it first. If someone suggests you let go of your dream, don't feel pressured to listen to them. Our dreams are too important to abandon while we still have a chance to realize them. For these same reasons, if you once had a hockey dream, but gave up on it without needing or wanting to, get it back! And if you aren't sure whether or not you have a dream, don't worry. Making it as a hockey player is a difficult, exceptional, and special ambition for millions of people. I expect that since you are reading this book, it's important to you. That intense desire that exists within you is the critical ingredient for developing a hockey dream of your own. And creating a powerful, inspiring dream is exactly what this book will help you do.

The Secret to Powerful Dreams

Creating your dream:

* When you think about your desire to make it in hockey, what is it that makes you most excited? Try to identify what feels special to you. It could be the thought of someday becoming a professional hockey player. It could be representing your country in the Olympics; to someday play Junior or College hockey; to one day make the highest level youth team in your area; or to become the best player in your family or town. It could be to grow up to be just like an idol you admire—the same way I wanted to be like Guy Lafleur. One youngster in our hockey school had the dream to someday have the hardest slapshot in the world! The beauty of a dream is that everyone can create their own, and not everyone's is exactly the same. Whatever yours is, a special wishing and longing for it must come to be present in your mind.
* Dreams commonly have several dimensions and variations. A dream doesn't have to be fixed or precise. From day to day, the focus of your dream could switch from playing in a certain league, to becoming just like a certain idol, to gaining the chance to have a certain special experience, and so on. Dreams can also change over time. For example, when Guy Lafleur retired, my dream found a new idol: "The Magnificent One"—Mario Lemieux. Changes in your life or career may force corresponding shifts in your dream. New facts or insights you gain as you go

along may also cause you to modify your dream. But amidst all variations and changes in your dream, there must be a general idea that remains definite and constant.

Once your desire to make it has these qualities, you have a dream.

Another secret is that not all dreams have the same power. By that, I am not referring to your *choice* of dream, but to the *way* you dream. The following *visualization exercise* uses your imagination and senses to amplify the power of your dream and all its benefits:

- Start with your dream as it currently exists. Close your eyes and imagine your dream as if it were real and present—yourself in the place you would like to be, as you would like to be. For example, let's say your dream is to be an Olympic Gold Medalist. Picture yourself standing on the ice with your teammates, having the gold medal placed around your neck. See the people you love in the crowd smiling. Hear the fans cheering. Smell that familiar smell of the inside of an arena. Taste the sweat dripping from your brow after a hard-fought game. Sense the weight of the medal resting against your chest. Feel the sensations of excitement, pride, and triumph. Stay with that feeling until a burst of energy and inspiration wells up inside you, and you can't wait to get started on working to make it happen!

To maximize the benefits of this exercise, you should repeat it regularly. You might do it each night before you go to sleep. Repetition will condition you to dream this way by default, even when you are not doing the exercise.

Setting Goals and Objectives

When you are first starting out, achieving your dream can seem pretty far off. You may not know exactly how to reach it. As a result, it helps to break down dreams into a series of *goals*. A goal is a target you will aim to achieve. It is in line with the general direction in which you need to move to reach your dreams, but is more immediate and precise. Specifically, a goal should have the following characteristics:

- can be clearly defined;
- is easy to remember;
- is able to be measured;
- has a fixed time frame in which to achieve it; and
- is a stretch, but is reachable within the above time frame.

Goal-setting is an exercise in itself. A series of goals are set, extending forward in time. Each goal in the series represents where you think you need to be at that point in time in order to someday reach your dream. Setting these goals pushes you to improve. Each goal is like a step up a ladder; the successive rungs allow you to gauge your progress toward the top of the ladder, where your dream will come true. Every time you reach the next step, you also gain confidence and build momentum.

I recommend setting a goal of where you want to be in five years, three years, and one year. Start with the five-year goal, which can be more general, and then work backward to the three-year and the one-year goals, which should be the most specific. Then, take the most immediate goal (the one-year goal) and break it into a series of *objectives*. Each objective should correspond to a particular area of your game or personal development. The objective identifies a targeted improvement you believe you need to make in that area to reach your overall goal.

PRO-file

Jennifer Botterill

My friend Jennifer Botterill has been a member of the Canadian Women's Hockey Team since 1997. She is a two-time Olympic Gold Medalist (2002, 2006) and a Silver Medalist (1998). She has twice been named MVP of the World Championships. Jennifer is a graduate of Harvard University, where she twice won the award for the top player in College hockey. She currently plays for Mississauga in the Canadian Women's Hockey League. Here is what she had to say about her dream: "I was always a kid that watched the Olympics on TV when I was young, and I knew that winning an Olympic Gold someday was my ultimate dream, but I didn't know what sport! I actually didn't start playing hockey until I was thirteen. My brother Jason played in the World Juniors, and I watched, and that's when I started playing, and hockey became my sport. So to actually win that Olympic gold medal was pretty incredible. I remember being lined up on the ice watching my teammates get the medals placed around their necks. And to come home and hear that

people watching the game stood and sang the anthem and had tears in their eyes made it that much more special, being able to share that experience with others."

Below are samples of how a player's goals and objectives might look. The objectives listed are just a few examples. To complete this exercise, you will need objectives for *every* aspect of your game or personal development. For example, you may have several objectives just within the area of your hockey skills.

Player: Jake, Age 13, AAA, Forward
Dream: To someday make the NHL.
Five-Year Goal: To win a scholarship to an NCAA Division 1 school.
Three-Year Goal: To make a Tier 2 Junior team.
One-Year Goal: To be in the top five in scoring in my current league.

One-Year Objectives:
Character Objective: To learn to control my temper so I am not getting in trouble off the ice as well as on the ice, where I've been losing valuable ice-time sitting in the penalty box.
Foundation Objective: To lose weight so I am in better athletic shape.
Skills Objective: To improve all my shots (wrist, slap, snap, backhand, one-timer, wraparounds, and deflections) so they are of the top calibre in my league.
Training Objective: To increase my foot speed and coordination so I can accelerate faster and change directions sharper and smoother.

Player: Gina, Age 10, House League, Defence
Dream: To someday make AA.
Five-Year Goal: To be called up to the AA team as a fill-in at least three times.
Three-Year Goal: To make A.
One-Year Goal: To be invited to play in my House League All-Star Game.

One-Year Objectives:
Character Objective: To bolster my commitment so that I put in the time and effort I need to actually improve at hockey, and not just wish I was a better player.
Foundation Objective: To improve my sleep patterns so I can get enough rest to focus and concentrate better during games (as well as at other times).
Skills Objective: To develop my skating technique (including forward and backward skating, stops, starts, and turns) to be in the top tier of the league.
Training Objective: To strengthen my legs so I can skate better and enjoy improved balance and body control on the ice.

As time goes by, goals must be reviewed and revised to ensure they are still serving their intended purpose. We recommend reviewing them at least once a month—say on the last day of each month. If something happens that dictates a goal ought to change, you are always free to modify goals at any time.

When this goal-setting process is new to you, it might be a challenge to come up with sensible hockey goals and objectives. For example, you want them to be realistic and attainable. Your goals shouldn't be so far out of reach that you are just setting yourself up for failure and disappointment—such as perhaps trying to go from the bottom of league scoring to the top, in one year. That can be a more distant goal. Your intermediate goals should have a more measured pace that will allow you to see progress and gain encouragement. In the beginning, goal-setting might be easier with input or help from a trusted parent, coach, or advisor who is familiar with you, your dream, and your current abilities. As you gain familiarity and practice with goal-setting, you will be better able to do it yourself.

Here is another exercise. This one will help strengthen your goals:

1. Make a list of all the things you will gain from reaching each of your goals. Be sure to relate the goals to your dream, and to what excites you about achieving it.

2. Make a list of all the things it will cost you or that you will lose out on if you don't reach each of your goals. Again, make sure to tie the goals to your dream, and what inspires you to reach it.

3. Read over the first list and feel as if this has actually happened.

4. Do the same for the second list.

By the end of this exercise, you should be bursting with enthusiasm to pursue your goals! This was a *motivational exercise*. Motivation is what spurs you to take the actions you need to take in order to reach your goals.

As with the dream exercise, the goals exercise is most helpful if repeated regularly. Keep the two lists you made from this exercise. Each morning, before you start your day, re-read the lists and repeat parts three and four of the exercise. This will keep you motivated throughout the day, and help you get the most out of it.

Can I have more than one dream?

Some people have one dream, which has a special significance for them above all else. Others can have multiple aspirations at a similar level. The question is not so much whether you can have more than one dream, but whether you can reach more than one dream. And the answer is: It depends. Sometimes it is possible. It's more likely when the different dreams have a "synergy" where one feeds off another. For example, Arnold Schwarzenegger could have dreamed of being one of the world's top bodybuilders, an actor, and a politician. Becoming a top bodybuilder made him a natural fit to play a starring role in action movies. Then, being a well-loved actor helped make him popular enough to win election to government. Other scenarios may have a logic that works too. In general, though, it takes an incredible commitment of heart, soul, mind, time, energy, and money to pursue a dream like making it in sports. So if you try to make it in too many things, you may not give yourself a chance to make it in anything.

What if I don't have a hockey dream?

Some readers may have ambitions in hockey, but a dream outside of hockey. Others may not have a dream at all. Both of these are perfectly normal and fine.

Many people do not have a dream. They can still pursue a field and achieve success in it, sometimes even a high level of success. Typically, they still use goals and objectives, because these tools help people achieve better success in any endeavour. Since you are reading this book, I would expect that you at least have a desire you wish to achieve through hockey. You can therefore still use goals and objectives to help you reach it. As far as dreams go, their tremendous benefits cannot be discounted. In a competitive field like sports, the higher your aim, the more difficult and unlikely it is to realize without the power of a dream. But dreams are not the type of things that can be forced, so don't lose sleep if you don't have one. Through our hockey school, I have met many players who participated in hockey for several years without a hockey dream, and then suddenly developed one later on. Likewise, if you currently have a hockey dream, but someday your dream changes to a different field, many of the principles and techniques from this book will still apply and serve you well.

Believing in Your Dream

It's fine to appreciate that doing so may be difficult, and that you can't know for certain in advance that you *will* achieve your dream. But you must believe without question that it is *possible* for you to achieve it.

Many successful athletes had been previously told that they never would make it. But these athletes didn't believe that. If they had, they would likely have only proven their doubters right. When you don't believe you can do something, part of your mind acts to stop you,

> The most important thing if you are an athlete is you have to believe in yourself. I've always had a belief in what I was doing and you need that if you are going to keep developing as a player and as a person.
> —MATS SUNDIN[3]

jock talk

and the thing becomes much harder to do. Your negative belief becomes a self-fulfilling prophecy. To achieve difficult things, you must guard your mind like a fortress. Do not let the doubts, criticisms, or negative opinions and attitudes of others enter and subvert your belief in your ability to succeed. Likewise, do not let negative experiences undermine your belief either. You will learn more about the power of beliefs, and how to strengthen positive ones, in Chapter 18. For now, accept that if you want to make it, you should first believe that you *can*.

Together, the things you learned about in this chapter—dreams, goals, objectives, and self-belief—should give your mind a *focus*: making it. That focus is key. It dictates what you do and how you do it, which strongly determines where you will end up.

EXPERTS' RECAP

Remember . . .
· A dream provides purpose, direction, inspiration, and motivation.
· Goal-setting helps guide you toward your dream.
· Believe in your ability to achieve your dream.

pursuing your dream with passion

CHAPTER 2

SCOUTS' PREVIEW
In this chapter . . .
· The importance of motivation
· The magic of fun
· The power of spirit
· Stoking your passion

DREAMING IT IS THE START OF MAKING IT. BUT MAKING IT IS A PROCESS—ONE THAT CONSISTS OF YOUR ACTIONS AND THEIR EFFECTS OVER TIME. SO HOW EXACTLY DO YOU GO ABOUT PURSUING YOUR DREAM?

To realize such a big ambition, you need a plan, which you will find in the succeeding sections of this book. The plan will involve many components: personal qualities, skills, training, strategies, and more. After reading about them, you then need to master them in action. Reading about fitness will help you learn how to train, but only actual training can make you fit. Making it takes many hours of sweat and strain on and off the ice. How will you get yourself to do it?

The Importance of Motivation

In Chapter 1, you took your goals and did a motivational exercise to strengthen your resolve to reach them. You can do a similar exercise with any task needed to make it: Think through and feel all the positive things you will get if you complete the task. Then consider and feel all the negative consequences you may suffer if you don't. Whenever you find yourself hesitating to do something you know you should, this can provide the motivation you need.

But exercises have their limits. If you found yourself stalled after each activity, having to redo the exercise to get going again, chances are you aren't moving forward very quickly. Besides, you can only do an exercise so often. A motivational exercise uses your mind to pull the levers of your emotions and manipulate yourself into action. If you do that too often in a short span of time, the effect starts to wear off. Or you begin to dread the exercise itself. Would you then have to do the exercise to get yourself to do the exercise? Clearly you don't want to get caught in that kind of vicious cycle!

What you need is a way to create and maintain a high level of motivation that will spur you to continually do whatever is necessary to advance toward your dream. Reliance solely on mental motivation exercises for each new task simply isn't sustainable.

So what means of motivation *is* sustainable? As it happens, your dream has some magic properties that can provide such means.

The Magic of Fun

One of the reasons a person has a dream is because that dream is *fun* for them. You have your dream because it's something you love, something that inspires you, something you enjoy. It's fun for you to imagine it, to think about it, and to strive to achieve it. Meanwhile, fun is one of the greatest motivators in existence. When something is fun, you don't need to think about why it would be good for you to do it—you simply do it because you enjoy it. When something is fun, you don't need to invoke the future's sake to get yourself to do it—you just do it because you like doing it. When you're having fun, hard work doesn't seem so hard. Arduous tasks can feel effortless. This is the "genius" of your dream: It aligns fun with the demands of making it, and fun then acts as a magical source of motivation to make it. It's automatic, constant, and comprehensive. No amount of exercises can match that.

This book won't teach you how to have fun. Having fun isn't something anyone needs to be told how to do. Chasing your dream *ought* to be fun. However, a few things can happen with fun.

Firstly, people can get the wrong idea of what sort of fun counts as good and useful. Fooling around, goofy behaviour, and being a prankster is not the right kind of fun. These behaviours undermine a player's focus and cause others who

the inside story

You would think that it would be no fun to be up against a rival like Alexander Ovechkin for the NHL scoring title or against a teammate like Sidney Crosby for recognition on your own team. But Evgeni Malkin has a very different attitude, according to my brother Dominic, who played with Malkin during his rookie-of-the-year first season.

Malkin's attitude is in fact playful, easy-going, almost carefree. This helps him handle all that pressure well, and maintain a healthy, energetic state of mind over the course of a long season. He loves the game, loves to win, and never loses sight of that. It shows through his exceptional—and consistent—performance.

can help them to lose patience with the player instead. The kind of fun that helps you make it is the fun that comes just from devoting yourself to playing the sport you love, and from the enjoyment that comes with improving.

Secondly, fun can be spoiled. It's a shame that this occurs at all in sports, but for various reasons it occurs much too often. Every athlete has people around them. When those people respect your dream and just want to share in it with you, it increases your enjoyment. However, if they have their own dreams for you that start to take precedence over yours, and you feel pushed against your wishes, your enjoyment will suffer, consequently hurting your chances of someday making it. Fun can also get lost in the shuffle when large groups of people are chasing the same dream. If rivalry gets carried too far, for example, sports can cease to be fun competition and become more like conflict, which is no fun at all. (Other group circumstances can also challenge fun, as you will learn how to deal with in Chapter 21.)

Finally, while making it requires dedication, some people take their sport or ambition so seriously that there is no place left for fun. They become their own "slave-driver"—pushing themselves unreasonably hard and being overly self-critical. Or perhaps there is someone around them that has this attitude and becomes the slave-driver who spoils the fun.

To prevent fun from getting ruined, simply make it a personal rule not to allow anything to take the fun out of chasing your dream. You can have fun while still working hard, competing hard, and recognizing the need to improve. Fun is too important a motivator throughout your long quest to sacrifice for a result that may seem worth it in the short-run. More importantly, since fun is central to why you chose your dream in the first place, your dream won't mean the same thing if you let the fun get taken out of it. Fun is one part of chasing your dream you ought to make non-negotiable.

Here are a few practical examples of how to keep the fun in your pursuit:

ATTITUDE: I will make sure fun and safety take precedence over competing and winning.

BEHAVIOUR: I will smile around the rink, even though I am competing hard.

SITUATIONAL: If other people are getting carried away, I will try to find an appropriate way to ask everyone if we are all losing sight of the fact that hockey is supposed to be played for fun.

FOCUS: I will make fun games for myself out of practice drills, training exercises, and other necessary tasks that are part of pursuing my hockey career dream.

PRO-file

Bobby Orr

Bobby Orr is the greatest defenceman in hockey history, and perhaps the greatest hockey player of all time. He controlled the game from one end of the rink to the other, using his skating ability, skills, and instincts to win the NHL scoring title twice (the only defenceman ever to do so). He won two Stanley Cups, two trophies for playoff MVP, and in 1976 with his injured knees almost at the point where he could no longer play, he dominated the Canada Cup, receiving the MVP trophy as Canada won the elite international tournament. He was voted the greatest athlete in Boston history. Orr has said he is most grateful that he was allowed to play the game in a way that he had fun playing. As part of the Safe & Fun program in partnership with Hockey Canada, Orr now spends time travelling across Canada each year

along with Hall-of-Famer Mike Bossy and Canadian Women's Olympian Cassie Campbell to teach kids and parents how to play the game and keep it enjoyable for themselves and others.

The Power of Spirit

Besides fun, your dream has another associated magic property that can help keep you motivated and moving forward: *spirit*. Spirit is a special experience of joy, excitement, and exuberance that can give you incredible energy and enthusiasm in whatever you are doing. And your dream is one of the rare things that can produce this special experience in you. Indeed, whether you realize it or not, that special experience is likely a big part of the reason you chose the dream you did.

Spirit is similar to fun in the way it feels and how it helps you. But unlike fun, spirit doesn't depend on the activity you are doing or any immediate outside circumstances. In that sense, spirit has an advantage over fun. Doing an activity you don't like or that you're not doing well can sometimes make it difficult to have fun. But you can still have spirit, because its source is within you; nothing outside is needed.

Spirit can transcend the activity at hand, the moment, and even yourself. For example, you've probably seen shirtless fans with letters painted on their chests standing next to one another in the bleachers of a freezing cold outdoor football game looking overjoyed! Are they crazy? Maybe! But more likely they are just filled with team spirit. Team spirit allows them to brave the freezing cold, the embarrassment, and the body paint, in order to do what they think will give a spark to their team and other fans. You may have had a similar experience—doing something that wouldn't be fun on its own, but which you did with great enthusiasm and excitement because of school spirit. Or think of winter holiday spirit. People in the holiday spirit have a sparkle in their eye and a jump in their step that isn't there the rest of the year—even while doing the most routine or boring tasks! When you have a dream, you have the opportunity to catch a "Chasing the Dream Spirit." This will give you the power to do whatever your dream demands and more, with untiring enthusiasm.

There is another key difference between spirit and fun: Unlike fun, spirit isn't something you just *have*, it's something you must *get into*. Take our example of holiday spirit: You've probably seen someone who just wasn't into it. Another person might say, "Hey, what's with Scrooge? He doesn't seem tuned in to the holiday spirit." In fact, accessing the spirit inside you *is* like tuning a radio dial. Your dream has special meaning to you, and can bring forth incredible energy and creativity from you. But just like searching for music on the radio, you have to tune in to the spot where the "Chasing the Dream Spirit" exists for you, or all you'll encounter is useless static.

The concept of spirit is difficult to explain, and the presence of spirit can be difficult to find at first. But if you remain patiently open to it, when you do find it, you will have tapped into an incredible source of motivation, energy, and creativity for pursuing your dream. A few illustrations of spirit include:

- A team is being bag-skated by their coach. Although not looking forward to it, a player knows the coach is doing it in order to help the team in the long run. The player is smiling, skating full speed on each sprint, and seems to be gaining energy rather than getting tired. Soon all the players are doing the same and the coach is pleased, knowing that this spirited kind of effort is just what the team needs.

- A team is down several goals in a game. But instead of falling silent on the bench, the players keep their spirit up. They continue to encourage each other and cheer on teammates on the ice. Soon they get back in the game. The opposing team can hear them and is intimidated by their spirit. As the game wears on, the team of spirited players eventually comes back to tie and ultimately win the game.

- Having music playing in the dressing room can both cue spirit before a game and express spirit after a game.

Stoking Your Passion

Together, fun, and spirit make a formidable combination. To pursue a dream with fun and spirit is to pursue it with *passion*. Passion is the ultimate motivation. It is activation. It is the awakening and focusing of your total energies and abilities at a given moment on achieving your goal. Passion is a state of being electrified with seemingly limitless energy and excitement in doing what you are doing. Passion is the burning desire that comes from being completely committed to and engaged in realizing a dream in an activity you love. You can see that fire burning in the eyes of someone pursuing their dream with passion. You can see it in the eyes of Maurice "Rocket" Richard in old photographs. I myself have seen it live on the ice from a foot away in the eyes of Mario Lemieux. Passion is so powerful that you don't possess it, it possesses you. Sidney Crosby plays like a player possessed. That's because he *is* possessed—by passion.

How important is passion? According to the famous philosopher of history Georg Hegel, "Nothing great in the world has ever been accomplished without passion." Passion is genius in the making. If you dream of developing athletic genius, or achieving great sports accomplishments, passion is a must.

So do everything you can to kindle your passion. Your dream is its source. Feel your love for the game, your favourite aspects of the game, your favourite moments. Feel your desire to reach your ambitions in hockey. Use the exercises you learned in the last chapter and the magic forces of fun and spirit you learned here to stoke your passion. And with the fire of that passion, pursue your dreams.

> **EXPERTS' RECAP**
> Remember . . .
> · Hockey should be fun, so don't let yourself or anyone else spoil that.
> · Try to tap the exciting spirit that flows from your dream.
> · When people pursue their purpose with passion, the results can be amazing.

2

CHARACTER
the personal qualities of great athletes

The most famous Canadian is not an NHL player; it was a phys-ed teacher with cancer named Terry Fox. Fox's character inspired all, including the Toronto Maple Leafs, who offered to finish his cross-Canada Marathon of Hope when cancer halted him after 5,373 km.

THIS SECTION TEACHES YOU ABOUT DEVELOPING THE GOOD CHARACTER THAT WILL HELP MAKE YOU A GREAT ATHLETE.

"A man's character is his fate."

HERACLITUS, ANCIENT GREEK PHILOSOPHER

character matters

SCOUTS' PREVIEW
In this chapter . . .
· What is character?
· How character can help you make it
· Real character versus caricature
· True character versus phony character

CHARACTER.

You've probably heard the word a thousand times. You've heard it from TV sports commentators during telecasts. You've heard it from athletes in interviews. You've heard it from coaches during post-game press conferences.

Outside of sports, you've heard of it from heroes and those who describe them. You may have heard about it from religious preachers, from teachers in school, or read about it in books by famed success coaches such as Stephen R. Covey.

When you hear a word invoked so often, you know it has to be important.

Character matters.

It matters a great deal.

But when you hear a word used by so many different people in so many different contexts, sometimes the meaning of the word becomes foggy.

And to make things even more complicated, the word "character" itself has more than one dictionary meaning.

So let's be clear: in this book, "character" does not refer to a letter or number on your keyboard, or to a being in a comic book or story! For our purposes, it is the other sense of the word that we are concerned with: *"Moral excellence and firmness."*

additional help You may have participated in the annual Terry Fox run, the world's largest one-day fundraiser for cancer research. For a $15 donation to the Terry Fox Foundation at www.terryfoxrun.org, you can get your own biography of heroic character role model Terry Fox.

What Is Character?

Character is the set of personal attributes that defines or *characterizes* a person. If those qualities are negative, a person has "bad or weak character." If the qualities are positive, the person has "good or strong character," or is simply "a character person."

If you look again at the dictionary definition above, you will see that character has two parts. The first is *"moral excellence."* This refers to a person's values—what they deem morally important. A person of moral excellence is a person who has a good set of values, a person with high standards of right and wrong. The second part is *"moral firmness."* This refers to a person's strength—not the strength of their muscles, but the strength of their personal resolve in sticking to their values. A person of moral firmness doesn't forget their values. They don't change their values every time circumstances change. They don't abandon their values when it's difficult to uphold them or convenient not to. Values and strength together create character.

Character isn't something that some people are born with and others are not. It can be learned by anyone who wants to learn it.

How Character Can Help You Make It

Above, we mentioned an expert on character: Stephen R. Covey. According to Covey, "Our character is basically a composite of our habits. Because (habits) are consistent, often unconscious patterns, they constantly, daily, express our character." In other words, our character is seen through our habits, and our character also determines our habits. Habits are just the countless choices we make and things we do every day without thinking. Now you see how the statement that began this section—*a person's character is their fate*—becomes true. Character is tied to the habits that take a person in a specific direction over time, and eventually to a destination or fate. If your desired fate is to make it, you can start by cultivating the character that can lead you there.

Many elements are required to make it: a clear sense of purpose, outstanding skills, rigorous training, sound strategies, and more. What is the role of character among these? It's the impact of all your basic personal qualities upon your chances of reaching your dream. In his studies, Covey found the personal qualities that make up character have been linked not only to moral excellence and firmness, but also to success.

From an individual standpoint, character helps you to do things that success demands but are not easy or fun. Character also guides you to do things the right way, rather than in a poor or counterproductive manner. You have probably heard from many sources how important it is in sports to have a proper *attitude*. But how do you know what the proper attitude is for each different situation that can present itself? It is the qualities of character that tell you. When you face critical decisions, character helps you make the right choices. Character helps you find or form environments that will support you in your quest. It carries you through the ups and downs and the twists and turns that will occur on the journey to reach your ambitions. And last but not least, good character makes you a good person. Placing stock in that, in its own right, protects you from feeling threatened by the possibility of failure. Every aspiring athlete *will* meet many failures. But a failure in sports doesn't dictate who you are as a person. As a character athlete, the type of person you are striving to be should provide you with a sense of self-worth that's as firm as a rock and will hold you steady even in the case of deep disappointments. When you are not on the line with the outcome of your every performance, you play with less pressure, do better, and endure longer. You are able to ride through bumps without being hurled from the track.

From a team standpoint, character is also important. Teams want character players. In the days leading up to the NHL Entry Draft, for example, teams interview potential draft picks. What are they trying to find out? They want to know the players' character. They use character to predict whether a player will continue striving to improve after they are drafted. Likewise, if a team is looking to sign free agents and is considering a particular player, they often speak to other players familiar with them. Why? They want the inside scoop on the player's character, to assess whether they'll fit in well with their team. Character is often a top factor for coaches when choosing captains and assistants to lead a team. But they want character in *all* their players, because a team is like a chain, and "a chain is only as strong as its weakest link." When strained, the *firmness* of character is what holds that chain together and makes the team strong.

the inside story

When my family runs a hockey school, the staff comprise a team. Guess what we look for first in potential staff? Character. The reason is simple—to run a program smoothly, we all depend on each other. We can't have a person who will let the rest of the team down. A character person doesn't let people down. In fact, they even do that little bit extra—without being asked—that circumstances sometimes demand.

Character doesn't just matter for success. It is a "Code of Conduct." Character makes you a good person: a person other people will admire and emulate; a treasured member of your family, your team, and your community; a person you can be proud of whenever you look in the mirror, regardless of how you did in your latest game or season.

Real Character versus Caricature

Given that people see character represented so differently by so many different sources, how do you know what character actually is and isn't?

Imagine a hockey broadcast: It's a playoff game, and a star player is being stymied by strong defence. Frustrated, he instigates a fight and is ejected from the game. A colour commentator may say, "It just shows his character. It shows his team he cares. And it shows his toughness." Is that so? No! The instigator penalty he took shows he was more concerned with his own frustration than with his team, that he hurt by leaving them shorthanded. It also showed his weakness; instead of continuing to battle to find a way to score, he gave in to his frustration and looked for an easy way out of a difficult game. Maybe the star player *is* a character person who most of the time perseveres and scores goals to help his team. But in this case, he did not show good character, and the colour commentator's claims, while entertaining, were misleading about what character is.

Let's now picture a movie: Every time the fictional hero gets stressed, he lights a cigarette, talks disrespectfully to peers, and smashes something in anger. Since he is the hero, his character is the one that viewers are meant to admire. So the unspoken message is, "The hero has grit. He won't give in. He is fighting back. The way this hero acts is character." Again, is that accurate? No! If the hero had more grit, he wouldn't need harmful cigarettes to help deal with stress. Through his disrespectful talk, he is giving in to his stress by taking it out on his peers. And by smashing things, he may hurt himself or an important piece of property, hampering his ability to fight back. The movie portrayal of the hero's character is compelling and entertaining, but not accurate in terms of what character is, in the sense used in this chapter.

It can be tempting to believe in the hyped or romanticized portrayals of character we see in stories, but often these are *caricatured* versions of character. They may fit well with their stories, but not with what you need in real life. Chances are the colour commentator and movie scriptwriter above both knew what *real character* was, used it to help get to where they are, and could teach you about it if you asked them. But when telling stories through media, their job is to be entertaining, and they portray character in that other sense of the term—a being in a story. So don't let messages created for purposes other than to simply and accurately teach you about character mislead you. In the real world, only *real character* matters, and only it can help you make it.

In the next chapter, you will learn precisely about what comprises real character. But simply reading about it doesn't magically imbue you with it. It takes considerable effort to acquire, and continuous action to preserve.

True Character versus Phony Character

Some people find that the building of character isn't easy. They may try to take a shortcut, developing instead what can be called *"phony character."* These people know the value of character, but aren't willing to pay the price to earn it. They think they can "cheat the system." Here's how they try to do it: They observe closely what real character includes, what it looks like to others, what it sounds like to others, and what it feels like to others. And then they try to display the same superficial signs of character to people they encounter, to fool those people into believing they have character when in fact, underneath, they did *not* develop true character.

Let's imagine a College hockey player named Veneer. In the dressing room, Veneer is always whining and complaining. But whenever the coach enters, Veneer shouts "rah-rah" encouragement to her teammates, so the coach thinks she is a positive influence and a leader. On the ice, whenever Veneer gets mildly bumped by an opponent or struck by the puck, she falls dramatically to the ice, labours to get up, limps to the bench wincing in pain, doubles over on the bench for a few minutes, and then hops back on the ice for her next shift and skates extra-hard. The fans cheer. "What toughness and heart!" they think. During a game, Veneer scores two goals, but doesn't back check, so her line gets scored on three times and the team loses. After the game, a reporter for the school newspaper is interviewing Veneer, and asks her to comment on her two-goal game. She replies, "I don't care whether I score goals; the only thing that matters is whether the team wins. I would gladly trade my two G's for one W." The next morning, the manager for the National Team reads her quote and thinks, "What great humility, what a team player." He invites her to training camp. The National Team recently lost its captain, Stone, a girl who was appreciated for her great character and who led them to many championships. When Veneer arrives at camp, she asks for the same number as Stone, wears the same equipment as Stone, and tucks her jersey in sideways the same way Stone did. A few scouts say to each other, "Veneer really reminds me of Stone. . . . Wouldn't it be great to have a player who could replace the character that Stone brought to our team?" After a couple weeks of camp, the coaches check with several trusted veteran girls on the team about what kind of presence Veneer is in the dressing room. They tell the truth about Veneer's two-faced act. The coaches know this will have a negative influence on the team, and they release Veneer. So Veneer goes back to her College team. The team had been doing great without Veneer, but after Veneer returns, the team goes into a slump. The College coach notices the sudden nosedive in team chemistry, and asks some trusted team leaders who had been there all year about what's going on. They are honest about Veneer. The coach cuts Veneer from the team. Suddenly Veneer's playing days are over. She can't believe it! What happened?

At first, Veneer's phony character ruse seemed to be working. She fooled her fans from beginning to end, and at one point, had everybody fooled. But to quote President Abraham Lincoln, a great historical example of character, "You can fool some of the people all of the time, and all of the people some of the time, but you can't fool all of the people all of the time." It was only a matter of time before certain people saw through Veneer's act, and once that happened, her jig was up. Phony character was a fake shortcut.

There are different types of phonies. A bully, for example, *acts* tough to get respect. But once someone calls the bully's bluff, the bully permanently loses all respect. They won't get it back again for being tough, or for any other reason. Here's another quote—this one from my father, Jack: "Whatever you profess, make sure you possess." People exposed as phonies often wish they'd never faked anything. Others resent having been deceived, and won't trust them, respect them, or take them seriously anymore.

There's usually no need to try to convince others of your character. *True character* helps you succeed, and takes you in the right direction—and other people should notice that on their own. It's also the only kind of character that can make you the kind of person you yourself would respect. As philosopher Ralph Waldo Emerson said, "Character is what can [suffice] without success."

Why do some pros seem to lack character, or even have "bad character"?

A few athletes are extraordinarily privileged in some way from a young age, and manage to make it without needing the guiding values and strength that come from character. In a sense, one might say that they were lucky. But in the big picture, are they really lucky if they aren't pushed to learn character for sports, and if that lack of character adversely affects other areas of their life? Also, there is a difference between a successful athlete and a great athlete.

A player can be so successful they make a Hall of Fame, but without good personal character, they won't make a true Hall of Praise. Being a great athlete takes being a successful athlete and a good person.

For most athletes who have made it, character was very important. So why do you sometimes observe pros who seem to exhibit bad character? In the majority of cases, I believe it is not that they made it without character, but that they *lost* their character after making it. Character is not something you learn once and own forever, but something you must work to preserve. However, some athletes, after making it, don't work as hard on their character as they did in striving to make it. They might let the perks of success (pride, adulation, money, celebrity, etc.) spoil the character they once had. But look what often happens: Those players' performance starts to slide, and young players coming up with unspoiled character take their spots away. In other cases, lapses of character lead players into off-ice trouble that may cost them their career or more. Preserving character is never easy, and never over. Everyone will make mistakes, but we must simply constantly strive to do our best.

EXPERTS' RECAP

Remember . . .

· Character = moral values + moral strength.
· Character is important to success and to being a good person.
· Don't fall for a storybook caricature of character.
· Phony character is a fake shortcut.

key components of character

SCOUTS' PREVIEW
In this chapter . . .
· The attributes of character
· The nine key character components
· "Character Combos"

FROM THE LAST CHAPTER, YOU MAY HAVE ALREADY GLEANED SOME HINTS ABOUT WHAT MAKES UP CHARACTER. THIS CHAPTER WILL TAKE YOU THROUGH PRECISELY WHAT CHARACTER CONSISTS OF, AND GIVE YOU A THOROUGH UNDERSTANDING OF THE CHARACTER ATTRIBUTES YOU ASPIRE TO ACQUIRE.

Bear in mind that since character consists of personal qualities, there are many adjectives we could use. Think of all the adjectives in the dictionary that describe people! If you've learned about character elsewhere, you may notice that different people or organizations prefer different words in describing character. But what they're getting at is still the same. The terms we've chosen are the ones we feel are most apt and useful for an aspiring athlete.

Also, try to get a sense of the whole picture of character, not just the parts. This will eventually make it easier for you to automatically respond to situations in a good character way.

In the list below, we will describe not only the attributes of character, but how a person with those attributes behaves. As you learned in Chapter 3, a quality must be reflected in a person's habitual behaviour in order to be *characteristic* of them. Character isn't just believing in the right qualities, but consistently acting in accord with them. We will also explain how each of the attributes below can help you make it in hockey.

The Key Components of Character

To help you make character a habit, we have arranged the components of character into an easy to remember form, for whenever you need it. The word "character" has nine letters and the following list has nine key character components. The first six components below all begin with the letter C, just like the word "character" itself. The last three components start with the letters P-R-I, which together form the beginning of the word "priority." To recall the attributes of character, memorize this sentence: "Character is my priority." It should be easy to recall the attributes that the Cs and P-R-I stand for.

1. **COMMITMENT:** Commitment is a decision to dedicate yourself to something that is important to you—in this case, your hockey career. It includes an ongoing, binding pledge to do whatever you can to see things through to a successful outcome. You will not settle for excuses. Being committed means working hard and doing your best. It means being deeply engaged in thought and emotion, and demonstrating dedication through action, including sacrifices when needed. A committed approach is one in which you take the pursuit of your dream seriously. It is a "sacred mission" that stays a pervasive and constant presence in your life. If a person is flaky, lazy, or half-hearted in their efforts, they are not committed. Commitment is crucial to excellence in sports. Without commitment, you would never be able to get yourself to do the many things required to make it. When you *are* committed, you do everything you can, do it your hardest, and do it your best—giving yourself the best chance to succeed. An example of commitment could be reading this book carefully and trying to learn every tip you can. It could be foregoing a trip to the mall with your friends in order to spend the time improving your shot in your garage.

2. **CONTROL:** The control we are referring to here is control over your emotions. If you don't control your emotions, your emotions will control you. They will not take you where you're trying to go; they will take you wherever they happen to feel like! You will be at their mercy, instead of having them at your service. Control means being disciplined about what you do, rather than being impulsive or only doing things you want to do. It means maintaining your composure, and not getting rattled or making rash decisions when faced with unsettling circumstances. Self-control prevents you from being self-destructive when you have such an urge. On the ice, control allows you to perform your best, and not get distracted by anxiety or sidetracked by anger. Off the ice, control allows you to keep to a schedule of what you need to do to improve—and get it done.

3. **CONSTRUCTIVENESS:** Constructiveness is the attitude of always trying to find the good in a situation or a way to make things better. Being constructive means having a positive attitude and being optimistic as opposed to pessimistic. It means being practical about how things might be improved upon in the future, rather than stubborn about who was right or wrong in the past. With a constructive attitude, you can make the best out of any situation. You can be resilient after a failure, instead of trapped

by unhelpful self-criticism. A constructive focus means being creative in finding new ways to solve a problem, rather than obstinate about why what *should* be working isn't. If you make a mistake on the ice and the other team scores, constructiveness can help you learn from your mistake and become a better player, instead of getting down on yourself and making things worse. If you have hours of homework to do at night plus hockey practice, being constructive can help you find a solution instead of focusing on the problem and complaining. (For example, try doing all the reading parts of your homework on the way to and from school and practice, and save the written part for when you are home.)

4. **CO-OPERATION:** Co-operation means working with others for the benefit of all. It means realizing you can't always do everything alone, and that sometimes two heads are better than one. It means being a team player and buying into your team concept, not being out for yourself or "on your own page." It means appreciating the value others can bring to a cause, rather than excluding them and losing out on what they can offer. Co-operation can mean agreeing to a compromise for everyone's sake, rather than perpetuating a conflict. Co-operation might involve agreeing to help your parents with chores on a day off, so they have time to take you to games and assist with your training. Co-operation could mean passing to your open teammate on a 2-on-1 and getting an assist when they score, instead of trying to score yourself and taking a low-percentage shot that gets blocked.

5. **CONSIDERATION:** Consideration is thinking and caring about people other than yourself, and not being overly self-centred. A considerate person is a thoughtful person. You understand that others are in many ways just like you, and therefore you treat them the same way you treat yourself. You realize they will have a chance to decide how they treat you and thus you treat them the way you would want to be treated back. Consideration includes having respect for others, even opponents. It includes being compassionate, not cruel. It includes being generous and giving of yourself, not being selfish and unduly demanding. On the ice, consideration could mean you don't hit a player from behind, even if the referee isn't watching. Maybe on another shift, an opponent will have the same chance to hit you, and hold up because you were considerate of their

teammate. Off the ice, consideration could mean you lend a spare stick to a teammate who broke theirs, and end up developing a friendship that has tremendous value to you over your career and life.

6. **COURAGE:** Courage is doing what is necessary even when you know it will be difficult, painful, or scary. It doesn't mean having no fear; it means doing what you need to do, even when you're afraid. It doesn't mean never getting weary; it means getting to the finish line even when you're tired. It doesn't mean never suffering; it means doing what's right even when it hurts. A courageous person is the opposite of a coward. A courageous person carries on whether circumstances are easy or not, and is tough enough to take whatever is thrown at them without abandoning their goals or their principles. Courage can mean that when other teams use intimidation tactics to knock you off your game, you keep playing— keep playing your game, and beating them on the scoreboard. Courage means that even though you are tired and bruised, you still go to practice and practice hard, earning the respect of teammates and coaches.

7. **PERSEVERANCE:** Perseverance is staying power. It includes the stamina to keep going over the long quest to reach your dream. It includes the determination to succeed and the willpower to face any adversity and not let it stop you. Perseverance is the tenacity to keep going, even when you are discouraged or things look bleak. A person who perseveres is the opposite of a quitter. Perseverance could mean taking a test over and over until you score high enough to qualify for a college scholarship. Perseverance could mean that after being cut by a team, you keep improving your game, and you make it the following year.

8. **RESPONSIBILITY:** Responsibility is holding yourself accountable for what you should do. It is caring about results, and not being satisfied with having someone to blame if things don't go well. Responsibility is being reliable for a team or others who are depending on you. When you're responsible, others develop trust in you and look to you for leadership. You take initiative, both in your own life and wherever you are counted on as a leader. Responsibility could include refusing to join friends engaging in off-ice trouble that could jeopardize your career. Responsibility includes making sure you are ready to play every shift of every game, so that your coach comes to appreciate your reliability and look to you as a team leader.

While teamwork is a big part of hockey, equally important to learn in order to accomplish any personal goal is self-reliance. Family, friends, coaches, and teachers can all help in important ways and every player who ever made it will point to several people who helped them get there. But no matter how much they might want to help, nobody can make it for you. There will be lots of times when you will need to count on yourself to do what needs to be done.

9. **INTEGRITY**: Integrity is telling the truth and doing what is right. A person with integrity plays by the rules and doesn't cheat to get ahead. A person with integrity is honest and doesn't resort to lying in order to get what they want or avoid facing the negative consequences of their own mistakes or misconduct. A person with integrity says what they mean, and does what they say. Their word is their bond. Integrity includes being fair in what you do, and not silently going along with any other injustice taking place. It means doing what's right, and making no exceptions. If your friends find a copy of an upcoming exam in your teacher's desk and intend to steal it, you could show integrity by trying to convince them not to. Or suppose you've already committed to play for one team, when another team offers you a better deal. If you go back on your word, you may acquire a reputation as someone who can't be trusted. On the other hand, if you have the integrity to be upfront and ask the first team for their consent, they may let you go as a courtesy, or work out a deal to let you play for the second team. If not, at least you've preserved a good reputation. And as you advance over a long hockey career, wherever you go, your good reputation will always precede you.

Character Combos

In your journey toward making it, you will encounter situations where you will need to apply not just one, but a combination of the above qualities. Let's say you are having a difficult season with a coach who often criticizes and benches you. As a result, you haven't played your best. How do you get through it and bounce back with a strong season the following year? To do it, you will have to draw upon a "character combo" of several attributes. It will take *control* to endure the criticism without talking back and being perceived as having a bad attitude. It will take *perseverance* to overcome discouragement caused by benchings, and to keep playing and doing your best. At season's end, it will be crucial that you take *responsibility* in recognizing it's your career at stake, and show initiative to change some circumstances that will allow you to succeed in the future. It will take *constructiveness* to identify what aspects of your game you can improve in that off-season, and *commitment* to making those improvements happen. A person of weak character might allow this adverse experience to damage their career or defeat them. A person of strong character will use it to motivate them to do better than they've ever done before. As the saying goes, "When the going gets tough, the tough get going."

You have probably heard from hockey leagues, officials, coaches, and others about the importance of demonstrating good sportsmanship in the way you play. Sportsmanship is itself another character combo. Sportsmanship means that although you want to win very badly—as all passionate athletes

---

PRO-file

Paul Henderson

In 1972, Paul Henderson scored "the goal heard 'round the world" in the dying seconds to snatch victory from defeat for Canada over the Soviet Union in the fabled Summit Series. A momentous event in Canadian history, the series was a contest in hockey, Canada's most defining cultural possession, against an opponent that defined Communism, the arch-enemy of the democratic political systems espoused by Canada and the United States. Every Canadian was deeply emotionally involved in the series. Down in the series, Canada would have to win the last three games, all on Soviet ice in a scary and hostile environment, to win the series. The players were under higher-stakes pressure than any hockey players ever before or since. Paul Henderson, an unlikely hero, scored the winning goals *in all three of the final games* as Canada successfully pulled off the improbable comeback. His performance in that series was an incredible display of character under fire. Al-

though he has long since retired, I have had the privilege of knowing Henderson off the ice and seeing first-hand his true and genuine personal character. As Don Cherry of *Hockey Night in Canada* said of Henderson, "You couldn't find a better role model. … There's not many around like him."

do—you will not lower yourself to trying to win at-all-costs. And that's based on your character. It involves having the *integrity* to play by the rules, and not resort to cheating in order to win. It involves having the *control* over your emotions to not hurt others, even if you are frustrated or provoked. When a game is over, character is what makes you a good sport. If you lost, it means being a good loser by taking *responsibility* and not complaining, making excuses, or blaming others. If you won, it means being a good winner by being *considerate* of defeated rivals, and not being arrogant, or bragging, or taunting them.

Countless other situations in your quest will require a combination of several character components. These personal attributes will be called upon constantly as you strive toward your dream. The way to meet that challenge is to know the character qualities called for, and have those qualities solidly in your possession whenever they may be needed.

But you can't buy character qualities off a store shelf. They must be developed and reinforced through experience, before they become characteristic of you. The next chapter will teach you how to use experience to build and maintain your character.

EXPERTS' RECAP

Remember . . .

- "Character" has nine letters, and nine key attributes.
- The phrase "Character is my priority" can help you recall the character attributes through their first letter (six start with C, and one each start with P-R-I).

how to acquire and preserve character

SCOUTS' PREVIEW
In this chapter . . .
· The secret to how and when character can be developed
· Traditions, real-life situations, and your environment
· Role models and how they influence you
· Exercises for building character

YOU KNOW CHARACTER MATTERS, AND YOU KNOW WHAT IT IS AND ISN'T. BUT HOW DO YOU ACQUIRE IT?

It's not as simple as learning a skill. Skills are just techniques you use, but character is a set of qualities that define your very person. And if you obtain these qualities, how do you keep them?

Once you learn a skill, you own it for the rest of your life. Personal qualities, on the other hand, can change. Over time or in response to pressures, qualities that once helped define a person's character can fade or be lost.

Developing character can *seem* like a monumental task. How can you possibly do all it requires in just a portion of the time you have available for hockey?

Luckily, you don't have to.

Unlike hockey skills such as skating, stickhandling, and shooting, the personal qualities that make up character are used throughout the rest of your life. You use them in dealing with family, school, jobs, and many other things. As a result, you can "practice" and develop your character not only through hockey but in your life outside of hockey.

In fact, "the rest of your life" not only *can* develop personal qualities that characterize you, it *will*. Your life is filled with situations in which you must choose how to react. You can respond to those situations either in line with the character attributes you've learned about, or in the opposite way. The way you typically respond helps define the qualities that characterize you. But it also helps develop those qualities. Each time you react a certain way, you condition that response to become more habitual; it becomes something you automatically repeat when dealing with future situations. And once your way of reacting becomes a habit, it defines your character. If your habit is to respond the right way, you will have developed good character. If your habit is to respond the wrong way, you will have developed bad character. Nearly *every* life experience can influence your character, strengthening or weakening it, based on the reaction you choose.

So the secret to how you develop character is hardly a secret at all! It happens on its own, through the way you handle every situation you encounter: big things, small things, extraordinary things, and ordinary things. Each time you handle one of them in a character way, your character grows. But certain kinds of experience can indeed be particularly relevant to developing character.

Traditions

Being part of a formal *tradition* can impart character. The most obvious case is a family tradition, in which parents raise their children to learn the character values held by their family. Likewise, cultural traditions can pass on a nation's or community's character values to youngsters. The world's great religious and spiritual traditions also include specific moral codes or personal guidelines to teach character. From traditions such as these, you can learn values, exercise them in action, and receive reinforcement from others who are part of the tradition. One benefit of these traditions is that they can begin teaching character early, even before a child has to decide to try to learn it. Being immersed in traditions also allows for rapid learning. As an added bonus, traditions can provide a rationale for why character is important, separate from its importance in sports. This gives character deeper roots for times of challenge.

By definition, a tradition has a history, so it should provide a means of developing character that is tested and true. At the same time, traditions are not always perfect or complete teachers of character, and not everyone has the same opportunity to learn character through traditions.

Real-Life Situations

A natural inclination toward character is already inside us. Every language on Earth has words for "right" and "wrong," which means every culture on Earth has a moral code. Character must therefore be a part of human nature. In other words, you don't create it as much as bring it out of yourself.

This can be done through *real-life situations*, everything you might face in the normal daily course of living. Because these activities and experiences make up your whole life, they offer countless chances to build character, *if* you respond the right way. They also have the benefit of not taking time away from pursuing your dream. And nothing makes as strong an impression as a lesson learned from what happens in real life. All of this makes real-life situations an ideal way to build character.

For example, suppose you accidentally knock over a glass and it shatters on the floor. Although you may be angry, if you stop yourself from cursing, you can develop *control*. By promptly seeking help to clean up the broken glass before anyone steps in it, you would be exercising *responsibility* and *consideration*. By moving other glasses to a place where they won't be knocked over as well, you are practicing *constructiveness*. From this common little situation came many opportunities to develop good character.

Everything can affect your character, but high-stakes situations have greater impacts. For example, suppose what you knocked over and broke was a priceless antique vase, and that you were fooling around when you did it, but nobody saw it happen. The owner will likely be quite upset to learn what happened to their precious vase! You might be tempted to discard and hide the broken pieces and wait for the owner to eventually notice the vase missing. When they ask if anybody knows where it went, you might be tempted to keep silent, or lie and say you broke it innocently, rather than admit you broke it by fooling around. But responding in any of those ways would significantly damage your character. And that would come back to haunt you when, in your hockey quest or in life, you need to call upon those character qualities you damaged. On the other hand, if you show the courage, integrity, and responsibility to approach the owner and tell them the truth about what happened, they might still be angry at losing the vase, but they'll admire the way you responded afterward. And later, when a challenge inside or outside of hockey calls upon your character, it will be much stronger than before. Facing tough situations is never easy, but it is the way you react to these situations that matters most in forming your character.

Helen Keller, who despite deafness and blindness became a world-famous author, activist, and example of character, said this: "Character cannot be developed in ease and quiet. Only through experiences of trial and suffering can the soul be strengthened, vision cleared, ambition inspired, and success achieved."

Your Environment

Another area of experience that can have a strong influence on the personal qualities you acquire is your *environment*. You can do much to foster and support the development of your character by managing the environment in which you dwell. No one completely controls their environment, but you do have control over parts of it, and you can use these parts to have the most positive impact possible on your character. Like real-life situations, your environment is something you're in at all times and that can develop your character without using up any time you've allocated to chasing your dream. In fact, you can think of your environment as *real-life surroundings*.

This includes your social surroundings. Part of the social surroundings you control are the friends you choose. Having friends of good character rubs good character off on you, whereas choosing friends who may be entertaining but are ultimately people of poor character will have the opposite influence. Likewise, people often join communities such as clubs and associations. Choosing ones where you perceive a positive character in the way the group members conduct themselves will positively impact your character. Another part of your social environment is the neighbourhood in which you live. Each neighbourhood comes with its own set of potential environmental influences. You will want to be aware of these potential influences, and be vigilant at thwarting the negative ones. Aside from the examples above, you will have countless interactions with other people for various purposes. It often won't be possible to decide your social surroundings, but it always will be possible to remain aware of them, and to manage how you let them influence your character.

Real-life surroundings also include your mental surroundings. Your mental environment consists of everything that enters your awareness. In the same way that food entering your stomach can impact the shape and strength of your body, what enters your mind is like "mental food" that can impact the shape and strength of your character. Again, you can't control all of that, but you can control major portions, such as: what you choose to read, what you watch on TV, and what activities you occupy your mind with. Pick ones that reflect good qualities, as these will influence your character positively.

Role Models

A special case within your mental environment is *role models*. A role model is someone you admire and are inspired to emulate. It could be somebody you don't personally know, but learn about and follow in the media. Or it could be somebody you do know, perhaps a relative or acquaintance. You could have more than one role model. When you have a role model, you think about them often, watch them closely, and imagine being like them. This makes them a very important part of your mental environment. Through the process of observation and emulation, you will keenly notice and naturally imitate the qualities they exhibit. Sometimes this can even happen unintentionally. Because of the special place they occupy in your mind, role models have great influence over you. If your role model exhibits poor personal qualities, this can have a serious detrimental impact on your character. If your role model's personal qualities are good, the influence on your character can be wonderful. This makes it important to choose role models carefully, and to pick *character role models*—people whom you don't just admire for their success or style, but for their highest standards of personal conduct, both in public and in private. If you know them or have a chance to meet them, don't be afraid to ask them for advice on developing character like theirs, or ask how to deal with a challenge you are facing that is unfamiliar, or especially difficult or complicated.

· Pick character role models. Beware of flashy choices that are all style and no substance.

heads up!

Exercises That Can Help Build Character

You can also hone your character through *character-building exercises*. These are situations in which you deliberately place yourself for the purpose of developing character. Unlike the other methods above, exercises *do* take time away from other things. Since you have only so much time, and lots to do to reach your dream, you should limit the time you spend on these exercises. This method of character-building should be only a supplement to the others above, not a replacement.

---

the inside story

My brother Dominic joined the New York Rangers as a rookie in 2005. The Rangers had missed the play-offs seven seasons in a row, and many expert analysts predicted they would finish the upcoming season last overall.

The Rangers had other plans, including a new approach. As part of Training Camp, the team went to the famous United States military base West Point for a character-building exercise. The players were placed in situations that were difficult and even seemed impossible, at first. The purpose was to test the players' mettle and see how they would respond. Coaches and management were on hand to witness the events. One of the most difficult tasks was for groups of eight players to push a massive military vehicle called a Hummer up a long, steep hill.

Dominic's group tried different formations and strategies, and it seemed there was no way to even budge it. Finally they found a formation where, in total unison, they managed to get the monster moving. That was the easy part. Once it was moving, they had to keep it moving all the way up the hill, or, the moment they stopped, it would roll back down to where they started. Through initiative, teamwork, a constructive search for a good strategy, and extreme exertion, they finally got the Hummer to the top of the hill. It was then they found out they had accomplished the task in West Point record-time. This exercise wasn't just a novel experience and a difficult challenge for Dominic and his teammates, but one that built character and confidence. The Rangers would make the playoffs for the first time in eight years.

Yet, even with exercises, you are still developing character in the process of doing other things. That's because the activities can have their own purpose and benefits, even though *your* purpose for doing them is to build character. For example, you may choose to go to a wilderness camp that is designed to develop character. At the same time, however, you will be getting physical exercise, learning canoeing and camping skills, and developing an appreciation of nature. Other potential exercises could be:

- completing character-instruction programs in schools,
- reading biographies of people who are great role models of character,
- doing volunteer work with charity organizations; or
- joining the Boy or Girl Scouts or similar groups, which have often been cited by people as having been instrumental in forming their character.

These aren't the only exercises you can do. You can design your own to suit your needs and preferences. But with any exercise, if you don't at least put commitment into it, you won't gain any other character attributes from it. Even if the activity itself seems boring, strange, or unimportant, remember that your purpose is to develop character, and that is extremely worthwhile.

Whatever combination of methods you employ to build character, always keep striving to improve yourself. There is never a time when you are finished, and can rest on your laurels—except maybe when you are asleep! Each new situation or potential influence will always either lead to a step forward or a step back for your character, depending on how you react. On the path to making it, you will face different types of character tests: adversity, prosperity, temptations, and threats can all pose challenges. The character you have at the moment of each test will help shape your response, and the response will help shape your future. Like the physical strength of your muscles, the moral strength of your character must progressively increase to handle greater trials as you get closer to the top. You never know how—or how much—your character will be tested, so the surest way to pass is simply to have developed your character as much as possible. If all of this sounds difficult, just remember: you can build unbreakable character merely through choosing the right responses in the everyday situations you face.

> jock talk
>
> " The character you want to develop will help you beyond hockey; it will serve you well in your life's experiences. "
> —STEVE MOORE, COLORADO AVALANCHE

The above methods will help you acquire and preserve character, which will help you in hockey. Plus, pursuing your dream in a character manner means that no matter the outcome, you can count on being able to look in the mirror and be tremendously proud of the person you see.

EXPERTS' RECAP

Remember . . .

· Every choice you make not only reflects your current character, it affects your future character.
· Real-life situations, formal traditions, and your mental and physical surroundings can all shape your character.
· Choose role models based not just on success and style, but on character above all.

3

ARE YOU READY?
a solid foundation for sports

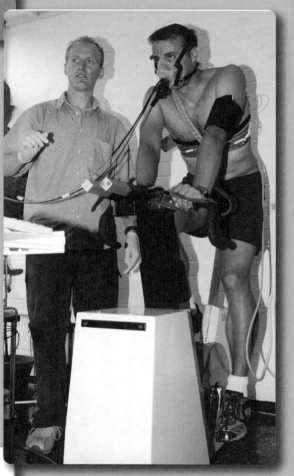

Good health is an essential part of the foundation you need to play.

THIS SECTION TEACHES YOU HOW TO LAY THE FOUNDATION FOR A TOWER THAT CAN REACH THE SKY.

Chapter 6: good health and balance

Chapter 7: avoiding pitfalls

Chapter 8: support, supplies, and equipment

"The loftiest edifices need the deepest foundations."

GEORGE SANTAYANA, HISPANIC/AMERICAN PHILOSOPHER

good health and balance

SCOUTS' PREVIEW
In this chapter . . .
- Why health is critical to your foundation
- Maintaining your medical, physical, mental, and personal health

WHEN WORK TO BUILD A TOWER BEGINS, IT IS THE FOUNDATION THAT IS CREATED FIRST. THE REST OF THE TOWER SITS ATOP THE FOUNDATION, SO THE FOUNDATION ITSELF MUST BE STABLE AND STRONG. PRESSURES WILL BEAR UPON THE TOWER AND WITHOUT A SOLID FOUNDATION, IT MAY COLLAPSE. THE TALLER THE TOWER, THE BROADER AND DEEPER THE FOUNDATION NEEDED.

Think of your game like a tower. There are a lot of different elements that go into it and each of these must be fit together securely to provide you with a strong foundation. Your foundation is that which needs to be in place before you play, practice, train, and compete.

This foundation starts with your health.

You may have heard the saying, "The most important thing to have is your health." The saying is true; without health, it's hard to have much else. That makes comprehensive good health the first, most basic layer of the foundation upon which your game should be built.

Without a strong foundation of health, many things could go wrong in striving to build your game. It may not be safe for you to play and train. It could be unduly difficult, or you might be prevented from playing effectively. You could be vulnerable to frequent injury. You may be on a track that leads to mental burnout. Or you may feel so off-balance as a person that you just can't continue on your quest.

On the other hand, with a healthy foundation in place, your game draws strength and resiliency from it. A clean bill of health can give you peace of mind and confidence to push yourself in play and training. Having your health properly taken care of can remove a limitation you may not have even known was there, allowing you to take your game to new heights. Good health can give you a head start in training and a high level of energy that you are able to sustain. A healthy foundation also helps you maintain a sense of personal balance to stay on track during the long trek to reaching your dream.

The Four Components of a Healthy Foundation

To provide the most expert health advice from an aspiring athlete's perspective, we sought the advice of sports medicine expert Dr. Anthony Galea of the Institute of Sports Medicine in Toronto. Dr. Galea has helped numerous NHLers and pros, collegiate athletes, Olympians, and other athletes start their athletic careers right and keep them underpinned by good health. There are four components of the healthy foundation you want in place for building your game.

MEDICAL HEALTH: Taking care of your health starts with regular checkups by a medical doctor. According to Dr. Galea, "It's a good idea for anyone who's going to be playing a sport to undergo a prior examination by their family doctor and pass a physical. With younger children or less intense sport regimens, this could be part of their general annual physical with their family doctor. For more advanced or intense athletic regimens, the screening should be a more detailed pre-participation screening exam. The reason to see a doctor before playing is to check out the heart, lungs, do a musculoskeletal exam, and identify any potential issues that need to be addressed or that may predispose them to injury or other health complications; for example, asthma, heart murmurs, or a joint problem. From a medical perspective, it would also be appropriate to follow up with their doctor at least once within the year. If you don't feel well or feel hurt, get it checked, make sure it's nothing to worry about. And don't wait and do nothing. Doing nothing is the

the inside story

Last winter, I was working one-on-one with a player whose father asked me to help improve a number of deficiencies in his son's game. The boy was an extremely good listener and a quick learner. After I explained how to perform a skill and demonstrated it, the boy would try, and get the hang of it very quickly. But as I asked him to repeat so it would "sink in" and stick, all of a sudden after a few repetitions his technique would fall apart. Skill after skill we worked on, the same thing happened. After a couple more sessions, I said to the boy's father, who was watching, "There must be an issue with your son's conditioning. He is getting abnormally tired, and that's when his technique falls apart." The father was at a loss, because the boy got plenty of exercise. The next time we worked together, the father said he had been to the doctor, and it turned out the son had asthma. The doctor gave him an inhaler. We went out and did our drills, and this time the technique remained perfect from the first repetition to the last.

worst thing. You have to be proactive and get it looked at, and if necessary, treat it, rehab it, and have the doctor and a trained physiotherapist help you keep fit while it gets better."

PHYSICAL HEALTH: While specific medical issues may require the help of a doctor, staying in general good physical health is usually within your power. Dr. Galea explains: "It's important to keep fit. The exercise you're getting just by participating in hockey will help, but it's sometimes also good to cross-train by playing other sports. This can give you a broader base of fitness and make you healthier overall. Other types of exercise include swimming, cycling, jogging, participating in school sports, and playing lacrosse in the summers, etc. You also need sleep and downtime to give your muscles time to acclimatize to the strain you're putting on them, and to recover. Sleep is especially important when you're still growing. Nutrition is important too. There are no nutrients in junk food that will help you recover and build on the exercise you're doing. Stay away from candy, chips, soft drinks, pastries, doughnuts, anything rich in sugar or high in fat. They can be tough to resist, but it's worth it. Choose healthy foods like chicken, turkey, pasta, and vegetables that can give you essential protein, complex carbohydrates, and vitamins and minerals. If you need something quick, instead of a chocolate bar or a candy bar, pick a good protein bar or meal-replacement bar. And of course, avoid smoking and street drugs. There is simply nothing worse for your health."

the inside story

My mother was a swim coach, and so even before I started playing rep hockey, I swam for my neighbourhood and regional swim teams. Swimming is a great exercise for general strength and conditioning of your whole body. When I first started rep hockey, most of the other kids didn't have the strength to shoot the puck very hard. Meanwhile, regularly I would shoot pucks in and out of the net so hard that unexpecting referees would think the puck couldn't have gone in at all, and allow play to continue. My coaches and parents would just shake their heads! A few times, when we went to tournaments, unfamiliar coaches and parents would see me fire pucks in the top corners while the other players could barely raise the puck, and allege that I must be over-age. Afterward, tournament officials would come to investigate, and see me in the dressing room with relatively big muscles compared to the other kids, who at that age, didn't yet have much. This made them "certain" that I was over-age, so they would angrily confront my coach, and demand to see my birth certificate! I wasn't over-age. And I wasn't superhuman. I just had a much stronger base of physical health for hockey than the other kids—from swimming so much.

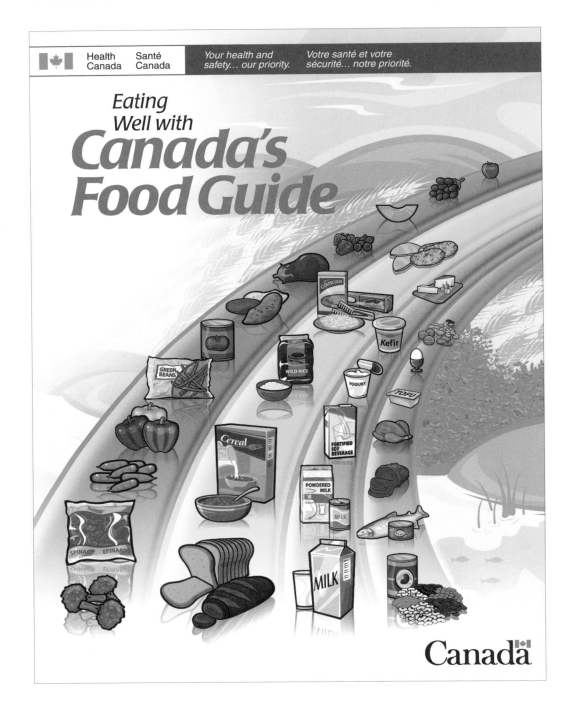

MENTAL HEALTH: Besides physical health, good mental health is equally important. The sense of purpose and inspiration you get from your dream will help keep your spirits up. Good character will help you maintain the best attitude for dealing with any adverse experiences. But here are some further tips from Dr. Galea: "Don't put too much pressure on yourself in hockey. There's probably enough pressure already, and you don't want to get to the point where you forget what it is just to play. If you're playing a lot of hockey, make sure to keep the hockey fun. Have some other hobbies that can take you away and give you a mental break from hockey when you need one. In terms of activities you spend a lot of time on, choose ones where you're doing things with friends and that are interactive, rather than ones that are passive or isolated that may cause you to withdraw. On the other hand, sometimes you can get overloaded with all the inputs and messages from the multimedia in our society—phone calls, text messages, email, advertising, and various activities. If you feel like your ability to focus is being sapped or you have no private space, it might be a time to turn those things off and get away, and spend some time in nature or in the countryside. For example, you could go on a hike with a group of friends, or just go to a nearby park. Also make sure your environment is positive and supportive. If there is a bully on your team or at school, or someone that is making you feel uncomfortable, that person may need to be confronted. Talk to your parents, and seek any appropriate help from authorities. If something is bothering you, make sure you talk about it with somebody who cares about you. You can't just suppress it and hide it, because then it only builds up even worse."

PERSONAL HEALTH: The last area of health needed for your foundation is personal health. By nature, there are several dimensions to what we are as human beings. We are creatures, first of all. And we aren't just any creatures, but ones with highly developed minds and powerful emotions. We also aren't solitary beings; our nature involves the need to interact with others. Everyone has these sides to them. In order for us to be healthy and happy people, we have to take care of the needs we have corresponding to each. If we ignore a dimension, our health and happiness as people will suffer, and our foundation for success can be weakened or broken.

For example, imagine a girl named Isola who enjoys time alone because it allows her to focus on her goals and work toward them without distraction.

This is fine, as long as Isola doesn't take it to the extreme, where she deprives herself of a sense of support and love from family, a chance to express herself with friends, and the opportunity to learn from others. Without all that, she is missing a great deal that can enrich her life and assist her aims. Neglecting the social side of her nature as a human being could cause a gap in Isola's foundation for success.

Becoming Well-Rounded

Good personal health requires us to maintain a *balance of activities* covering the different sides of our nature, within our regular life routine. If we do this, we are *well-rounded individuals*, with a foundation of health, happiness, strength, resilience, and versatility that's ideal for enabling success.

So what are the different dimensions? There are *six sides to our nature* as people. Think of them like the six faces of a cube.

1. **INTELLECTUAL SIDE:** Humans are very intelligent creatures. Your mind needs to be exercised through stimulating intellectual activities such as school, reading, mental puzzles, or learning new things. Look for opportunities to develop your critical thinking and problem-solving abilities. Your mind also has a capacity to become a powerful tool to help you succeed and find happiness. Include activities in your routine designed to help you understand yourself and your world better, and the processes that lead to success and happiness. Doing so leads to your growth or *personal development*.

2. **CREATIVE SIDE:** Everyone has an inner urge to be creative. You express creativity through the choices you make, and you can express it through the way you play hockey. It's also good, however, to include activities in your routine that are specifically designed to encourage the self-expression of your creative impulse. These might include art (music, sketching, painting, poetry, graphics, etc.), creative writing, and projects or special events you undertake. When done safely, additional creative activities can include imaginative play for younger children, and for older ones, coming up with little inventions or innovations.

3. **EMOTIONAL SIDE:** Also important is your emotional side. Our minds act to bring us positive emotions. Negative emotions like fear and anger can serve a helpful purpose too, if they mobilize us into action that will bring greater happiness in the future. But driving yourself too hard with too

many of them, or simply allowing them to dominate your emotional life, can sap the energy you need to succeed. Pay attention to your emotions, and strive to keep them in a healthy balance. Don't allow yourself to feel so satisfied that you stop striving toward your goals. But at the same time, incorporate appropriate activities in your routine to balance the emotional drag of the unpleasant things you have to do. This could include simple, fun activities (playing a game, watching a comedy, going to an amusement park, etc.); it also includes a regular dose of inspiration (by reading, watching, or experiencing whatever it is that inspires you).

4. **PHYSICAL SIDE:** Humans are not meant to be couch potatoes. Luckily, as a hockey player, you have picked an activity that covers a tremendous part of your physical side. Young people, however, naturally need a great deal of physical activity in their life. Unless you are on the ice multiple hours a day, every day of the week, you may still not be getting enough physical exercise. Playing that much formal hockey is not the solution either. You need to add variety to your physical activities. When you are younger, variety can help stimulate and develop your physical nature the most broadly. It's true that high-level sports require specialization, but a broad athletic base must be in place first. So at younger ages, outside of hockey, choose play and recreation activities that have a physical component. And at older ages, include cross-training and hobbies that have a physical component, such as:

- other sports such as soccer, basketball, swimming, cycling, jogging, road hockey, racquet sports, etc.
- outdoor activities like hiking, canoeing, and camping
- activities that exercise your dexterity such as table tennis, juggling, playing catch with a ball, Frisbee, or manually constructing things

5. **SOCIAL SIDE:** Be sure to spend time with family and loved ones who share an intimate bond with you. Develop friendships with people you respect, can be yourself around, and make you feel understood and appreciated. Join clubs, associations, or other groups that give you both a sense of belonging and a positive purpose. And seek to interact with teachers, coaches, and others who inspire you and can help you reach your potential.

6. **SPIRITUAL SIDE:** Your spiritual side is the part of you that seeks to understand life and make sense of it. Whether your spiritual sense comes from a

religious tradition, a feeling of connection to nature, or other personal beliefs, it's important to tend to this side of you. That includes allowing time for whatever activities you may pursue related to it.

Especially when you are younger, a broad spectrum of activities and experiences *within* each dimension can help you discover where, within each dimension, your interests and talents lie. This allows you to gradually develop hobbies or areas of special interest outside of hockey. When you are older, you may often choose activities related to those, within each dimension. Your activity choices can also be guided by an overarching focus you have in mind at any given time. For example, at some point you may pick intellectual, creative, and social activities that will help you work toward a potential future fallback career, as you will learn about in Chapter 28.

ask the AUTHOR-ity

To stay balanced, within what time frame should I aim to do activities for each of my different dimensions?
Try to include activities covering each side of you at least once a week.

How can I remember the different dimensions?
You may have heard the saying "variety is the spice of life." The first letter of each of the six dimensions together spells "spices." Remember the saying above, and then recall which of the six sides of "the cube of you" each letter of the word "spices" stands for.

EXPERTS' RECAP
Remember . . .
· You must be in good health before you can play and excel at hockey.
· Have your medical health properly monitored by your doctor.
· Preserve good physical and mental health by remaining physically and mentally active.
· Maintain your personal health through a balance of activities that keeps you well-rounded.
· The phrase "Variety is the spice of life" can help you recall "the six sides of the cube of you" (they start with the first letters of the word S-P-I-C-E-S).

avoiding pitfalls

SCOUTS' PREVIEW
In this chapter . . .
· The hidden peril of pitfalls
· A simple method for spotting pitfalls
· Managing your time and attention
· Other common pitfalls and how to avoid them

IN ADDITION TO GOOD HEALTH, ANOTHER IMPORTANT ELEMENT OF YOUR FOUNDATION IN PURSUING AN ATHLETIC CAREER IS YOUR ABILITY TO SPOT AND AVOID PITFALLS.

Pitfalls are traps that can ensnare people who fail to recognize them. First your attention is caught by something that seems appealing or intriguing. Then the ground gives way beneath you, and you wind up in the trap.

Most of the pitfalls you will read about in this chapter are not tied exclusively to sports, and many could in fact more readily capture a non-athlete than a committed athlete. The issue is simply that in the competitive world of sports, an athlete with a dream can ill-afford to be caught in a needless pitfall.

Cheating, using drugs, not knowing your priorities, and associating with the wrong people are just a few examples of pitfalls that can hurt hockey careers. A list like that can make it seem obvious that such things should be avoided, and make it seem simple to do so. Yet pitfalls such as these and others somehow claim countless careers. Every pro player could probably tell you of several people they knew who had what it took to make it, but got caught in pitfalls. The reason it happens so frequently is that the danger isn't always obvious until it's too late, but the appeal is up front and clear from the beginning.

Spotting Pitfalls

The foundation you build your ambition upon should include an ability to spot potential pitfalls and steer clear of them. But how can you do this?

The easiest way to avoid pitfalls is not to be lured in by whatever attractive or interesting angle they present. As you read in Chapter 1, having a dream gives focus to your actions. When younger, you can often decide a course of action by answering one straightforward question: "Will the proposed course take me closer to my dream, or not?" If the answer is "no," then you can dismiss it as a distraction, no matter how appealing or intriguing it may seem. When older, certain propositions that may seem good might be worth a few additional questions, as you will learn in Chapter 29. But if answering those questions still leads to a thumbs-down, you can again dismiss the idea. These questions alone should help you avoid many potential pitfalls.

If the answer to the questions above was thumbs-up, you must ask yourself another question: "Does the proposed action fit with the character attributes I've learned I need?" If the answer is "no," dismiss the idea. Even if it seems like the action may bring you a step closer to making it, it's not worth sacrificing your character. Besides, in the long run, any action that negatively impacts your character will not take you closer to where you need to be, regardless of how it may seem in the moment. This additional question should help you avoid even more potential pitfalls.

If the action *will* take you toward your dream, and *does* fit with your character, then by all means feel free to do it! It is not a pitfall, but a legitimate opportunity to move in the right direction.

Managing Your Time and Attention

You might have glimpsed above the importance of managing your time and attention. *Mismanagement of time and attention* is in fact a pitfall, and by far the most common in preventing the realization of ambitions.

You only have so much time—in each day, each week, each month, and each year. A big chunk of that time is spent simply sleeping and eating. Then comes family, school, and other obligations, taking up a whole lot more of your time. All of the requirements for reaching your dream must come out of what's left. As you can see, if you intend to make it, you must devote a large proportion of your free time to it—especially as you get older and are competing at higher levels. This means that there is not a huge amount of free time left for things unrelated to your dream. You simply can't do everything. While you might enjoy other activities from time to time, they don't compare with the passion you feel for pursuing your dream. And to succeed in your desired area, you must make sacrifices in others.

Similar circumstances apply with regards to your attention. Your attention consists of what you occupy your mind with. Attention exists only while you are awake, and much of it is preoccupied with fulfilling your obligations.

As with your free time, much of the free attention you have left must be devoted to the pursuit of your dream. There is not a massive amount of attention you can spare to let drift, or apply to random topics that are intriguing but unrelated to your dream. To succeed, you must focus your attention where it is needed.

The way to recognize the pitfall of mismanagement of time and attention is to notice when you find your mind wandering, or wondering: "What do I feel like doing right now?" In merely asking that question, you are mismanaging your attention. And if you use the answer to decide what to do, you will mismanage your time as well. When you hear the question in your head, it seems reasonable and doesn't readily set off alarms, which is what makes it such a common pitfall. The problem is, we are meant to use thoughts to shape our feelings. So if your thoughts are asking your feelings what to do, your attention is not doing its job. It is missing in action! Without guidance from thoughts, your feelings at a given moment could be just about anything. And if you frequently decide what to do based on them, your actions will be all over the place, rather than in line with your aims. If you use the question above to routinely decide what to do, your chances of making it are almost nil.

Setting Priorities

Avoiding the pitfall of mismanagement of time and attention is so important, and such a widespread need, that specific systems and tools are designed and used to help with it. The simplest of these is to set *priorities*. Priorities are a ranking of the most important areas for your time and attention. They are dictated by your obligations and life aims. An example of a person's priorities might be:

1. health (including balance of activities for personal health)
2. family, faith, or other obligations
3. schoolwork
4. hockey
5. hobbies
6. leisure activities

You can create and maintain your own personal sports-related schedule at www. sportsmaster.TV. Plot your official games and practices, your other life commitments and obligations, and then plan when you can fit in the personal hockey training initiatives you'd like to do.

Priorities are then used along with the goals and objectives you learned about in Chapter 1 to create a *schedule*. Your schedule plots out what you will do and when, in order to give sufficient attention to your priorities and progress toward reaching your objectives and goals. Many people use tools such as computer-based, electronic-based, or paper-based organizers to facilitate creating and following their schedule. Following your schedule allows you to take care of your obligations, and advance toward your goals. It helps you know when you have done so, and when you can plan some break-time to devote to something else. Sometimes it happens that we lose our schedule or for whatever reason end up knocked off of it. In those cases, you can help manage your time and attention by asking yourself the question, "What do I need to do right now to realize my aims?" This redirects your attention to your obligations and ambitions. And the answer that comes to mind will be one that allows you to make good use of your precious time.

The methods above don't just prevent the pitfall of time and attention mismanagement, but can help you avoid many other pitfalls as well. When you are focused and occupied with obligations and aspirations, you simply don't have a lot of extra free time and attention for other propositions—including those that turn out to be pitfalls.

Common Pitfalls and How to Avoid Them

While clear priorities and good time and attention management can help you avoid many pitfalls, it is still helpful to learn about some of the pitfalls that have adversely affected athletes before you. Understanding the threat they pose, and knowing what to watch for, can help you avoid them.

ADDICTION: Addiction refers to the compulsive need and use of something to a point where it becomes detrimental to your best interests. People who are addicted can have trouble ceasing to use what they're addicted to, even after they realize it's harming them. The addiction compels them to continue as it pulls them in the opposite direction of their goals. Examples of harmful addictions may include:

- DRUGS AND ALCOHOL: By making people temporarily feel good or by numbing pain, these substances can lure people into addiction. Negative consequences may include harm to health and fitness, impaired judgment, destructive behaviour, being in dangerous environments, and breaking the law. The safest thing for a young athlete to do is stay completely away from them. If someone offers them to you, just say no. If peers pressure you, remember the consequences: a future in hockey is your dream; a future in drug addiction would be a nightmare.

- ENTERTAINMENT: TV, video games, the Internet, and other entertainments can be engaging to the point of becoming an addiction. When that happens, people struggle to pull themselves away, even though they know the activity is taking essential time away from fulfilling their obligations and pursuing their goals. Make sure your entertainments fit into your time-management schedule. And if you find a particular entertainment becoming an addiction, summon your courage and ban yourself from it entirely, before it goes any further.

- SOCIAL GRATIFICATION: People can pursue social experiences or relations with others—for purposes of gratification, attention, or adulation—in ways that are a harmful addiction. This can cause them to make irresponsible and dangerous choices, and lose valuable time needed for meeting their obligations and pursuing their dream. Use your character as your guide for each social decision. And beyond that, follow the same plan as for avoiding the pitfall of an entertainment addiction.

- YOUR SPORT ITSELF: In many ways, a dream is a healthy kind of obsession. You need to be driven, dedicated, and relentless in its pursuit. But sometimes an athlete can enjoy their sport so much that they play and play, seemingly without end. This leaves not enough time to develop other aspects of what they need in the long run to reach their dream. Remind yourself that you need balance to sustain yourself long-term, and that by playing less now, and also spending time on other important things, you give yourself a chance to play more later on.

the inside story

For Christmas one year, someone gave me as a gift a computer hockey video game. It had all the NHL teams and players and arenas, and was just like the real thing. You could even create your own players. I created myself and my brothers and put us on a line. We scored goals assisted by one another, the PA announcer would announce them, and there the three of us were atop the "official" NHL scoring standings!

There was a whole season set up, and it was so thrilling, I couldn't wait to play again and again. But then I realized I was losing more and more time, drawn into working toward a whole separate reality that wasn't reality. Did I want to make it in the video game, or in real life? I didn't have time for both. The game was tempting, and I couldn't take a risk of losing more critical time to it, so I got rid of it completely.

DEPENDENCY: The pitfall of dependency is similar to that of addiction; it involves a person continuing to rely on something that has become harmful. The difference is, the object has no addictive property—the compulsion comes only from the person's *perceived* need for it. Such dependencies could be on:

- OTHER PEOPLE: In their quest to make it, athletes can feel dependent on people who have helped them in the past or have the power to help them in the future. Believing another person has control over their fate can make an athlete ignore their basic wits about acting in their own best interests. A few worst-case situations have seen another person abuse an athlete's trust or personal welfare, knowing that the athlete's sense of dependence would prevent them from stopping it. Always value the help of others in the form of guidance, support, approval, or opportunities for advancement. But never feel dependent or beholden to them to the point of accepting actions that are against your best interests.

- SUPERSTITIONS: In sports, superstitions are common. The pressure to perform, the uncertainty of outcomes, and the role of luck can induce athletes to seek "aid" or "control" through superstitions. Often, these aren't a problem. If an athlete becomes literally dependent on one, however, it is. Instead of being focused on the many important factors within their control, they are ceding control over their fate to the object of their superstition. This can perpetuate an anxiety that undermines personal happiness and sports performance. Superstitions can also sometimes become detrimental themselves, yet athletes may still cling to them. Examples could be wearing a lucky piece of equipment that no longer fits or provides proper injury protection, using a lucky stick in big games even though it is cracked and weak, or needing a sweater number already held by another player on what would be the most suitable team to join. Superstitions can be okay if you don't take them too seriously. No superstition can dictate luck, the future, or control outside forces. Their only real benefit is as a "ritual" that helps you feel mentally assured that you are ready to succeed. Knowing this, you can avoid feeling dependent on superstitions, and dispense with them if they become detrimental.

- METHODOLOGIES: Athletes experiment to see what brings them success, and take note of a method that consistently does. Sometimes they start to think that a particular methodology is *"the key,"* and they become closed off to other possibilities. When there is a new circumstance in which this methodology no longer works, they are unable to adapt. In other cases, an athlete's faith in their methodology can become so great that they focus exclusively on following their method, and lose sight of its purpose. As needs and goals change over the course of a career, that method may no longer be useful, yet they fail to notice. Avoid this pitfall by remembering that there isn't one key, there are many. Do what works for you, but do not be closed to other possible methods or be rigid about changing when needed. It is your methods that should be dependent—dependent on the aim at hand.

Besides the items above, dependencies could exist on almost any object. Notice when one is developing. If it is harming you, breaking the dependency is typically necessary. Since that can be difficult, sometimes it's easier to do a "trial" without it, while telling yourself you can go back if needed. Once you see you can manage without it, you won't need to go back. Another way to break a dependency is to find something appropriate to replace it with, and not get to the point of dependency on the replacement. In any serious case of dependency, seek help in dealing with it from a trusted personal advisor, sports psychologist, or professional counsellor.

CHEATING: Breaking the rules is another pitfall. The lure of cheating is that it seems like a shortcut to making it, a way to get ahead or gain an advantage over the competition. At first, this may be true. In the end, though, cheating is a dead end. In some manner you *will* be caught, and the penalties can take away all that you've ever worked for. Worst of all, it sacrifices your character. When you cheat, you are cheating yourself out of being the kind of person you aspire to be. Some examples are:

- CHEAP PLAY ON THE ICE: Some players constantly break the rules with illegal rough play or cheap shots, through which they hurt and antagonize opponents and hope to gain an advantage. However, playing dirty can cause them to make enemies who will be looking for an opportunity to get back at them. Playing this way, and having others play the same way, can take away from the ability to enjoy playing. Over time, this can dry up a player's passion and induce them to abandon their dream. So play your hardest, but play fair, and don't cheat yourself by trying to cheat the game.

- FALSIFYING ACHIEVEMENTS: This may include things like cheating on a test or exam, lying on an application, or exaggerating achievements or assets in an interview or profile. If you find yourself considering this, ask yourself, "If I have to misrepresent myself in order to get somewhere, what will happen once I get there and people see something else? What will happen if my lies or exaggerations get caught? Why take the chance?" Honesty is the wisest policy.

- PERFORMANCE-ENHANCING DRUGS: Using banned performance-enhancing substances is another form of cheating. For example, some athletes use steroids as a way to build stronger muscles that will recover more quickly. Others use stimulants such as ephedrine to improve concentration or lose fat. There are many other banned substances as well. But there is a reason why substances are banned: They are known or suspected by scientific experts to be hazardous to health. Steroids, for instance, can cause depression, paranoia, violent anger (roid rage), increased risks of heart disease and strokes, and vulnerability to catastrophic joint injuries that can end a career in one instant. Ephedrine, likewise, can increase heart rate and sweating, leading to risks of heat stroke or sudden heart attacks. Risking or compromising your health in order to get ahead is the worst way to cheat yourself. Avoid this reckless pitfall, and stick to good nutrition, water, and safe nutritional supplements as your performance-enhancing substances. That way, you will have the pride of knowing that whatever successes you achieve come from your abilities, not from the effects of some chemical or pill.

the inside story

Marion Jones was a star at the 2000 Olympics. She won five track and field medals, and became a household name back home in the United States. But in 2007, after an investigation, Jones admitted she had used steroids. The chairman of the U.S. Olympic Committee demanded that Jones return her medals. Results were disqualified; she was suspended for two years, spent six months in jail, and lost the millions she had earned, paying for legal fees. Her steroid use didn't just cost Jones—her teammates on two relay teams that won medals were stripped of their medals as well.

REBELLIOUSNESS: At a certain age, a rebel attitude may be popular with your peers. But it will not go over well with parents, teachers, instructors, coaches, or scouts. Not following instructions, talking back, questioning and criticizing authorities, mocking procedures, and horsing around will all land you squarely in their bad books. In the short term, that can impede your development both on and off the ice. And in the long run, it can adversely affect your chances of realizing your dream. If your parents have been helping you pursue your dream, you may lose their support. Teachers or instructors with valuable tips that can help you improve may instead focus their efforts on aiding others who are respectful, attentive, and ready to learn. Coaches may hesitate to choose you for their team if they feel your attitude might undermine their authority, be a bad influence on others, or interfere with their plans. Among scouts, you might develop the reputation of "talented and skilled, but bad attitude, immature, not coachable." Prospective rebels should ask themselves whether short-term popularity with peers is worth the potentially dream-ending price.

TIES WITH TROUBLEMAKERS: As important as not making trouble yourself is not associating with people who do. When troublemakers get taken down, they often get taken down very hard. And people who are perceived to be tied to them—even those who are innocent—can go down with them. Inside and outside your sport, try to avoid being associated with people who fiddle with the pitfalls above, get involved in frequent altercations, stir controversy, or break the law. While those people are easy to spot, occasionally people of typically good judgement can also get a bad idea in their head and cause trouble. When this happens, don't be part of it, and don't go along with them. Landing even once in the wrong kind of trouble can seriously harm your chances of reaching your dream.

> **EXPERTS' RECAP**
> Remember . . .
> · Stay focused on your dream and stay true to your character.
> · Manage your time with diligence and your attention with vigilance.
> · Keep clear of potential trouble and avoid foolish risks.
> · Don't be afraid to seek help from loved ones and experts.

support, supplies, and equipment

CHAPTER **8**

SCOUTS' PREVIEW
In this chapter . . .
· The right support
· The right equipment
· Useful supplies

IN STRIVING TO MAKE IT, PART OF THE PROPER FOUNDATION INVOLVES THE RIGHT SUPPORT, SUPPLIES, AND EQUIPMENT.

The Right Support

For a youngster in hockey, having the right kind of support is key.

It starts with parents or other support people knowing, understanding, and respecting the child's wishes when it comes to hockey. Clear communication in both directions is key. If a child has a dream, has been given some realistic appreciation as to what's involved, and is committed to it, I personally believe that it's important to support them in it. Not supporting them in pursuing their dream can create resentment in a relationship, and leave the child with a lifelong sense of deprivation, causing regret to both parties. On the other hand, if hockey is not the child's dream, I don't believe a parent should try to force a dream that is theirs upon a child that is not embracing it. The child will inevitably feel they are being pushed against their will, again straining the relationship. Plus, they won't enjoy playing and will eventually quit when they get the chance.

It does certainly take some time to see what a child's wishes truly are. Trying something once or twice is not a good measure, particularly in an activity that requires as much technical skill to properly play and enjoy as hockey. Sometimes desires also change with the passing of time or new circum-

the inside story

In my experience of seeing and dealing with hundreds of hockey players and their families, I have noticed a great irony: The pushiest parents are often people who as children felt deprived of the opportunity or support they felt they needed to pursue the hockey dream they'd had. And the parents who are most dead-set against their children seriously pursuing hockey are often people who as children felt as though they were being forced to pursue hockey beyond their wishes.

stances. So it is perfectly reasonable to introduce a child to hockey, and have them participate to a point where they have acquired enough experience and competence at the sport to make a fair decision as to whether they enjoy it. It also makes sense to provide similar opportunities, experience, and information for alternative pursuits, to give children a chance to compare. Then it is a matter of taking cues from the child. If they have a dream, they need support. If they don't, they might still want to play hockey in a less intense way, just for fun. It doesn't have to be all-or-nothing from day one.

At the same time, if you have a hockey dream and are being supported by family or others, you must do everything you can to support those people in return. Assisting a child in pursuing a hockey dream requires major time and financial commitments and an emotional engagement as well. Have and show genuine appreciation for this, and share your enjoyment of playing, pride in progressing, and recognition for your successes with those supporting you. Support your supporters in whatever practical ways you can. This could include helping with chores at home, being open to sharing rides with teammates to decrease the travel burden on all the parents, and making some sacrifices in hockey and outside of hockey to allow your family the freedom, time, and means to pursue other interests or commitments.

The Right Equipment

Equipment serves two important purposes for a hockey player: it provides tools to play the game with, and it provides protection from injury.

In choosing equipment, the following are typically some of the main factors by which to evaluate choices:

PERFORMANCE: equipment that doesn't restrict or interfere with your abilities

SAFETY: equipment that protects you from injury

---

the inside story

Sometimes the biggest, bulkiest, hardest equipment is not the best protection if it restricts your ability to move freely to avoid injury. Plus, hard, squared, or angular equipment surfaces can hurt fellow players when you collide. So if every player is wearing that equipment, just like an arms race, every player is less safe. Unfortunately, a lot of recent equipment is being made that way. But, wherever you have a choice between different styles, this is another thing to keep in mind.

COST: the right equipment based on your budget and hockey needs

DURABILITY: equipment that will last until you choose to replace it

SIZE & FIT: the right size equipment, and equipment that fits your body shape

COMFORT: equipment you feel "at home with" and feel good in

For leading-edge information and details on equipment choices and care, we sought the advice of equipment expert Wes Huether of Canadian hockey-specialty store chain Pro Hockey Life.

According to Huether: "From our perspective, what's most important is the fit of the equipment. The mistake we most often see parents make is they buy equipment that's too big. They want to get the most out of their dollar, and so they buy equipment to last more than one season. The problem is, if it doesn't fit properly, there's a lack of protection, and it hurts performance."

According to Huether, the task of figuring out the right equipment for you is not as bewildering as it may seem, at least in one respect: "The various manufacturers are producing equipment that is primarily the same. They're carrying different models within their product lines at different price points. But within price points, the construction of pads is very similar across the makers, just different colours and logos."

additional help

Pro Hockey Life stores deal exclusively in hockey equipment, and are a good source for both equipment and equipment expertise.

Below is a list of the different elements of hockey equipment, and what to consider in making your choices.

Equipment for Skaters

• BASE LAYER (UNDERGARMENTS)

"You have two basic types. Compression fits tight like a second skin. And loose-fit, sort of like a T-shirt. It comes down to personal comfort."

- ### JOCK/JILL

"There are three main types. You have a traditional straight up strap. You have some that come with garter belt attached that you hook your socks onto. And you have some that come built into shorts, which the socks attach to using Velcro. We're tending to see as a trend players wearing the shorts style more."

- ### PROTECTIVE EQUIPMENT (SHIN, SHOULDER, AND ELBOW PADS)

"You have one style built for agility and maximum movement that are a slender, sleek style of pad. The other style is more for power and maximum protection, for playing a crash and bang style and fully absorbing impacts."

- ### PANTS

"These come in the same two style choices. The belt of the pants should be worn at waist level (like with regular pants). The bottom of the pants should go no further than the middle of the kneecap, and the top collar of the pant should extend up to the bottom of the shoulder pad to protect the kidneys and lower back."

• HELMETS

"Too many players do the 'mirror test' in picking a helmet, but it should be based on fit. Different brands and models are shaped differently, and you want one that fits snugly on your head and doesn't move. Different types of foam are available inside the helmet, which create the protection in the helmet. I would recommend everyone go for maximum protection, but it does come at a significant price point. In terms of replacing helmets, they have an expiry date on them. But if they get cracked, broken, or the foam starts coming off, then they have to be replaced right away."

• FACIAL PROTECTION

"Some players prefer a full visor, but a cage has the advantage that it doesn't scratch or fog, which reduces sight and can put a player in danger. Cages are also made of metal which is stronger than plastic."

• GLOVES

"Gloves come down to comfort primarily. Anatomical gloves fit snug and mimic the movement of the hand. Tapered-fit gloves are anatomical in the hand area, but the collar and cuff are wider to allow more wrist range of motion. Traditional gloves fit loose and boxy and have a wide open collar and cuff."

● SKATES

"Skate sizes are about one and a half to two sizes smaller than shoe sizes. For growing kids, buy skates no more than a size too big, maximum. Otherwise you run into major problems. Fit, comfort, performance, weight, stiffness, and durability are factors to consider. In terms of skate blades, stainless steel won't rust, whereas carbon steel will rust and pit. The blade should also be contoured to suit a player's style. This includes moving the balance point forward for a player that skates low with a forward lean, and moving it backward for a player that skates upright or does a lot of backward skating. And having more blade on the ice for a power skater and less blade on the ice for a player who turns a lot and needs more agility."

● MOUTH GUARD

"Junior mouth guards are for younger players who haven't got their adult teeth, whereas players with a mouth full of adult teeth wear a senior mouth guard."

● NECK GUARD

"The standard is a neck collar. Some have a bib as well, and some attach to your base layer shirt."

● **STICKS**

"Wood sticks are the cheapest. Most players today are using a one-piece because of superior perform- ance and consistency as they don't warp or soften. And then there are two-piece sticks with a compos- ite shaft and a wooden or composite blade, which gives the player freedom to change the blade. Stick height should generally be maximum at the base of the nose. There are different stick lies. High are for more upright skaters, and low are for more bent-over skaters. One thing we see is that players buy sticks that are way too stiff, probably because of the 'macho factor' and wanting to seem strong. But ac- tually, you need to be able to get good flex in the stick to get a whip on it and increase your shot power. In terms of curve, more helps get the puck in the air, whereas less is better for passing and back- hands."

Differences in Equipment for Goalies

● **PADS**

"You have the butterfly style, which are very stiff, rigid, flat-faced pads for goalies that are constantly down low, kicking out rebounds. And you have the hybrid style for up-and-down goalies who want softer pads that can move with them. The amount of customiza- tion a pad allows is another factor."

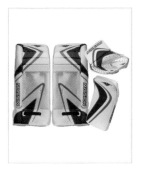

PANTS

"You want a good fit with the internal belt. Beyond that, it's about maximum net coverage, generally about eight to ten inches out."

CHEST PROTECTOR

"One type is built for maximum protection and net coverage. The other type is for maximum mobility, and is sleeker and slimmer for a more mobile goalie."

GLOVE AND BLOCKER

"It comes down to fit, feel, and comfort, primarily. Also flex, in that the goalie needs to be able to easily close the catcher."

● NECK PROTECTION

"Goalie neck guards typically come with a bib that tucks inside the chest protector. Goalies also often wear throat guards, which is a plastic piece that hangs from the bottom of the mask to deflect pucks, skates, or sticks away from the neck area."

● HELMET/MASK

"The right fit is number one. There are different internal foams available, which depict the amount of protection. There are also different external materials ranging from plastics to fiberglass to graphite and Kevlar for maximum impact protection."

" The right equipment is important, but the most expensive pieces aren't always the best. And never use equipment as an excuse. "
DOMINIC MOORE, TORONTO MAPLE LEAFS

In terms of maintaining equipment, Huether advises: "Take equipment out of your bag after playing, and hang it to dry it, so moisture and bacteria aren't trapped in it. We recommend having the equipment sanitized two to three times a season with a sani-sport machine (kept in stores) which kills 99 per cent of the bacteria found in equipment."

Also, don't worry too much about fashion or what others are wearing. Huether says: "Everything is generated from the NHL level when it comes to hockey. Kids want to wear what the pros are wearing, and what everybody else is wearing. ... The biggest thing we always try to do is identify what type of player we're outfitting, see what their skills and abilities are and what level they're playing. A high-level player generally is going to want maximum perform-ance models, but a more recreational level player just needs equipment that will get them out on the ice and allow them to play and be protected."

When appropriate, one way you can sometimes save a bit of extra money is through used equipment. In addition to relatives or friends, some used-equipment stores have practically new pieces for sale that another player for whatever reason didn't like after buying. Of course, you can also sell your old equipment to these stores when you grow out of it, to help defray the cost of your new equipment.

additional help

Useful Supplies

Actual hockey equipment aside, other supplies can be needed for playing or training.
Here are a few supplies you may want to keep on hand for playing:

* hockey tape (for socks, and sticks)
* personal water bottle
* spare screws and screwdriver (for your helmet)
* towel to dry your skate blades after playing
* skate-guards to protect your skate edges whenever your skates are not being worn

the inside story

My cousin Laura DeMarco was playing her first house league game in her hometown of Windsor. Many of the kids had brand new skates fresh from the store, while Laura had a pair of used skates that looked a little worn.

Some of the other kids took to making fun of Laura's skates. So Laura held her skates up, and on the bottoms, the other kids read the name of the previous owner: local NHL star Kyle Wellwood. The critics were silenced.

Here are a few supplies certain players might be interested in for training purposes:

- in-line skates (for playing street hockey)
- for fitness training: rubber bands, weighted balls, balance boards, agility ladders, and "reaction balls" (a multi-shaped ball that bounces unpredictably)

EXPERTS' RECAP

Remember . . .

· Parents and children should respect and support each others' needs, desires, and limitations.

· Choose equipment thoughtfully, as it can affect your safety and performance.

· Choose supplies that make sense based on your needs, budget, and level of commitment.

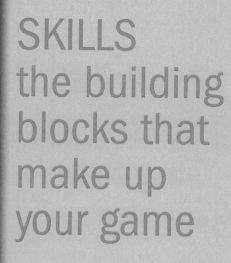
4

SKILLS
the building blocks that make up your game

In his day, Jean Béliveau was the most skilled player hockey had ever seen. Béliveau got his name on the Stanley Cup a record seventeen times, including ten as a player.

IN THIS SECTION, YOU WILL FIND THE VARIOUS SKILLS THAT ENABLE YOU TO MASTER HOCKEY.

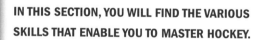

It is possible to fly without motors, but not without knowledge and skill.

WILBUR WRIGHT, CO-INVENTOR OF THE AIRPLANE

all about skills

CHAPTER 9

SCOUTS' PREVIEW
In this chapter . . .
· What skills are and why you need them
· The way to build skills
· Skills ≠ Talent
· The principles of ideal skill development
· The categories of skills for hockey

ONCE YOU HAVE THE PROPER FOUNDATION IN PLACE, IT IS TIME TO BUILD UP YOUR GAME. YOUR GAME IS MADE OF BUILDING BLOCKS CALLED SKILLS.

What Skills Are and Why You Need Them

According to the dictionary, a skill is "a learned power of doing something competently." Skills must be learned; no one is born with them. People are born with *talents*, which are like raw potential. Talents are an aptitude, and when you add instruction and practice, you can create a skill, also described by the dictionary as a "developed aptitude." In order to be a skill, an aptitude must be developed to a competent level. These skills then fit together to make up your game as a whole.

The Way to Build Skills

There are two main parts to building skills—instruction and practice. Instruction is how you learn the technical knowledge needed to execute a skill. One type of instruction is *direction and explanation*. This means that someone describes to you what to do and how to do it. This could occur in a written format, or verbally through coaching. The other type of instruction is *observation and imitation*. In this method, you observe an expert demonstrating a skill, and create a mental impression of it, so that you can try to copy it yourself. Similar to the role modelling you learned in Chapter 4, this is sometimes also called *skill modelling*. The difference is you don't emulate all the personal qualities of a skill model, you just try to copy the given skill.

Once you have had instruction, *practice* is the process of actually trying to execute a skill. Practice usually involves some trial and error before you are eventually able to perform a skill correctly. It is typically done in a controlled environment, which is more suited to learning than the competitive environment of games, where you don't want to risk error. You have heard the expression "practice makes perfect." Repetition is another element of practice. It is almost impossible to perfect a skill on the first try. Typically, skills are mastered by practicing them over and over within a session, and over many sessions, through which you gradually improve. A practice sequence for a skill is called a *drill*—because executing it correctly and consistently has to be "drilled" into you.

Skill development occurs best through a coordinated *skill-building project*, which targets a specific improvement in specific skills through a strategically chosen combination of instruction and practice. Each project is to be completed in a set period of time.

There are five main categories of skills relevant to hockey and covered in this section: physical skills, mental skills, social skills, safety skills, and skills of the stars. In order to reach your hockey goals, you should have a *separate* skill-building project for each of the above categories each year. At the end of the year, your goal changes, your skill-related objectives change, and so you will need to create five new skill-building projects to replace the five from the year before.

Each skill-building project should include the following elements:

OBJECTIVES: As you read in Chapter 1, your one-year goal for hockey necessitates a set of objectives that are part of what should help you reach that goal. Some of those objectives correspond to skills you think you will need to develop, and the level you will need to develop them to. The skill-related objectives you've identified across each of the five categories of hockey skills become the targets of your five skill-building projects for the year.

DIRECTION-AND-EXPLANATION INSTRUCTION: For each project, scan the corresponding chapter in this section, and find where it discusses the particular skills you have targeted within that category. Carefully review that material, and try to get as clear an understanding as you can of those skills and how to execute them with proper technique to use when you practice. You can also get additional instruction in person through a skill-development program.

OBSERVATION-AND-IMITATION INSTRUCTION: For each skill you have targeted, find a skill model you can observe demonstrating the proper technique in that skill. Create a mental impression of it, so that you can try to imitate it when you practice.

PRACTICE: With the proper technique in mind, thanks to your instruction, apply yourself to practice drills designed to help perfect your technique in each skill.

FEEDBACK: Try to get feedback on your practice, to help you make refinements in how you execute your skills, and improve them. Sometimes you can tell on your own. If you can videotape your practice and watch it later, this can help. You can also get feedback from someone watching your practice who is familiar with the proper techniques of the skills you are trying to develop. A quality skill-development program should have an expert on hand to provide this support.

Beyond the elements above, the details of your skill-building projects can be decided according to your own schedule, resources, limitations, and preferences.

Here is an example of a skill-building project:

SKILL-BUILDING PROJECT #1: PHYSICAL SKILLS

Player: Ethan, Age 13, AA, Defence

One-Year Goal: Make AAA

Physical Skills Objectives: Improve skating, passing, shooting, puck control, and checking skills to the level of the AAA players currently one year older.

Skating Development Initiatives

Direction and Explanation: Review portion on skating in Chapter 10 of this book.

Observation and Imitation: Observe NHLer Jay Bouwmeester skating on TV/video once a week, and create a mental impression of his skating technique.

Practice: Go to public skating at local arena each week.

(A similar set of initiatives would be employed for passing, shooting, puck control, and checking.)

To help with all of these skills in one fell swoop, one more project component:

Feedback: Attend a top-notch summer hockey school where I can get instruction, drills, and feedback from an expert hockey instructor in all of these skills.

In order to be able to climb the ladder in hockey, you will need to progressively develop your proficiency at hockey's various skills. Recall that the dictionary said skill involves doing something "competently." If Ethan completes his skill project as hoped, he will be able to skate, pass, shoot, check, and control the puck competently at the fourteen-year-old AAA level. Those abilities, however, would obviously not be competent at the Division 1 College level. From the vantage point of that level, he is not yet skilled, and must continue to work on his skills, likely through a series of additional projects, before he could be considered skilled at that level.

Progressively developing skills could mean improving the technique, accuracy, speed, power, or time it takes you to execute skills. As you move up, subtle differences in skill can make a big difference in outcome. For example, at a higher level, an extra fraction of a second to put home a shot could result in the goalie being back in position to stop it. It's important to set high standards. Raising your skill level could also mean developing more and more *subskills*—specialized variations within a more general skill, often necessary at higher levels. For example, suppose over time Ethan develops his skating to the point where he is quite proficient at forward and backward skating, starts and stops, all types of turns and pivots, and gliding on his edges. He is now eighteen, and his one-year goal is to make that Division 1 College team. To play defence successfully at that level, Ethan will need to develop a special skating subskill called *shuffling*—which is used to maintain position in front of the net, and move out opponents, while facing the play. Learning the skill of shuffling will be an important part of his Physical Skills project that year.

For more on the skill of shuffling, visit my website.

the inside story

My brother Steve, during his College career, was one of the best centres in the NCAA. But when he faced off against Chris Drury of Boston University, he could rarely seem to win a faceoff against him. Later Steve joined the Colorado Avalanche, and Drury was one of their other centremen.

Steve asked Drury, one of the top faceoff men in the NHL, for some advice on faceoffs. Drury helped him, and Steve continually practiced the tips Drury gave him. Later, after Drury had been traded away, Steve faced off against Drury again. This time Steve was often able to beat him.

Progressive skill development should flow automatically from the renewal of your goals and objectives each year, including skill-related objectives that serve as the aims of your skill-building projects. The key is to design each project well, and follow through on carrying them out.

To carry out projects and enhance your skills obviously takes energy and patience. But the power to improve as a player *is* in your hands. And that fact really is great and exciting news!

Players who have the skills have a chance to make it. To scouts watching, skills are what separate players with the potential to play at high levels from the rest of their peers. As you will learn in Section 5, skills alone are not enough, but they are a must.

The Principles of Ideal Skill Development

EXPERT INSTRUCTION: Getting the most expert instruction you can is very important. It's hard to do something right if you are given wrong instructions. And, if you practice a skill wrong, you are only ingraining a defective skill. You might then have to unlearn the defective skill before you can relearn the

---

ask the AUTHOR-ity

Isn't how good a player you are mostly a matter of talent?

No. In seeing deficiencies in a player's skills, some people mistakenly conclude the player just does not have an aptitude for the game. For example, they may look at a player with weak skating ability and say that the player "just doesn't have the talent to skate well enough to succeed in hockey, and should try some other sport or activity." But in most cases, this is wrong. The player does have the potential to skate better, but just hasn't yet developed the skills. And even if a player has a less-than-perfect aptitude for skating, they may have superior talent for other key hockey skills they can compensate with. For example, two of the six players in NHL history who have scored 700 career goals are Phil Esposito and Brett Hull, neither of whom were strong skaters by NHL standards. Yet Hull had one of the great-est shots of all time, and Esposito mastered skills for the critical net front area where many goals are scored from. Exceptional talent might allow an athlete to learn a skill faster than normal, or reach a high level of proficiency in it, but they still need to apply themselves to developing it. And that involves time and hard work, regardless of the extent of one's talent.

The truth is, many more players have enough raw potential to make it than is commonly believed. Some of hockey's greatest players did not have an obvious, innate set of talents geared to hockey, but they had the desire, and they used it to build the skills. Talent helps, but skills are what you play the game with. Skills are what count. So if anyone tells you that you don't have the talent to make it, you don't need to listen to them. Just concentrate on working extra hard on your skills.

correct version. Of course, you can't sit around waiting for some legendary guru to show up and perfect your technique before you try anything. But it is crucial to have expert instruction, so that your efforts yield positive results and develop the skills you intend. This section contains an expert overview to help you get pointed in the right direction.

PROPER PRACTICE: To build the skills you want, you must practice properly. Proper practice means being ready to practice. It means putting 100 per cent of the effort in. And it means being conscientious throughout, attentive to what you're trying to do, to what you are doing, and to feedback you may get through results or from an expert observing.

REPETITION . . . REPETITION . . . REPETITION: The only way to master skills is to repeat them over and over. The more you do, the better you get at automatically recalling how to execute them right. This allows you to perform them consistently and to progressively refine your technique.

UNDERSTANDING: In our hockey school, we have found that most players, if given the opportunity, prefer to not only be told what to do, but also to understand why that works and how it will help them. And when they have such understanding, their skills develop much faster because more of their mind is involved in helping them. Throughout this book, we have tried to adhere to this philosophy as much as space allows. In live hockey development programs, if you don't know the purpose of a drill, or the reason for a part of a technique, don't be afraid to ask the coach or instructor.

DON'T GET BY, GET IT RIGHT: Early on in the process of learning a new skill, it is often frustrating and difficult to get it right. It can be tempting to instead "get by" with a semi-effective version of the skill you can do more easily. But if you don't push yourself to get it right, you'll pay a price for that later. You get attached to your "get-by" version, and then when it is no longer enough to get by, like any bad habit, it is difficult to change. So don't quit working on a skill when you feel it's good enough to get by for the moment. Get it right from the beginning, even if it takes longer and is harder. It will pay off in the years to come.

FUN: Like every other part of pursuing your dream, skill development should be fun. Make games for yourself out of your practice, and mark your progress so you can see it and feel good.

Mark your progress so you can see it and feel good. You can track and record your progress in developing your skills using tools designed for this purpose, available at www.sportsmaster.TV

The Categories of Skills for Hockey

As mentioned earlier, this section contains five categories of skills that can help you build your game, and give yourself a chance to make it in hockey:

1. **PHYSICAL SKILLS** are the pure physical movement skills you need to be able to execute in playing the game. These include skating, puck control, passing, shooting, and checking.

2. **MENTAL SKILLS** involve the sense and strategy that go into playing the game, and deciding what to do in different game situations. These skills range from anticipation to positional play to give-and-go's and one-on-one's.

3. **SOCIAL SKILLS** are very important in a team sport like hockey. They include skills for dealing effectively with teammates, opponents, coaches, and others as well as in a team environment and in the competitive arena.

4. **SAFETY SKILLS** help you to avoid and deal with injury, to maximize the health and longevity of your career.

5. **SKILLS OF THE STARS** features a few special skills of some of the world's top hockey players—a crucial group to study, for anyone whose goal is to make it.

Building skills is how you build your game. And the skills that can help you make it are waiting for you in the following chapters.

EXPERTS' RECAP

Remember . . .

· You aren't born with skills, you have to learn them.
· Skills are the building blocks of your game.
· Progressively develop your skills through a set of annual skill-building projects corresponding to the five categories of skills contained in this section.
· Skills are learned through expert instruction, observing and imitating skill models, plus lots and lots of practice.

physical skills—your arsenal of on-ice abilities

CHAPTER 10

SCOUTS' PREVIEW

In this chapter . . .

· What Physical Skills are
· The five fundamental skills for skaters
· Supplemental skills for skaters
· Physical Skills for goalies

PHYSICAL SKILLS ARE ALL THE PURE PHYSICAL MOVEMENTS YOUR SPORT CALLS FOR.

Hockey's Physical Skills are broken down into two categories: *fundamental* and *supplemental* skills.

FUNDAMENTAL SKILLS are the most important building blocks of your game. Every player needs the fundamentals and uses them regularly. The fundamentals of hockey are skating, puck control, passing, shooting, and checking. You can hardly take a shift in a game without being called upon to employ each of these.

SUPPLEMENTAL SKILLS are used less frequently. They're no substitute for the fundamentals, yet the supplementals can be important additional skills for use in specific game situations. There are many different game situations, and therefore many supplemental skills. A few examples include dekes, blocks, clears, and wraparounds.

The Five Fundamental Physical Skills for Skaters

1. **SKATING:** As a skill, skating involves much more than forward strides. It includes the balance, control, and comfort level you have on your skates. It is a big part of every physical movement you make in hockey, including all the other Physical Skills. Most experts would agree that skating is the most important Physical Skill in hockey. Here are some key components of the skill of skating:

STANCE

In this photo, I am demonstrating the basic stance used for almost all skating in hockey. Notice my knees are bent sharply, not my waist. My chest and head are facing up, and I can see the play. I am leaning slightly forward, as though sitting on the very edge of a chair. This stance allows for maximum balance, power, and stamina in hockey skating.

STRIDING >

"Running on the ice" is no way to skate. The best forward skaters use powerful strides. The stride starts with feet close together, then a long hard push back into the ice with one leg, which thrusts you forward while gliding on the other foot. Bring that foot back to the middle, then push with the other foot. Arms move forward and back, not side to side.

>

STARTS + STOPS **forward start** >

Here, Women's Olympic star Jennifer Botterill, who you read about in Chapter 1, demonstrates a Forward ("V") Start. Begin by twisting your feet outward to form a V. This allows you to dig

>
your skate blades into the ice and push back so you can jump forward with a few short hops to get going before settling into your normal stride.

STARTS + STOPS **crossover start**

A crossover start is often used when you need to stop, and go back in the direction you came from. Facing sideways to where you plan to go, push your front leg back, and leap your hind leg overtop, hurling yourself forward in the direction you want to go.

STARTS + STOPS **stop**

Here, Jennifer demonstrates a forward stop. Notice she straightens up to lessen the pressure she is placing on the ice, so that she can pivot sideways. Then immediately she bends her knees sharply, leans back in the direction she is coming from, and digs both feet into the ice as sharply as possible. Notice she remains perfectly balanced at all times.

EDGES

Often in hockey you are not skating in a straight line. Such other skating requires you to be comfortable gliding on your edges—the sides of the bottom of your skate blade. In this picture, Jennfer is turning on one leg at a time to practice balancing on just her inside edges. At www.sportsmaster.tv you can find a similar exercise for outside edges.

TURNS **simple turn**

For all turns in hockey, lean forward on the toe-portion of your skates. For a simple turn as pictured here, spread your feet a little wider than usual, and keep your stick out in front. This allows you to stay balanced through the turn, so you can maintain your speed. A tight turn is the same, only you dig your heels in to turn sharper (but lose speed).

TURNS **crossover turn**

A crossover turn is a great way to pick up speed. Whichever way you are turning, your inside leg does the pushing—back and underneath. Push hard with a long stride, just like forward skating. Your outside leg does the steering—stepping over and in front in the direction you want to go, and then gliding until you are ready to push again.

>

BACKWARDS SKATING

As a former pro defenceman, I am especially attuned to backward skating technique. A common mistake I see is young players leaning too far forward. You must balance on the heels of your skates. Each stride is a C-cut or half-moon arc, while the other leg stays straight to steer you straight back. A deep knee bend is crucial to balance and to speed. The fourth photo frame shows a backwards stop.

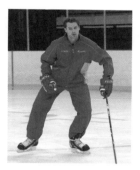

PIVOTS

First, straighten up a bit. From forwards to backwards, gliding on your front foot, quickly pick your back foot up, twist it backward in the air, and put it back down. Then quickly pick up your other foot and put it back down facing the same way. From backwards to forwards is exactly the same thing in reverse. Start at the last frame and move to the first.

2. PUCK CONTROL: Being able to control the puck with your stick, and make the puck do what you want, is probably the next most important Physical Skill after skating. Components of the skill of puck control include:

CARRYING THE PUCK straight-ahead

To carry the puck as fast as possible with no checkers around, use one hand on your stick. The puck should be off to the side on your backhand. With your arm and stick out of the way, you can skate fast pushing the puck straight forward. Your stickblade should be slightly ahead, so you can keep your head up and still see the puck without looking back.

CARRYING THE PUCK on forehand turns

Carrying the puck on forehand turns, always keep two hands on your stick. A backhand turn can be done with one or two hands. The key in either case, as Jennifer shows here, is to keep your stick and the puck in front of you at all times. Carry the puck on the heel of your stick, as the toe may come off the ice as a result of you leaning forward to turn.

CARRYING THE PUCK on backhand turns

STICKHANDLING side-to-side

When stickhandling side to side, cup your stick blade over the puck so the puck doesn't slide off. Extend your arms out to the side, keeping your top hand close to your body, and rolling your bottom wrist over and under as you extend out. When stickhandling forward and back, use the heel of your stick close to you, and the toe of your stick when outstretched.

STICKHANDLING front-and-back

PROTECTING THE PUCK

Here, Pavel, a Junior age player, tries to get the puck from me. Notice how I keep my body between him and the puck. If he tries to come around one side, I extend my knee on that side to fend off his stick, and my shoulder on that side to block his body from coming around. By bending over, I can create a greater distance between him and the puck.

CONTROLLING THE PUCK ALONG THE BOARDS **securing the puck**

To secure the puck, drop one hand off your stick so you can enclose the puck along the boards between your skates in a V-formation. You will need to straighten up to get close to the boards. Place your free hand against the boards to brace yourself in case you are shoved or hit into the boards, and to maintain your balance.

CONTROLLING THE PUCK ALONG THE BOARDS moving the puck with your skates   >

To move in either direction, kick the puck away from the checker, and then turn sideways and move after it, trapping the puck again, this time with your stick, using two hands. If you've made room to get away, now is the time! Otherwise, fend the checker off with your body as you learned earlier. You may need to re-secure the puck, and then try again.

>

"SEPARATING" YOUR UPPER AND LOWER BODY

Here, I am demonstrating some advanced stickhandling which comes in handy for maneuvering the puck in traffic, and also allows for more convincing dekes. By being able to have your legs move in one direction while your arms simultaneously extend in the other, you can keep the puck far out of reach of checkers and confuse them too!

3. **PASSING:** In working together with your teammates, giving and receiving passes is fundamental to hockey. The skill of passing includes:

FOREHAND PASS   >

Take the puck back behind you, roll the puck from the heel of the blade towards the toe, and sweep your stickblade forward. The motion finishes with my blade pointing up and directly at the target I'm passing to—in this case Jennifer's stickblade. This helps ensure the most accuracy and consistency.

>

>

PASSING backhand pass >

The technique is the same as for the forehand, as you can see. Note how I finish with my stick pointing straight at the target. Many young players' follow-through swings across their body. This can cause the puck to go off in any direction. Also notice how Jennifer receives the pass, taking her stick back and cradling the puck, as she did on the forehand.

>

>

DROP PASS

A drop pass is the one to use when there is a checker is in front of you and your teammate is behind you. Here Jennifer employs a through-the-legs drop pass, whereby her legs will fend off any stick lunge by a checker. Notice she also skates to one side, so as to draw the imaginary checker that way, while leaving the puck such that I can take it the other way.

4. **SHOOTING:** Hockey games are measured in goals, and you need to be able to shoot to score. The fundamental skill of shooting includes:

WRISTSHOT

A wristshot starts off the same as a pass. But on the foreswing, as the puck goes through the middle of your stance, quickly snap your wrists over the puck, so that you finish with your stick blade facing downward. Shift all of your weight onto your front knee on your follow through, and point the stickblade precisely where you want the puck to go.

BACKHAND SHOT >

A backhand is the same technique as a wrist shot, only from the backhand side. Many young players wrongly use a flick shot motion instead. They start with the puck in the middle of their

>

stance, and just shovel upwards, so their stickblade finishes facing the ice. This produces no power. Notice Jennifer's backswing and correct follow through.

SNAPSHOT

Position the puck roughly in line with your front skate. There is no rule that your backswing must stay on the ice, it just has to be quick! Snapping your wrists through the shot as fast as

>

possible is what generates most of the power. After that, the most critical thing for both power and accuracy is to follow through all the way, same as above.

SLAPSHOT >

A slapshot is essentially the same as a snapshot, only with a full backswing, taking your stick back over your head and behind you. Try to not to take an arc on your backswing as in golf.

>

This complicates your motion, and makes consistency more difficult. Instead, take the stick straight back, and follow through straight forward, same as above.

ONE-TIMER

>

The first key to one-timers is to get your body in the right position where you can shoot the approaching puck without stopping it first. Also lean forward in the direction the pass is coming from. And because of the moving puck and the power of your swing, shoot the puck off the heel of the stick—the most stable part of your stickblade—for extra control.

>

>

5. **CHECKING:** The fundamental skill of checking is used to prevent an opponent from scoring, and to retrieve the puck so that you can score. For boys, it's also important to know how to absorb a bodycheck, to avoid being knocked off the puck, knocked down, or hurt. The skill of checking includes:

BODYCHECKING **shoulder check**   >

Bend your knees, spread your feet a little wider than usual, and lean your weight into the check. Drop your shoulder into position to make contact with it, but keep your elbow tucked in, and your head out of the way. Don't let up as you make contact. Rather, keep pushing with your legs and shoulder to ensure you drive the opponent off the puck.

>

BODYCHECKING absorbing a shoulder check

In the first two frames, Pavel comes to hit me. I lean my weight and shoulder into the check, as if I were checking him. The result is, even though I was stationary and he was moving fast, he fails to budge me. In the 3rd, 4th and 5th frames, Pavel tries to absorb a check from me. His (wrong) instinct is to lean away from the check: You see the result!

>

>

the inside story

Many talented male players stop playing competitive hockey at a certain point because of their unease with bodychecking. If only they learned proper skills for absorbing bodychecks, they wouldn't have to make that heart-wrenching decision. Even a very small player can learn how to deal with checking so it isn't a discouragement. When I started hockey, I was a big kid. But I went through puberty very late, so that during my teen years, I was often one of the smallest players on the ice. For a few years in particular, I was like a child playing against adults. The only way I could survive in rep hockey was to learn superior checking skills—especially absorbing checks. Later, once I physically matured and became one of the biggest players again, these checking skills allowed me to become excellent at making checks.

BODYCHECKING hip check >

A hip check is all about positioning and timing, especially the element of surprise. First you position yourself to one side, to force the puckcarrier to skate the other way. Once he does, as quickly as possible, spin your body that way sideways until you strike the player with your hip. Again, be sure to keep your own head back and out of the way.

>

>

BODYCHECKING absorbing a hip check >

Having done a somersault in the air after getting hit with a hip check before, I've learned to diffuse one properly! Bend your knees, lean down, fold your arms, and block the approaching hip with forearms. Keep pushing with your legs and arms so the

> hit straightens you up. In the last frame, Pavel wrongly leans away from the check, and will fall backward. He is lucky that I wasn't a smaller player: Had my hip made impact below his waist, he would have done a forward somersault!

BODYCHECKING pins >

Here, you can see from both sides how to properly pin a puck-carrier to the boards. Notice I am not facing him, cross-checking him in the back. Instead, my knee wedges against the

> boards between his legs, so he can't move. I face the same direction he is facing, and keep my shoulder in front of his body so he can't squeeze loose or get at the puck.

CHECKING poke check >

Keep your stick close to your body to lull the puckcarrier within range. Then quickly lunge your stick directly at their stickblade. Tilt your blade back so that your blade goes under their blade

> and knocks their blade off the ice, and off the puck. Lunge with only your stick, not your body, so if you miss, you're not off balance and easily skated past.

>

CHECKING **sweep check**   >

Here, Jennifer's stick sweeps across in an arc to knock the puck off Pavel's stick. Notice how she doesn't lean off balance in the direction she is sweeping. That way, if she had missed, Pavel

>

could not have skated around her. She would just sweep back the other way, and continue sweeping back and forth until she got the puck.

CHECKING **lift check**

When approaching the puckcarrier from behind, a useful check is the lift check. Drop your bottom hand lower on your stick, and lift up hard, knocking the other player's stick off the puck, with yours underneath, where it will come back down to the puck before theirs. Make sure you follow through—don't stop lifting at the instant you touch their stick.

CHECKING **slide check**   >

Here Pavel is on a breakaway, and I am chasing, so I have to resort to a slidecheck. Dive forward, and with one hand on your stick, swing hard in front of their stick. Again, don't stop where your stick touches theirs. Follow through so you knock their stick off the ice, and finish with your stick in front of their skates, in the way of them skating.

Because the fundamentals are so important, it is especially important to develop solid techniques in them. Shortcuts or makeshift versions might allow you to succeed early on, but as you reach higher levels, these might impede your ability to advance. Strong fundamentals should be a priority for any player who wants to make it far.

>

ask the AUTHOR-ity

How did I learn such strong fundamental body-checking skills?

Those skills you read about earlier, I actually learned not from a coach, but from my younger brother Steve. Steve was a smart player, and he developed an astonishingly advanced set of balance and bodychecking skills. By the time he reached College and the Pros, his specialized skills in this area were far beyond those of any player I had ever seen before (or, for that matter, since). I was able to learn a few of these from him. After accidentally (and unfortunately) breaking two players legs with bodychecks, I myself was often mentioned for my checking abilities at those levels. But Steve's skills were in a league of their own. Although bigger, I couldn't even budge Steve

in practice. In games, whether he went to finish a check on an opponent, or an opponent charged at him, he would run over them like a tank. While I was with the Penguins and Steve was with the Avalanche organizations, we played an exhibition game against each other. At one point, I rushed into the corner to knock an opposing forward off the puck. At the last second, I realized it was Steve! It was the only time in all my years in hockey that I was truly terrified: What would my teammates think the next second when they saw me, the biggest player and the best bodychecker in our lineup, get flattened like a pancake? Luckily, I just managed to stop before I got to Steve, and then simply held him against the boards instead. Phew!

Supplemental Physical Skills for Skaters

1. **DEKES:** The purpose of a deke is to fake out or confuse an opponent, making it easier to get past them (or to get the puck past the goalie.)

Here are some examples of good dekes (and a few fun ones) for deking past players:

PLAYER DEKES **simple fake**

On a simple fake, I take my stick and the puck to one side, and also lean my knee, shoulder and head that way so that the defender mistakenly thinks I am about to go that way. When I cut back the other way, he is caught by surprise, and that moment lost leaves him too late to recover.

>

>

\>

PLAYER DEKES puck-through-stick

Similar to the simple fake, Jennifer starts off this deke by taking the puck out to one side. When the defender reaches for the puck, Jennifer doesn't have the space to pull the puck around the defender's stick, so she slides it through the defender's stick to the far side. She then skates around the far side, just as with the simple fake you learned earlier.

\>

>

PLAYER DEKES spinorama

In a spinorama, you actually begin skating to one side of the defender, so that they lunge or turn that way. Then you quickly stop with your back to them, push off the opposite way, and

>

pivot around the far side of them. By the time they recover their balance, it's too late. You've already made your highlight reel move, and pulled it off!

>

>

PLAYER DEKES puck-past-opponent

In this deke, you send the puck past the defender one way, while you skate around the defender the other way. You hope that the defender is tempted by the "loose puck" and turns that way, only to find that the puck is already by them. Meanwhile, you have gone around them while they turned the wrong way—as you see happened to Pavel here.

>

>

Here are some examples of good dekes (and a few fun ones) for deking past goalies:

GOALIE DEKES **forehand deke**

As Jennifer perfectly demonstrates, on a forehand deke, you first want to freeze the goalie with a fake shot, then pull the puck to your forehand side. As you do so, the goalie will have to move laterally, opening up the five-hole between their legs. Typically, you want to then immediately put the puck through that gap in the goalie's legs before it closes again.

>

GOALIE DEKES **backhand deke**

Like Jennifer, I begin by coming down the middle so the goalie has to stay frozen ready for a shot at any moment. At the last second, I reach the puck wide to my backhand, turning sharply to skate to that side. The goalie will react by sliding over to that side. But if I successfully raise the puck over his pads and blocker, there is nothing there but net.

>

GOALIE DEKES **sweep across**

>

You often see this move in shootouts because it is tough for a goalie. By sweeping across in a wide lateral arc, you force the goalie to move a lot to stay in the right position. At any moment they aren't, you could simply shoot it where an opening arises. Otherwise, you continue all the way around the far side, and try to roof it over their glove.

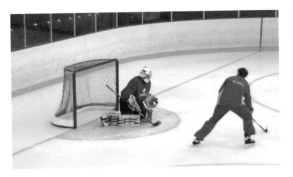

>

>

GOALIE DEKES backside slide

Wanting to impress? This deke starts off the same as the sweep across. About halfway across the net, as you keep skating the same way, you let your stick fall back with the puck with one

>
>

hand on your backhand. Then let the puck go, and it will slide in, as the helpless goalie is unable to stop their momentum sliding the other way.

>

2. **SQUEEZE-BY'S:** When you are close to the boards and have little room to move or make dekes, sometimes the best way to get by a defender is to squeeze yourself by, along the boards.

Here is the proper squeeze-by technique on both your forehand and backhand sides:

BACKHAND SQUEEZE-BY

Reach the puck out in front and by the defender, with one hand on your stick, on your backhand. Keep your front foot forwards, but pivot your back foot backwards. This way you can use your edges to power yourself by the defender, while remaining flat against the boards, making it tough for the defender to pin you even if they make contact.

>   >

>

>

FOREHAND SQUEEZE-BY   >
The technique is almost the same on the forehand side. The only difference is that on your forehand side, you have to drop your top hand off the stick, temporarily. On this side and the

>

>

backhand side, if necessary, use your free hand to block the approaching defender from pinning you, and push yourself by them.

>

3. **WRAPAROUNDS:** The usual place to score from is in front of the net. But sometimes it's tough to get open there with the puck. A wraparound allows you to instead score from behind the net.

Here is the proper wraparound technique from both the forehand and backhand sides:

BACKHAND WRAPAROUND >

Jennifer is skating as fast as possible, so she can try to beat the imaginary goalie across to the far side. Notice she also makes a sharp turn at the far post, and comes all the way out in front, so that she has a better angle to hit the net and can also apply more force on the wraparound.

>

>

>

FOREHAND WRAPAROUND

By staying tight to the net, Jennifer ensures that if a defender was chasing her, they couldn't cut her off before she completes the wraparound. On the follow through, notice how her stick actually slams into the post. A wraparound is like a dunk in basketball—you are slamming it in. If the goalie is there, you want to jam it through the goalie and in.

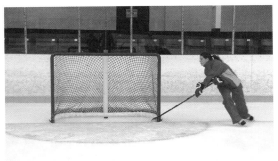

>   >

>

4. **CLEARS**: When you need to get the puck out of your zone, and you have no teammates open or no time to make a safe pass to them, a clear is how you safely get the puck out.

Here are some common types of clears you should learn:

>

FLIPOUTS

In the first two frames, Jennifer demonstrates a forehand flipout. She just makes a shovel motion, and the puck goes high in the air over defenders heads and out of the zone.

>

In the last three frames, I demonstrate a backhand flipout. Note, the flick shot used in a flipout is the same shot you on offence to roof the puck from in close over a sprawled goalie.

BANK-OUT

I learned this shot from a player I played pro hockey with. As a right shot stuck playing left defence, he used this clear a lot. You essentially bank the puck hard off the boards just above the bottom runner on an extreme upwards angle. The puck will then rebound high in the air like a flick shot, but stay close to the boards—out of harm's way.

5. **BLOCKS:** A block is the skill you use to stop the puck when your opponent takes a shot, tries to dump the puck in your end, or tries to clear the puck out of their end.

Here are some common types of blocks you should learn:

BATTING THE PUCK DOWN   >

Here you can see me demonstrating how to bat a puck down that is in the air, and control it. I don't try to catch it or knock it down, I just hold my hand in front of it, and it will then fall straight down to the ice. Then I quickly use my stick to corral it, in case it lands on its side or is bouncing or rolling.

>

TRAPPING THE PUCK

To stop a puck coming around the boards, wedge your body flush against the boards, and put your feet in a V formation, heels together, with no gaps. If you can, angle your feet slightly towards the boards, so that if it bounces off, it will stay on the boards. If the puck is on the ice, it will get trapped in your V or nearby. Then just kick it up to your stick.

STANDING BLOCK

Assuming the person taking these photos is standing where the player taking the imaginary shot would be, notice Jennifer skates from her net straight toward the shot, blocking the shooter's lane, and thus possibly deterring the shot. She also compacts herself so that the puck won't squeeze through her while she is screening her goalie.

SLIDING BLOCK

Let's say an uncovered player just received a pass in the slot, and is about to shoot from that dangerous spot—and I have a chance to block it. My only chance from where I am is a sliding block. Always slide feet first in the line of fire, because you don't want to get hit in the head or neck. Also face the puck, because that's where your equipment is strongest.

PRO-file

Sudarshan Maharaj

My friend Sudarshan "Sudsie" Maharaj has served as the goaltending coach of the NHL's New York Islanders for five seasons. He has been actively involved in scouting prospects worldwide and developing goaltenders in the Islanders system. He has also worked with Hockey Canada, serving as co-director/instructor of their inaugural National Goaltending Development Camp in 2006 and 2007, and a member of Hockey Canada's Goaltending Curriculum Writing Team. Recently, Sudsie served as a lead instructor for the OHL's Goaltending Development Camp. Previously, Sudsie served as a goaltending scout for the New York

Rangers and Phoenix Coyotes, and ran Goaltending Scouting Services, an organization that evaluated draft eligible goaltenders for NHL clubs.

Remember that your skills are developed through skill-building projects, as described in Chapter 9. Each year, you will have new skill-related objectives and projects through which you can progressively develop your skills in order to keep up with higher levels of hockey. To help you identify suitable practice drills and other skill-building suggestions beyond this book, check our website.

Physical Skills for Goalies

To help provide expert information on the physical skills required for goaltending, we sought the counsel of professional goalie coach Sudarshan "Sudsie" Maharaj:

"The main fundamental skill for goaltenders is *skating techniques*. It all starts with your feet. There are two basic elements—your *shuffle* and your *T-push*. Those are the two main ways of moving for goalies. You have to be able to master both of those in order to move yourself laterally into position in a smooth fashion. A *shuffle* is where you step sideways. The shuffle is used for moving shorter distances. It's also used when there's a potential shot on the way, so that your pad face stays facing forward as you move with the shooter. The *T-push* is used when you have to move longer distances, and usually when there's no shot potential.

SHUFFLING

Dan Bellissimo, who has served as a goalie instructor with my family's hockey schools, played College Hockey for Western Michigan and now plays goal professionally in Italy, as well as for the Italian National Team, thanks to his dual citizenship. Here he shows shuffling: a series of tiny sideways steps, front foot first, ready for a shot at anytime.

>

>

T-PUSH

When he has to move from post to post quickly, Dan uses a T-push instead of shuffling. He pivots his front leg to face the direction he is going. Then he pushes off his hind leg, and glides across on his front leg. When he gets to the far post, he digs in his front foot to stop, and then readies himself for a potential shot from that far side.

>

>

"The next fundamental component is the *save techniques* you have to be able to execute to make the save. Modern goaltending relies heavily on the *butterfly technique*. In the butterfly, the goalie sits balanced with both knees to the ice, legs facing laterally with pads rotated forward, and the five-hole closed as much as possible. Smaller goalies and younger goalies also use a *half-butterfly*, because their leg length just isn't enough to reach the two posts and cover the bottom corners with a full butterfly. In a half-butterfly, the goalie rests on one knee, with the other pad face facing out toward the shot. So for example, if they shoot to your glove side, your blocker-side knee would be down on the ice, and your glove-side leg would be extended, with the pad facing the puck. Then there are the glove saves, where you're just using your hands to make saves with the catcher and on the blocker side."

BUTTERFLY
Here is the butterfly goaltending posture. Notice how Dan's legs are flared out wide, as opposed to behind him, to ensure that both bottom corners are blocked. He also keeps his upper body nice and upright and tall to cover net.

HALF-BUTTERFLY
In the half-butterfly, one leg is in the butterfly posture, and the other leg is upright, as pictured here. As Dan is demonstrating, it's important to keep your pads as flush together as possible. Otherwise, the half-butterfly has more holes a shot could sneak through than a full butterfly.

GLOVE SAVES
From the butterfly, Dan shows a blocker save (1st photo) and catcher save (2nd photo). He doesn't overreact or leave his posture. He stays compact, and readies his glove to meet the approaching puck. This way, if the puck gets deflected, he is in good position, the puck will hit him, and he still makes the save.

BUTTERFLY SLIDE

Let's say the puck is passed from one side to the other, and the goalie knows a shot will be coming from that side right away—maybe even a one-timer. The butterfly slide gets the goalie across the net and set to make the save all at the same time. Dan has to push hard with his hind leg, and then quickly get it down into the butterly as he slides over.

"These two fundamentals sometimes combine, when you need to move while a potential shot is coming. You use either a *butterfly slide* or a *half-butterfly slide*. Basically, you're simultaneously pushing yourself into the shot, and closing your body up into a butterfly or extending your lead leg into a half-butterfly."

In terms of supplemental skills for a goalie, here are a couple of important examples:

"Another important skill is *rebound control*. For a higher shot, if the puck hits you in the body, sweep your catcher in from underneath and gather the puck with it as it comes off your body. For shots on the ice, you can use your stick or pad to direct the puck to one of the corners of the rink."

TRAPPING REBOUNDS

From a goalie's perspective, the best rebound is no rebound. Here, Dan shows how to swallow up a puck, as Sudsie described. The puck has hit him in the chest, and instead of letting it fall to the ice, he uses his catcher to gather it into his chest, so no opposing skater can get a second shot.

REDIRECTING SHOTS **blocker**

>

It's typically easiest to redirect shots to the far corner from where the shot originated. Here Dan demonstrates a redirect to the blocker side (first three photos) and glove side (next three photos). From the butterfly, he extends his stick out to meet the puck, and tilts it like a wedge, so the puck will glance off into the corner. After making contact with the puck, Dan keeps his stick in front of the puck long enough to ensure it is headed away from the net.

REDIRECTING SHOTS **glove**

PUCKHANDLING reverse grip

standard grip

"For *puckhandling*, wrap your catcher around where the paddle and the shaft meet on the goalie stick. You have a choice of two basic grips. A *standard grip* is where the catcher hand faces forward. This grip is easier for handling the puck, especially when you're starting out. With a *reverse grip*, the catcher hand is wrapped forward and around the stick so that heel of the hand is pushing downward. The advantage is that you can force the stick to bend into the ice, and get more whip and power on your shot, as opposed to a standard grip where you're just pushing the puck. But the reverse grip takes more time to learn in terms of puckhandling proficiency. Each goalie typically uses only one of these grips."

> jock talk
>
> " Guys are getting run. That takes a toll on your players. If I can take [the puck] and shoot it out, now my defencemen don't get hit. "
> —MARTIN BRODEUR[4]

the inside story

Like many sports, hockey is specialized to varying degrees by the different player positions. Although I have played all five skater positions at every level up to the American Hockey League, I can't say that I've ever laced on goalie pads—not even as a kid!

Young netminders need specialized goalie skill instruction, and Sudsie has that world-class expertise.

EXPERTS' RECAP

Remember . . .

- Master the fundamental Physical Skills of hockey, as they are constantly needed.
- The fundamentals for skaters are: skating, puck control, passing, shooting, and checking.
- The fundamentals for goalies are: skating techniques and save techniques.
- A number of supplemental skills are also important to learn for use in special situations.

mental skills—tactics of how to play the game

CHAPTER 11

SCOUTS' PREVIEW

In this chapter . . .

· What are Mental Skills?
· Mental Skills of the game
· Mental Skills for offence, defence, and neutral situations
· Mental Skills for goalies

MANY ASPIRING HOCKEY PLAYERS TODAY HAVE WELL-DEVELOPED PHYSICAL SKILLS. FAR FEWER HAVE COMPARATIVELY WELL-DEVELOPED MENTAL SKILLS. AND THAT MAKES MENTAL SKILLS ONE OF THE KEY FACTORS INFLUENCING WHICH PLAYERS MAKE IT TO HIGH LEVELS.

What Are Mental Skills?

You have probably heard people use the term "hockey sense." If it is said that a player has good hockey sense, this means that the player has a sharp mental understanding of the game, knows the right plays to make in reacting to each game situation, and consistently makes the right plays. To call this a "sense," however, implies inaccurately that it is a matter of instincts, which players are either born with or not. Of course, if a player does not have an opportunity to get expert instruction about the mental tactics that underlie the game and how to play various game situations, then all they will be able to rely on are instincts. But the truth is, that hockey sense—along with the ability to execute what that hockey sense tells you to do—are in fact skills, the Mental Skills of hockey. They enable you to mentally master the game itself, through expert individual tactical responses to each game situation that may arise.

Mental Skills are more complex than Physical Skills. In fact, using one Mental Skill typically involves using several Physical Skills as part of it. For example, the Mental Skill of cycling (which you will learn about later in this chapter) involves the Physical Skills of skating, puck control, passing, and perhaps shooting. But it also requires some thinking. For example, you need to recognize when during a game you should use this cycling skill. And while you are cycling, you must watch your teammates and the defenders, and decide when to skate, when to pass, and when to shoot as part of the cycle. You also need to recognize when the situation calls for ending the cycle and deploying a different Mental Skill instead. All of that thinking is what makes cycling a Mental Skill. Physical Skills are like *weapons* you utilize as part of *tactics* for playing the game. And the tactics are your Mental Skills.

At high levels, the tactics of how you play the game are sophisticated, and comparatively few people have a lot of expertise in teaching them. Certainly far fewer youth coaches and hockey school instructors have the high-level experience and expert understanding of the game to teach the more advanced Mental Skills than Physical Skills, which are more widely understood and mastered at lower levels. As a result, most aspiring hockey players do not receive as much quality Mental Skill instruction. By the same token, Mental Skills require more explanation, and therefore more concentration is required from a player to learn and develop them. Players who don't pay close attention as Mental Skills are being explained, or are impatient to leave the "coach's huddle" to skate off and play with the puck or take a shot, won't develop their Mental Skills as much as they could. The same is true for children whose parents want them in hockey schools where they are in non-stop motion, doing drills, whenever they are on the ice, without the necessary time to stop and teach those Mental Skills that are necessary to learn in order to play at higher levels. All of this helps explain why Mental Skills are underdeveloped compared to Physical Skills. Yet, the truth is a player may be a perfect skater, shooter, passer, puckhandler, and checker, and still have no chance of making it without mastering the tactics of hockey.

In this chapter, you will learn about hockey's Mental Skills. Although there is a limit to how many game situations we can describe the tactics for here, you can find extra information on my website www.sportsmaster.tv.

For each group of skills in this chapter, there are some mental *concepts* you should understand first. So put your thinking cap on: these concepts guide the way you want to play that portion of the game, and why you should use each Mental Skill at the time suggested.

On the next page are the Mental Skills for skaters. At the end of this chapter is a separate segment covering Mental Skills for goalies.

Mental Skills for the Entire Game

CONCEPT #1—TEAM PLAY: HOCKEY IS A TEAM SPORT. You can't win a game on your own, and if you try, you will likely only increase your team's chance of losing. Smart hockey means playing in a coordinated fashion with your teammates. Team play includes the following skills:

TEAMWORK: This is the basic skill that allows you and your teammates to work together to help your team play better. This includes:

- recognizing when passing the puck to a teammate will move your team closer to scoring, and executing those passes;
- figuring out where to go when your teammates have the puck so that you are putting your team in better position to score; and
- helping a teammate on defence when they need help, and otherwise letting them do the defensive job they are trying to do, while you figure out what other way you can help your team defend.

POSITIONAL PLAY: Hockey's positions allow teams to divide up the regions of the ice for players at different positions to cover. For each position, here are the regions you might cover as part of the Mental Skill of *"playing your position."*

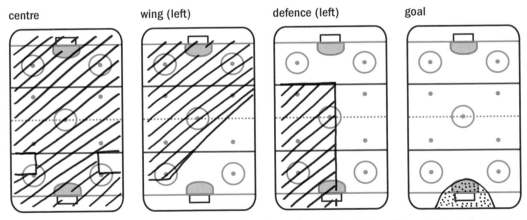

centre   wing (left)   defence (left)   goal

In each diagram, the shaded region shows the area of ice that a player playing that position would typically cover. This is only a general guideline. There are, of course, exceptions.

the inside story

While skill instruction often focuses on Physical Skills for when you are on the puck, an important set of skills are the Mental Skills of how to play *away from the puck*.

COMMUNICATION: If you have ever been down rinkside during a professional game, you will have heard constant chatter between teammates on the ice, relaying information to each other while playing. Here are a few examples of the Mental Skill of communication:

- calling for a pass when you are open, or warning a teammate when you are covered so that they don't try to pass to you;
- telling a teammate whether they have a lot of time to make a play, or whether an opponent is closing in on them;
- goalie warning teammates a penalty is expiring, by banging their stick; and
- defence telling the goalie what to do with the puck once the goalie has stopped a puck dumped-in behind the net.

CONCEPT #2—VISION OF THE ICE: Expert commentators often mention a star's "vision of the ice." This means seeing as much as possible of what's going on, on the ice, so that you can see the best play that might be available, and make it. Vision of the ice involves the following skills:

FACING THE PLAY: You need to know what is happening with the play in order to know what you should do. On offence, you might need to briefly look away to see where you're going and what space is open, but then turn back and follow the play. On defence, if you are guarding a player without the puck, you might need to "keep your head on a swivel" and alternate between watching your check and watching the play. But always keep close tabs on the play.

SEEING THE WHOLE ICE: When you have the puck, keep your head up, and try to see the whole ice. Don't look down at the puck or fixate on making one certain play and get "tunnel vision." This way if that play is closed off, you will notice. And if another play opens up, you will spot it.

ADVANCE GLANCE: At high levels, the game moves fast and there's not much time to make plays. Smart players, just before they might get the puck, use the mental skill of "advance glance" to do a quick survey of where the other players are on both teams. This saves them time in the event they do get the puck, because they already saw what to expect and decided what to do, and now can just do it.

CONCEPT #3—ANTICIPATING: Anticipation is predicting what is about to happen in the play, or where the play is likely headed next. This puts you in position to direct the play, instead of chasing the play and never catching it. It involves the following Mental Skills:

PATTERN RECOGNITION: By paying attention and making mental notes over time of patterns in how game situations often unfold, you can build up a mental database of familiar patterns. That way, when one of those situations is about to unfold again, your mind will recognize clues that will pull from your database what is going to happen next, and you can be a step ahead of it.

READING AND REACTING: The other kind of anticipation just involves some on-the-spot quick thinking to figure out what the shape of the play might force the puck carrier and other players to do. For example, if an opponent is about to retrieve a puck behind their net and has no space to skate with it and no opening to pass it, you can read that their *only* real option will be to fire the puck around the boards. So you react by skating straight to the boards to wait for it, instead of skating first toward the player, and then after the puck, a step behind.

Mental Skills of Offence

CONCEPT #1—PUCK RETENTION: If you lose the puck to the opposition, offence is over. In order to score, you have to retain control of the puck long enough to be able to develop a chance to score. This involves the following Mental Skills:

PUCK PROTECTION: As an individual player, your first objective when you have the puck is to keep possession of the puck, and not turn it over to the opposition. The key is to only try dekes or passes when you have an opening, and otherwise, protect the puck by positioning your body between the puck and nearby checkers. If the checkers approach from a new angle, turn so that you are still between them and the puck.

the inside story

Jaromir Jagr was famous for his puck protection skills. He would use his big body to box out defenders trying to reach around him and get the puck, and patiently wait for an open play. In 2005, my brother Dominic was a rookie with the New York Rangers, and Jagr was at the time the top player on the Rangers and in the league. After games, players would go to a family lounge in the arena to meet up with their families. One day after a game, my mother was in the lounge getting some grapes from a snack table that was set up. Jagr came in, and was eager to get some grapes himself. But my mother was taking a while because she has paralysis on one side of her body from a stroke she suffered. So Jagr tried to reach around her to one side and then the other, but my mother kept moving as she tried to get some grapes with her good hand, inadvertently blocking Jagr, who she never saw behind her because she is also blind in one eye from the stroke. Eventually Jagr gave up, and turned to look at his teammates who were all having a good laugh at him because my mother was foiling him with his own trademark skill!

SUPPORT: If you hold on to the puck too long, you may be cornered or surrounded, and be unable at that point to avoid losing the puck to the opposition. The key to avoiding this is the Mental Skill of support passing. This involves frequent, short, low-risk passes to nearby open teammates. By keeping the puck moving like a hot potato in this way, it is tough for the opposition to put the squeeze on any one player on your team, and get the puck from them before they get it to a teammate.

CONCEPT #2—MANEUVERING INTO SCORING POSITION: Once your team has established puck possession, the next step of offence is maneuvering yourselves along with the puck into a position your team can score from. This involves the following skills:

HEADMANNING THE PUCK: In moving the puck up the ice toward the opposing net, teams usually want players to headman the puck to teammates further ahead, and then skate to catch up. Remember the puck moves faster than you do, so doing this can help advance the puck quickly and catch the opposition off guard.

GIVE-AND-GO'S: Getting by opposition players is often accomplished by isolating and outnumbering one of them at a time, one after another. The simplest way to do this is a give-and-go. As a checker approaches, you make a quick pass to a teammate, skate by the opponent, and get a quick pass back from your teammate. Now you are past the opponent.

AREA DUMPS: When you have nowhere to skate and no one to pass to, often the best offensive play is to dump the puck to a certain area where you or your teammates can race and try to get it back. Pick an area where there is the highest chance of your team getting to the puck first, or where if you do regain control of the puck in that spot, you are closest to a scoring position. For example, when teams play "dump-and-chase," they dump the puck in the opposition end, so that if they can retrieve it, they have the puck close to the opposing net. If you have a teammate streaking up the ice fast, another area to dump the puck would be just behind the opposing defence, where your teammate can skate past them and get it first.

CONCEPT #3—INITIATING OFFENCE: When your team first gets the puck (typically closest to your own zone), offence involves certain Mental Skills:

BREAKOUTS: These are organized setups and passing sequences that allow your team to start offence "on the right foot." Here are a few common breakouts.

Note: For all rink diagrams, see legend on page 153.

breakouts [a]   [b]   [c]

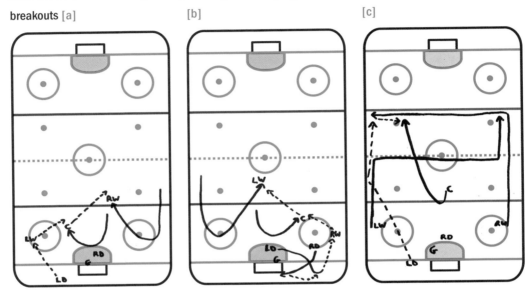

[a] SIMPLE BREAKOUT: Let's say our team's LD gains possession of the puck in the left corner of our end. The LD passes the puck straight up to the LW, positioned on the near hashmarks, by the boards. The C, facing the play, watches where the puck goes, and then curls to the left side to provide close support, eventually receiving a pass from the LW. The RW starts by heading to the hashmarks on their side boards. Once seeing the puck is going up the other side, the RW curls that way, to provide more support. Ultimately, the RW receives a pass from the C in the middle of the ice, outside the blueline. Now the puck is in good position, and all three forwards are on the attack. The RD stays in front of the net, for safety, in case a pass is missed and the puck is lost.

[b] REVERSE BREAKOUT: If RD retrieves the puck with a forechecker in hot pursuit, a good move is to draw the forechecker after them behind the net, and then bank the puck back into the corner they just opened up. The LD then leaves the front of the net to retrieve the puck (as the RD will eventually circle the net and take LD's spot in front). The rest of the breakout is then the same as the Simple Breakout, only this time the puck is coming up from the right side in our diagram.

[c] STRETCH BREAKOUT: On a powerplay, or sometimes if an opposing team is forechecking too aggressively, a team will employ a stretch breakout, sending some forwards outside their zone, beyond the forecheckers. In the diagram, the RW skates up the boards, and across the far blueline, where they retrieve a long bank pass the LD fired off the boards. The C curls to the side the puck is going, for support, and receives a tip pass from the RW. The LW skates up and across the redline, ending up on the right side. Again, our forwards are organized and on the attack.

REGROUPS: Regroups are similar to breakouts, except typically they are simpler and are used to get moving on offence quicker when there's a chance to catch the opposition off guard before they can get into defensive position. Here are a few common regroups.

regroups [a]   [b]

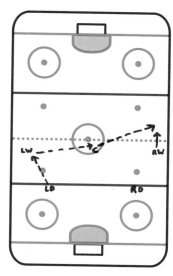 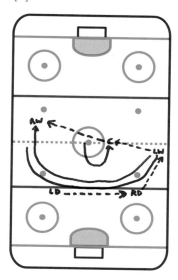

[a] STRAIGHT-UP REGROUP: Let's say our D recovers a turnover at our blueline. Our three forwards come back in their lanes and stop in close proximity to the D, to allow for an easy pass. Here the LD has the puck and passes it straight up to the LW. All three forwards then take off straight up the ice in their lanes. The LW immediately makes a pass to the C, the C passes to the RW, and a quickly organized attack is underway.

[b] CRISS-CROSS REGROUP: In this regroup, the W's crossover all the way across the ice in order to maintain their speed, and provide a safer passing angle for the D, before taking off up the far side. Here the LD passes to the RD while waiting for the W's to make their cross. Then the RD passes to the LW who has crossed over to that side. The C makes a hairpin turn to be in position to receive a support pass, then passes it across to the RW. A coordinated fast-moving attack is now in progress.

LEGEND FOR RINK DIAGRAMS:

C: Centre
LW: Left Wing
RW: Right Wing
LD: Left Defence
RD: Right Defence
G: Goalie

Solid Line: Movement of a player skating forward
Parentheses Line: Movement of a player skating backward
Dotted Line: Movement of the puck (e.g., a pass)
Double Line: Shape of the formation a group of players are in
A: Attacker
D: Defender

CONCEPT #4—ATTACKING: Once you've got the offence moving, you want to attack toward the opposing net, where you have a chance to score. This involves the following Mental Skills:

INDIVIDUAL RUSHES: Beating players one-on-one is one way to attack. A rush is when you get past several players in a row, moving toward the opposing net. Speed is usually key. It's also important to pick your spots. If there are five opposition skaters in proper defensive position in front of you, your chances of beating them all are low, and chances of losing the puck are high.

MULTI-PLAYER RUSHES: On a multi-player rush, you and your teammates pass the puck among yourselves as you skate up ice, and sometimes criss-cross in order to confuse the defence. Multi-player rushes have better odds than a solo rush.

OUTNUMBERED RUSHES: When the players in your rush outnumber the opposition players defending it, the odds of a good scoring chance are very high.

outnumbered rushes [a]

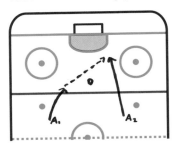

[b]

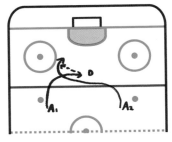

[c]

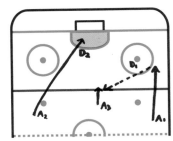

[d]

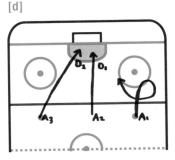

[a] SIMPLE TWO-ON-ONE: By skating full speed to the net, A2 makes it difficult for the D to mark A2 while simultaneously guarding A1, who is higher up. As a result, A1 can make a pass behind the D to the streaking A2 who receives the pass all alone in the crease, in prime position to score.

[b] "PICK-AND-ROLL" TWO-ON-ONE: If there was one play I hated trying to defend when I played as a defenceman, it was this one! Here, A1 starts with the puck and skates on an arc directly at the D, while doing a drop pass to A2 who is crossing over behind A1. Now A2 has a breakaway, and the D will have a hard time getting at A2 to stop them, because A1 is directly in the way.

[c] CENTRE-TRAIL THREE-ON-TWO: A simple but effective 3-on-2 attack is shown here. A1 carries the puck in down the boards, while on the far side, A2 drives full speed to the net, pulling D2 with them. A3 hangs back as a trailer in the middle of the ice, uncovered, and receives a back pass from A1. Now A3 is in prime position to shoot with A2 and D2 both screening the goalie.

[d] PUCKCARRIER CURL THREE-ON-TWO: Here, just inside the blueline, A1 curls towards the boards, seemingly out of scoring position. A2 and A3 drive full speed to the net, forcing both D to go with them to prevent them receiving a pass in the crease. Now A1 completes the curl, turning to face the net again, and moving into the slot for a great angle shot.

PLAYING DOWN LOW: Deep in the offensive zone, attacking takes a different shape. The earlier skills of puck protection and give-and-go's are important. So are Cycling and Triangle plays.

cycling

triangle plays

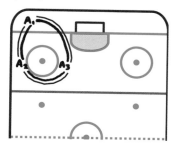
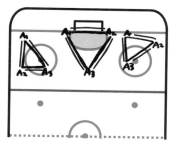

CYCLING: This diagram shows a cycle out of the left corner. A1, A2, and A3 spread out as shown on the puck-side of the ice, making it difficult for the opposing D and C to cover all three of them. If one of them is chased, they can move in either direction along the circle, drawing the checker after them, and then dropping the puck past the checker to their open teammate, following a distance behind. The goal is for one of the attackers to eventually get the puck with enough time and space to attack the net.

TRIANGLE PLAYS: Triangle plays operate on the same principles as the cycle. The triangle at left is the one that applies to the cycle. Another setup would be, as pictured in the middle, two forwards behind the net on either side, and one in the high slot. A third setup would be as pictured at right, which is similar to the first triangle, only two players are low, and one player is high, as opposed to vice versa. Passing around such triangles is designed to eventually stretch the defenders too thin, allowing one attacker a clear shot or play at the net.

POINT PLAYS: If you have the puck in the opposing zone and your defence are open at the blueline, getting the puck to the defence opens another form of attack called point plays. Forwards head to the net. They can screen the goalie while the defence shoot. Or they can get open in front for a pass from the defence. For the defence, it's more important to make sure you get the puck through to the net area than to shoot it as hard as you can.

the inside story

My brothers Steve, Dominic, and I used to train in the summers with other pros. One of those pros was Daniel Briere, one of the most accurate shooters in the NHL. One time, Dominic asked Briere a question: When he was shooting, was it his habit to look at the net or at the puck? Briere's response was that he actually looked in between, so that, using his peripheral vision, he could see both at the same time.

CONCEPT #5—FINISH: Once you have a scoring chance, finish is what will turn it into a goal. Here are the Mental Skills involved:

SMART SHOOTING: Nowadays, almost all goalies play the same style. Except at very young ages, this leaves the same spots typically open for a shot from a scoring position (medium-distance away). Have a look at the diagram below to see the common scoring spots.

scoring spots

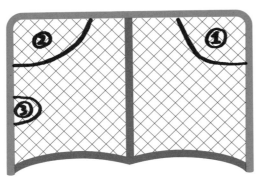

THE SCORING SPOTS: If you recall from Chapter 10 what the butterfly position looks like, the spots it leaves open (for a left-catching goalie) are as follows. Spots 1 and 2 are open in the top corners, over the goalie's shoulders. Spot 3 is open above the goalie's pad and below their blocker, about a foot-and-half off the ice off the left post. On a right-catching goalie, spot 3 would simply be on the other side.

GETTING THE GOALIE MOVING: When the goalie has the angle on you, and your chance of scoring on a regular shot is low, you want to try to get the goalie moving to create an opening. Moving your body or the puck laterally forces the goalie to move as well. Then a quick shot or deke might get by the goalie before the goalie has a chance to get set again.

DRIVING THE NET: The most reliable way of scoring is to drive pucks to the net as often as possible and drive players to the net as hard as possible (within the rules).

- If you are skating in wide, try hard to cut in on goal on the close side and take the puck straight to the net.
- Keep player "traffic" in front of the opposing net during point shots by your defence.
- Stay in front of the net and look for rebounds off initial shots.

You can get a copy of the official rulebook from Hockey Canada by downloading it from their website at www.hockeycanada.ca.

additional help

"GARBAGE GOALS": A lot of goals are scored within a few feet of the net. This includes the following Mental Skills: deflections, rebounds, tap-ins, and stuff-ins (see page 157).

deflections, rebounds, tap-ins, and stuff-ins

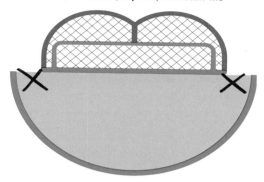

DEFLECTIONS, REBOUNDS, TAP-INS, AND STUFF-INS: For a deflection, you want to position yourself in front of the goalie (serving as a screen) and in line with the shot. Just outside the arc-shaped line marking the top of the crease is the ideal depth to stand, so that you don't get a goaltender interference penalty, plus have enough room to change the trajectory of the shot significantly before it gets to the goalie. The X's in the diagram apply to rebounds, tap-ins and stuff-ins. When carrying the puck in from a tough angle, try a stuff-in when you get to one of the X's. When waiting for a pass, stand on the X's for a tap-in. When looking for a rebound, stand on the X's, so that if a puck bounces out sideways, it will leave you an open net.

Mental Skills of Defence

CONCEPT #1—DEFENSIVE POSITIONING: One of the keys to good defence in hockey is your positioning with respect to your opponents. You must stay "in good defensive position." This means:

STAY BETWEEN YOUR OPPONENT AND YOUR NET: If you were to draw a line between the player you are checking and your net, you want to stay on that line between the two. This allows you to block the player from getting to your net or from taking a shot at your net. If you move off that line or get on the wrong side of the player, they will have an open lane to go to your net or shoot toward it.

GAP CONTROL: When guarding an opponent, don't leave too much space between you and them. Stay about a stick length away, or less when you are closer to your net. A large gap gives your opponent space to execute dekes or make other plays.

TAKE THE SHORTEST ROUTE BACK TO YOUR NET: If your check gets by you, don't chase them, skate in a straight line toward your net. They eventually need to move toward your net to score, so you may have a chance to head them off when they do.

CONCEPT #2—SEPARATING THE OPPOSITION FROM THE PUCK: If you knock the puck away from the opposition, you've successfully defended, and now have the puck to go back on offence. This involves:

PLAYING THE BODY: Since staying between your opponent and your net is key, the way you eventually stop them is through body contact. Playing the body just means engaging them physically on their way to your net, stopping their progress, and dislodging the puck from them. In boys' leagues where it is permitted, you can use a bodycheck to make body contact. But don't rush at the player in doing so, as this makes it easy for them to sidestep you.

INTERCEPTING PASSES: If you are guarding the puck carrier, keep your stickblade in front of where their stickblade is facing, to prevent them making a pass without you intercepting it. For other cases, keep your stick on the ice so you can intercept any pass attempted by the puck carrier to your check.

CONCEPT #3—FORECHECKING AND BACKCHECKING: Furthest from your net, defence takes the form of forechecking. If the opposition is already moving up the ice, various players on your team could be forechecking or backchecking. This involves the following Mental Skills:

HUSTLING: You don't want to give your opponents time to make plays. This doesn't mean chasing without thinking. It just means hustling when making any play that smart defence calls for.

PUCK PRESSURE: Taking away opposition time with the puck, and trying to retrieve the puck for your own team, are both helped by having defenders stay on the opposing team member with the puck. But not all five defenders can do this, or other opponents will be left wide open. Usually your team system (as below) will dictate which player pressures the puck; otherwise the closest player should do so.

ANGLING: When preparing to make body contact with an opponent, it is crucial to take an angle of approach that cuts off their ability to escape the contact. With the wrong angle, your opponent can avoid the check and get by you. Usually you take an angle that forces the opponent progressively toward the nearest boards. See page 159 for some examples of the proper angle in different situations.

angling [a] [b]

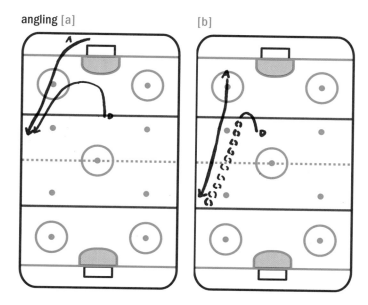

[a] FORWARD ANGLING: Here, the forechecker, D, skates forward on the correct path to gradually angle puck-carrier A, into the boards, without allowing A the chance to escape.

[b] BACKWARD ANGLING: Here, the defenceman, D, gradually inches over backwards from the middle of the ice towards the boards, until A runs out of room and D squeezes A into the boards. Notice D took the ideal angle, so as to prevent A from gaining the offensive blueline before being stopped.

HOLDING THE LINES: The zones of the ice and the rules of hockey make the centre redline and two bluelines particularly good places to try to stop the opposition.

- *Pinching:* Stopping the opposition at your offensive blueline allows you to keep pressure on them in their end, and not have to clear your players out before you can bring the puck back in.
- *Step-up:* Halting the progress of the puck carrier before the redline prevents them from dumping the puck in your end, as this would be icing.
- *Stand-up:* Halting the progress of the puck carrier before your blueline can cause them to go offside, and prevent them from getting in your end where they can apply pressure to score.

TEAM FORECHECK AND BACKCHECK SYSTEMS: Teams coordinate defence by dividing up the responsibilities for different players. See below for some common systems used.

forecheck [a]

[b]

backcheck [a]

[b]

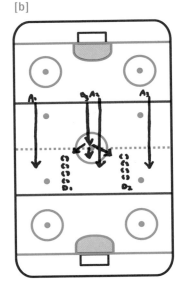

[a] 2-1-2 FORECHECK: Here, two forecheckers, D1 and D2, both pressure the puckcarrier, A. One forechecker, D3, hangs back in the high slot, ready to retreat if need be. And the two forechecking defenceman, D4 and D5, await even further back—D4 on the puckside, just inside the blueline, to try and keep any clearing attempt in, and D5 usually back a little bit outside the blueline as a safety valve if the opposition does get out.

[b] NEUTRAL-ZONE-TRAP FORECHECK: Here, lead forechecker, D1, steers the puckcarrier, A, to one side, and begins angling A to that boards. The forechecker waiting on that side, D2, steps up to further close off A, and create a turnover. D3 retreats to the middle of the ice to cut off any attempted pass across. And the forechecking defenders, D4 and D5, slide into positions as indicated, to cover open men and retrieve loose pucks.

[a] BACKSIDE COVER: This backcheck is used only if D3 is certain they can get back on time to cover one of the attackers. In that case, whatever side the puck is on, D3 takes away the far-side attacker, in this case A3. This leaves the defencemen D1 and D2 to stop the two attackers closest to the play.

[b] DEFENCE-DIRECTED: If the backchecker, D3, is not sure they can get back on time to cover any of the attackers, the two defenceman can't count on them doing so, and must at least initially stay in the middle, playing the opposing attack as a 3-on-2. D3 skates straight back toward their net, which is their best chance of getting back on time to help. If the defence then feels that D3 has gotten back fast enough to help, they will then point D3 to which player they want D3 to cover.

CONCEPT #4—DEFENDING: When the opposition has the puck in your zone, they are a high threat to score, and your overwhelming concern is defending. This involves the following Mental Skills:

DEFENDING RUSHES: Aside from the skills mentioned earlier, it's important to have ample speed moving backward as you defend a rush against fast-moving opponents.

- *One-on-one's:* Watch your opponent's chest or logo crest, and keep yourself in front of it. Don't get drawn into watching or chasing the puck.
- *Multi-player rushes:* On an equal-numbered rush, the defenders must communicate, based on the shape of the rush, what each defender will do.

OUTNUMBERED RUSHES: A rush where the opposition attackers outnumber your defenders is the most dangerous. See below for some common outnumbered rushes and ways to defend them.

outnumbered rushes 2-on-1 [a]   **3-on-2** [b]

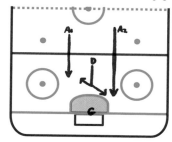 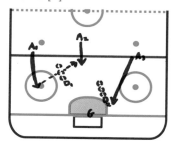

[a] DEFENDING A TWO-ON-ONE: The defender, D, should try to stay in the middle of the two attackers initially, as chasing one of them would simply leave the other attacker wide open to receive a pass from the other, and attack the goalie completely unimpeded. Once the puckcarrier gets close enough to the net that they would have a high chance of scoring if they shot (e.g., in the slot), the defender must then stop staying in the middle and make a choice. If they are certain they can check the puckcarrier or block the shot, they should do so. Otherwise, they should go the other player, and take away the pass option, leaving the goalie clear on which player will be shooting, so the goalie has the best chance they can to make the save.

[b] DEFENDING A THREE-ON-TWO: Using the centre-trail 3-on-2 you learned about earlier, the D on the far side opposite the puck must go with the far-side winger A3 to the net, and cover them. This leaves D1 to effectively play a 2-on-1 on the puck side of the ice. D1 should then use the principles for defending 2-on-1s described above, to give themselves the best chance of not being scored on.

COVERING OPPONENTS: In your end, stay within no more than a stick length of your check, with your stickblade in front of theirs. In front of your net, you must be actually engaged with them, and use your stick to lift their stick off the ice.

TEAM DEFENSIVE ZONE SYSTEMS: See below for how defensive responsibilities are typically divided up in the defensive zone.

team defensive-zone systems

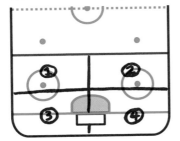

TEAM DEFENSIVE-ZONE SYSTEMS: Hockey teams typically play zone-defense in their end. The zone is divided into quadrants. As diagrammed, the LW has quadrant 1, the RW has quadrant 2, the LD has quadrant 3, and the RD has quadrant 4. The C goes wherever the puck goes within quadrants 3 or 4, and usually does not enter quadrant 1 or 2 unless an opposing puckcarrier takes the puck there, while both opposing defence simultaneously remain in those quadrants as well.

DEFENDING DOWN-LOW PLAY: Don't get sucked into rushing after a player and ending up out of position. Stay in position, and keep a close gap on your check. Eventually this should allow you to either intercept a pass or pin an opponent to the boards, freeing the puck up for one of your teammates to retrieve.

CLEARING THE NET FRONT: Opposing players should be moved away from the front of your net, to avoid them screening your goalie, deflecting shots, or getting rebounds. This doesn't mean cross-checking them in the back. Legs are what players use to move. Place your stick in the gap between their legs, and while making sure you stay centred toward them, skate them away from your net, pushing from around waist-height.

PUCK LANES: For opponents without the puck, keep your stickblade between their stickblade and wherever the puck is to prevent them receiving a pass. If they have the puck, you can keep your body in front of their stickblade to deter them from shooting.

CONCEPT #5—EVACUATION: Even once you've checked them and retrieved the puck, you are still in danger while the puck is close to your goal. Turning the puck over to the other team near your net would leave you very vulnerable to being scored on. Smart defence calls for immediately evacuating the puck far away from your net. This involves the following Mental Skills:

GETTING THE PUCK TO SAFE AREAS: If the puck is in front of your net, get it away from there as soon as possible! This often means evacuating the puck to the nearest corner, where you can retrieve it again, and then deal with clearing your zone.

GETTING THE PUCK OUT: Once the puck is away from your net front, the next priority is getting it out of your end. Waste no time, but look to see where the opposition is before choosing the appropriate clear.

DEFENSIVE DUMP-DOWNS: If you have a lead late in a game and don't need any more goals, or are tired after a long shift and need a line-change, the safe play is to dump the puck in the other team's end as a defensive measure, rather than risking a turnover by being checked closer to your end. The key is to get by the centre redline first, to avoid an icing.

Mental Skills of Neutral Situations

CONCEPT #1—PUCK POSSESSION: When a team has the puck, they're able to score and the other team is not. So when the puck is free, aside from a few special circumstances (which you can learn about at www.sportsmaster.tv), the aim is generally to try to win possession of it. This involves the following Mental Skills:

LOOSE PUCK RACES: Whenever there is a loose puck, try to get it to it first.

PUCK BATTLES: When battling with an opponent for a loose puck, get inside position on the puck. Try to lift their stick or knock it away from the puck, and get your stick in between. Or try to get your body in front of theirs, to shield them off, while using your feet to corral the puck. Then try to get away with the puck in whatever direction is open.

CONCEPT #2—GETTING INTO POSITION: When the puck changes hands from one team to the other, you must quickly change your positioning. This involves:

DEFENCE-TO-OFFENCE TRANSITION: Get open and start the attack as quickly as possible before the opposition can set up their defence.

OFFENCE-TO-DEFENCE TRANSITION: Race to get back into defensive position between the opponent and your net, and read where your teammates are to find your place in your team's defensive system.

You can find tips on playing these situations on my website.

There are additional Mental Skills of special situations (numeric advantage situations, 4-on-4, 3-on-3, faceoffs, etc.).

Remember that your skills are developed through skill-building projects, as described in Chapter 9. Each year, you will have new skill-related objectives and projects, through which you can progressively develop your skills to keep up with higher levels of hockey. For additional practice drills and other skill-building suggestions, check our website.

Mental Skills for Goalies

Here, again, are professional goalie coach Sudarshan Maharaj's insights into the Mental Skills for goaltending:

SAVE PREPARATION
Our goalie, Dan, is square to the puck and has moved up to the top of the crease. The only spot that looks open for Jennifer to shoot is the five-hole. But of course, as soon as the puck leaves her stick, Dan will be dropping down into the butterfly, and that five-hole will disappear before the puck reaches the net.

"There are really three phases to what you do as a goalie. You're going from preparing for the save, to executing the save, to recovering from the save.

"The first category is *save preparation.* Moving into the right position is key. This means aligning yourself to the player, and making sure you're aggressive enough to that player. You have to monitor your depth based on the situation. A general benchmark would be to stand at the top of the crease. The basic strategy is this: Let's say a player's coming down the wing. You're standing up, and you push across so that you're lined up square to the puck with proper depth. You have your catcher up high. Your legs are in a wide stance so that the corners are covered. The player looks up and sees one spot to shoot at—the five-hole between your legs. Then he drops his head and shoots.

---

the inside story

In overhearing professional goalie coaches talking to their goalies, one piece of advice I've often heard is for the goalie to position themselves to take away the main (middle) part of the net. As a goalie, that means that sometimes, if a player makes a great shot, you will have no chance. But overall, you are playing the percentages. And the percentages are that, more often than not, they won't hit that shot, they'll hit you.

"Next comes *save execution*. When the player is about to release the puck, you drop down, catch the shot in your chest, and freeze the puck. The strategy is based on luring shooters. Now, shooters adjust, and may try to go top-shelf, but it's a tough target to hit. The idea of the butterfly is you are covering a much higher percentage of net than standing up and trying to do a skate save. Modern goaltending is all butterfly, and it's based on percentages. Now sometimes for extra reach or height, you can use a half-butterfly. But the drawbacks are it takes more time to position one leg down than to just drop into a full butterfly, plus the five-hole is more exposed, whereas in a full butterfly it is more closed.

"Next comes *save recovery*. Let's say you're down on your knees in your butterfly, and you want to move to your glove side. You pick up the blocker-side leg, and push with it, rotating on your other knee like a hinge pin. So you always get up on the leg you're going to push with. That's called back-side recovery and it's important for basic biomechanical efficiency reasons: If you got up on the other leg, you'd have to transfer your weight before you could push, which wastes precious time. You also want to develop your edgework so that instead of picking a leg all the way up, you can plant your edge, push, and slide over while the legs remain on the ice. For example, let's say the puck squirts out two feet left. You don't want to get up, push, and drop again. By that time the puck's in your net. Watch how goalies like Roberto Luongo or Marc-André Fleury just plant their blade, jam on it, and push themselves over in order to get centred to the puck again. Then if the puck gets moved to a safer area, that's when they get up.

SAVE RECOVERY
After a save on Jennifer's initial shot, a rebound heads across the netfront, where I am waiting for the puck to arrive to shoot it in. Dan pushes himself across, while staying in save position, so that by the time I am ready to shoot, he is across in his butterfly, and has the net covered once again.

>

>

"In terms of playing the puck, traditionally you play the puck if you have time, but it depends on your comfort level in doing so. If a puck is shot in around the boards, you always play the puck off your near post, and come back to your net off the near post. Never go to the far post, you don't have time. Normally the goalie stops it and holds it for a teammate. If they can't get to it, the goalie should rim it around the glass, or if they're strong enough, fire it off the glass by the blue-line so it can't be kept in. If those aren't options, chip it to a corner where there is no opponent waiting.

PLAYING THE PUCK

Dan watches the puck heading around, but proceeds cautiously in case it should take an unexpected bounce on net. He places his body behind the puck, and traps the puck against the boards. Then he fires the puck around the boards, away from the net and from trouble. He skates back into the net the same way he came, getting ready for any shot.

>

>

"At more advanced levels, there are a variety of goaltending philosophies which have some differences. But the above are general guidelines that apply in most situations."

EXPERTS' RECAP

Remember . . .

· Mental Skills are the tactics of how to play the game (sometimes called "hockey sense").

· Advanced Mental Skills are key to success at high levels, and help set players apart.

· The first step to building strong Mental Skills is understanding the concepts behind them.

· The second step to building strong Mental Skills is knowing the right tactic for each situation.

· The third step to building strong Mental Skills is mastering executing them as intended.

· Only this third and final step is accomplished by doing drills on the ice.

social skills—respecting the human face of sports

CHAPTER 12

SCOUTS' PREVIEW
In this chapter . . .
- What Social Skills are, and why they're important for hockey
- Social Skills for making a good impression
- Social Skills for striving for favourable outcomes when interacting with people
- Social Skills for dealing with various contexts within hockey

HUMAN BEINGS ARE SOCIAL ANIMALS. WE LIVE, WORK, AND PLAY IN GROUPS.

In order to accomplish what we hope to in any of these scenarios, we have to develop Social Skills for dealing successfully with other people.

Hockey is no exception. Participating in hockey involves countless *social interactions*. A player striving to make it must deal with teammates and opponents, referees and linesmen, coaches and managers, doctors and trainers, scouts and player agents, family and friends, fans and media, and others. Each may demand a different kind of social interaction. The activity of hockey also includes several different social processes occurring within it, including: bonding, cooperation, competition, conflict, apprenticeship, judgment, and negotiation. As a result, hockey players find themselves in many different *social contexts* just within hockey itself. All of this gives hockey a perhaps surprisingly active and complex social side to it.

For this reason, aspiring hockey players need not only the skills of the game covered in the last two chapters, but also skills for handling the "human face" of the sport. You must be able to interact successfully with others, and operate successfully in the game's various social contexts.

The first group of Social Skills important to realizing hockey ambitions are those that enable you to interact successfully with other people. These can be used in any hockey dealings with people such as those mentioned above as well as in interactions with people outside hockey.

Making a Good Impression

In any activity in which you deal with others, it's important to create a good impression. Never forget that advancement in hockey is a subjective process, which relies upon the opinions and decisions of other people. You can't get to the top through your play alone, as you could in golf or tennis, for example. In hockey, you rely on others to pick you for teams, to put you on the ice, and to place you in a position to succeed. When people like and respect you, it can benefit you. Conversely, creating a negative impression makes realizing your ambitions more difficult. It's a simple fact that people are more likely to want to assist you in reaching your goals if you've made a good impression on them.

Here are some key Social Skills for making a good impression on people:

1. **BE POLITE AND COURTEOUS:** Making a good impression starts with the simplest advice and the smallest gestures. Talk respectfully, not rudely, to others. Be sensitive about the words you choose and how they may affect others' feelings. The use of appropriate manners such as saying "please" and "thank you" and holding doors for people can all affect opinions of you. Aspiring athletes want to gain the reputation of being a class act, and being polite and courteous goes a long way toward that.

2. **SMILE AND ACKNOWLEDGE OTHERS:** When someone walks right by you without acknowledging you, it can seem like they haven't noticed that you even exist. To avoid giving others that impression, all it takes is eye contact and a nod as you pass by. Of course, a smile does much more: It tells people that you are friendly, and sets them at ease around you. If you know them, it can help convey that you like them. When people feel respected and liked by you, they are in return likely to form a good impression of you.

3. **BE POSITIVE:** If someone trashed you, would you keep a favourable impression of them? Probably not! So, to make good impressions on others, don't criticize them or complain about their decisions or actions. Even if they don't hear you do it, word may still get back to them. Generally it's wise to bite your tongue and keep negative opinions to yourself: "If you don't have anything good to say, don't say anything at all." On the other hand, if you do have something good to say, then say it! It is a thoughtful thing to do, and people appreciate having their efforts recognized. False flattery is easy to see through, but genuine praise that is deserved helps make a good impression. Keeping a positive attitude will help you see positive things worth praising in others and what they do.

4. **TAKE INTEREST IN OTHERS:** Attention makes us feel good. It's nice knowing that someone finds us interesting or important. Part of being polite is to not talk only about yourself, but also show an interest in others. By doing this, you will likely find out interesting things about others, or their experiences or opinions that you will want to know more about. Asking them about those and listening to what they say is taking an interest in them. In response, they will likely develop a favourable impression of you.

5. **TALK IN TERMS THEY UNDERSTAND:** It's hard to make a good impression without establishing good communication first. Different people have different backgrounds, personalities, outlooks, and manners of communicating. Learning the way they operate and how to "speak their language" in dealing with them helps assure them that you truly understand them. This in turn gives them a comfort level in letting you get closer into their inner circle. It also helps them get a "read" on you, to feel safe in forming a solid good impression of you.

In order to see exactly how these skills might apply to various hockey situations you may face, practice them in similar *low-pressure situations*:

1. For an example, here are a few hockey situations where you would use these:

- meeting a new teammate;

- being introduced to a coach;

- entering or leaving an arena or a full dressing room; and
- sitting down to talk with a scout, etc.

2. Outside hockey situations where you could practice these:

- meeting a new student at your school;
- being introduced to a friend of your parents;
- entering or leaving a store or a birthday party; and
- applying for a job, volunteer position, or student council role you might not otherwise apply for, where you will be interviewed by a decision-maker.

Notice when you see the desired reaction from others, and when you don't, and refine your skills accordingly.

Striving for Favourable Outcomes When Interacting with People

Many situations will arise in your hockey career (and outside it) where in interacting with someone you will be hoping for a specific outcome. It could be getting a tryout, being picked for a team, gaining more ice time, having a linemate pass the puck more, securing help with your training, or any number of things. In such situations, if you've already made a good impression, the chances are much greater the person will make a decision that will please you. Some other Social Skills, however, can specifically help in these kinds of situations:

1. **START ON SAFE GROUND:** Begin your interaction in a friendly way. This encourages the other person to interact in a friendly way with you too. Before you get into any points of contention, be positive about the other person, as you learned earlier is appropriate. As the discussion moves toward the matter at issue, find common ground where the two of you will agree. Find things to say to which they will reply "yes." This helps remind both of you how much you share in common, and puts in perspective any single matter of possible contention that may be discussed afterward.

2. **MINIMIZE CONFRONTATION:** Arguing may be the natural thing to do when presented with a position you don't agree with, but it is tricky to argue in a way that doesn't have negative effects on dealings. As with criticism, it is often best to avoid direct confrontation. Even if you disagree with another person, you should still show respect for the other person's opinions, which they are as entitled to as you are to yours. Be humble and honest about instances in which you have been wrong. This will show them you are not trying to prove you are superior and they will be less defensive about the possibility of their being wrong in the matter you plan to discuss. Now that you have given them a chance to be receptive, you can sensitively outline your perspective.

3. **DISCUSS THINGS FROM THEIR PERSPECTIVE:** Try to truly see things from the other person's point of view, appreciating their personal situation and sympathizing with their feelings. Doing this will help you understand what, if anything,

would make them support the favourable outcome you seek. Only from their perspective can you see a case for how that outcome could address their needs, desires, and concerns. If you hope to have them support your desired outcome, this is the case you will need to help them see. If you are successful at doing this, you may not only have their agreement, but maybe their gratitude as well.

4. **GUIDE OTHERS TO INDEPENDENTLY CHOOSE YOUR WAY OF THINKING:** When possible, let people come to the conclusions you hope they will on their own, without you telling them what to think. This allows the other person to feel confident in their own thinking and comfortable with the conclusions they may end up coming to. You can encourage the process through a series of questions that lead down the same path as the direction you are thinking. Allowing them to arrive at a conclusion on their own enables them to quite legitimately feel that their conclusion was their own idea. And this can make them more enthusiastic to implement it.

5. **ADD MEANING TO THE DISCUSSION:** Besides practical aspects of the matter at issue, remember that other people have a sense of personal character and their own dreams. If you know what theirs are, then when you discuss things from their perspective, as in number three above, consider whether the outcome you hope for has a genuine bearing on the dreams they hope to achieve and the reputation they aspire to live up to. If it does, help them see this in a sensitive way, as these are matters of overwhelming importance to them. Just as you know how important it is to support yourself, express support for their aspirations and their possibility to reach them. If a person feels something is important to their dreams or character, the practical costs involved can shrink in comparison.

In order to see exactly how these skills might apply to various hockey situations you may face, I suggest asking a parent or mentor to read the above, and then join you in a *role-playing exercise*, which you can repeat from time to time to practice these skills:

1. Pick a common hockey situation where you might need these skills, such as talking to a recruiter about getting a tryout, a coach about getting more ice time, a linemate about passing the puck more, a teacher about writing a letter of recommendation for you, etc.

2. Your parent or mentor will assume the role of this other person, and act as if they really are that person.

3. You must also act as if they are that person, and then practice your skills above in dealing with them, and responding to how they react to you. Notice when you see the desired reaction from them, and when you don't, and refine your skills accordingly.

You can apply all of the Social Skills above both inside and outside of hockey. A different group of Social Skills apply specifically to the various social contexts in hockey.

Working within a Team Environment

Operating effectively within a team includes interactions with peers. This involves the following Social Skills:

BEING COMFORTABLE IN THE PRESENCE OF A GROUP: A hockey player must be comfortable enough in the presence of a group (their team) to play their best. This includes:

- being self-assured about who you are and your rightful place in the group;
- projecting a *presence* that conveys this assurance to others, yet also your welcoming of them;
- not being overly self-conscious or worried about what others think of you, but also not projecting any disdain for their opinion;
- being able to adapt in order to fit in with the group, while still staying true to yourself; and
- not allowing any group social issues to detract from your ability to perform the tasks you must perform as a player.

GETTING ALONG: It's important for players to be able to get along with as many teammates as possible, as much as possible, as often as possible. You want to be a player who is good for "team chemistry," not a "cancer" that teams don't want around. This often involves:

- being easy-going (not as a competitor, but in social interactions with teammates), and not being outwardly judgmental;
- avoiding contentious discussions, keeping conversation topics light, and joking around in a playful and harmless way;
- being versatile in the way you talk, act, and interact so you can develop *rapport* with players of very different types, backgrounds, outlooks, and personalities;

- being upbeat, positive, and encouraging of teammates;
- being humble, not arrogant or egotistical;
- being liked and respected by your teammates. In other words, making friends with every player you can; and
- not being drawn into any cliques of players that don't get along with other groups of players on the team. Cliques hurt team bonding and chemistry.

BEING A TEAM PLAYER: For everyone's benefit, it's important to be able to work together effectively with teammates to help the team compete well. This includes:
- making clear in word and deed your commitment to the team's goals;
- accepting on-ice roles assigned by the coach, and not trying to do other players' tasks or do everything yourself (which won't work anyway);
- supporting others and making appropriate sacrifices for the team;
- leading through play and positive example, not setting yourself up as a leader by self-pronouncement or being condescending to everyone else; and
- helping the team, and not being a selfish player whose actions benefit themselves at the expense of the team.

DEALING WITH PEER PRESSURE: You must be able to resist pressure from peers urging you to do something you're not comfortable with. This means:
- accepting the general rule that you can't please everyone, and that if you try, there is one person you surely won't please: yourself
- considering whether others' positions have merit, but otherwise not being concerned with what others say about you or your decisions or actions. The secret to being "cool" is to just be yourself, and at the same time, be self-assured about who you are;
- likewise, knowing there is no pressure on you to do anything peers bug you to do, or even to justify to them why you won't. Try, however, to do things in a way that doesn't invite unnecessary attention or confrontation.

Working with Authorities

Hockey players play under the authority of coaches, and according to the rules of the game as administered by league officials and referees. In addition, young players live under the authority of parents or guardians. And they may learn under the tutelage of expert hockey instructors and school teachers. Interacting effectively with these authorities is essential and involves these Social Skills:

GIVING AND GETTING RESPECT: This includes:

- treating authorities with the respect and deference they expect;
- being obedient to directives given by authorities; and
- showing eagerness in following instructions.

In doing the above, you should earn the respect of the authority. But if they don't give you respect, respectfully request it. You can't succeed long-term in a relationship where respect only flows one way.

If an authority respects you, you should receive from them an appropriate balance between compliments and constructive critiques.

GIVING AND GETTING TRUST: This includes:

- trusting that authorities know what they're doing in how they direct you, unless a situation arises where it becomes clear otherwise;
- being responsive to what authorities appropriately ask from you; and
- displaying leadership in reliably executing what they expect or more.

All of this should earn authorities' trust in you. If not, ask them what you can do to earn greater trust from them, and if it makes sense, try to meet that challenge. You want to be someone who is counted on.

LEARNING TO LEARN: You don't just want to deal effectively with authorities; you also want to learn from them. This involves:

- having a good attitude about what you can learn from each authority figure, and being committed to learning those things;
- figuring out *how* to learn what there is to be learned from each authority;
- listening intently to instructions and explanations;
- being humble and receptive to the possibility of improving, including through their suggestions. In other words, being *coachable*; and
- asking questions or asking for assistance when needed in order for you to learn and improve.

PROTECTING YOUR IDENTITY: While respecting the power of authorities, you must still stay true to yourself and your values, first and foremost. This means never letting threats or promises by an authority figure induce you to do what your conscience tells you is wrong, or that you are not comfortable with as a person.

Operating in a Competitive Environment

Another social context you must be able to operate effectively in as part of hockey is competition. Sports are competition, and advancing to higher levels involves competition. That includes interactions with rivals and opponents. This involves:

BEING COMFORTABLE IN A COMPETITIVE SITUATION: You must be comfortable enough in competitive situations and even conflict to do what you need to succeed. This includes:

- not letting anything shake your sense of self-worth, or your determination and pride in competing your hardest, no matter the results;
- not being mentally unsettled or intimidated by competitive situations;
- not being thrown off by others' emotions or responses to a competitive situation (including hostility or jealousy); and
- acting *professional* by not taking any competitive run-ins personally, which will only distract you from doing what you need to do to succeed.

DISARMING AND DEFYING OPPONENTS AND RIVALS: Between competitions, it can help to have Social Skills for disarming your opponents and defying their ability to catch on to your game's tactics. This involves:

- being gracious and friendly to opponents and rivals when off the ice;
- being humble and respectful—not arrogant or dismissive—when you win;
- not being a sore loser by making excuses or complaining when you lose; and
- learning from them what you can about them, their approach, their game, and their tactics.

Meanwhile, don't disclose too much or be too predictable and allow them to do the same to you. You don't want to tip your hand, you want to leave them guessing.

CONTENDING WITH OPPONENTS AND RIVALS: In competition or conflict on and off the ice, you must be able to hold your ground. This includes:

- knowing your purpose. In a game, the object is to win, to defeat your opponent. In any off-ice situation, you must bear in mind what your purpose is as well;
- being fiercely competitive when the game is on. Within the rules, hold nothing back, regardless of your feelings toward a person outside competition; and

- being assertive and aggressive when called for. Don't let yourself be intimidated on the ice, or bullied off the ice. Sometimes standing your ground in a firm but appropriate way against aggressive behaviour is necessary, and doing so early on can prevent having to do it more later.

Dealing with the Surrounding Environment

At every level, an environment surrounds the game. At higher levels, that environment becomes larger and more complex, with the presence of fans and media. You must be able to operate effectively in your sport's environment, and interact positively with external observers. This requires the following Social Skills:

BEING COMFORTABLE UNDER SCRUTINY: Wherever hockey is played, people watch and will express opinions on what they've seen. You must be comfortable playing under scrutiny and at higher levels, in the public eye. This includes:

- having a thick skin for criticism—*Crocodile Skin*, as it's called. Don't let negative opinions of outsiders affect your accurate perception of your game or your focus on playing your game; and
- taking compliments from outside observers with a grain of salt. Outside opinions don't count when it comes to making it. You don't want to develop a "big head" and let your attitude or play suffer in the eyes of those whose opinion does count—the people deciding who will advance.

EARNING A GOOD REPUTATION: Spectators and the media may not be officially involved in hockey, but they are close to it. So:

- be respectful. The way you treat them can affect your reputation with people in hockey; and
- be careful. Assess what you might gain versus what you could lose, and don't say or do something you may regret.

---

the inside story

If you make it far, high-level hockey is supported by fans. A request for an autograph or photo may seem like a small thing to you, but means a great deal to a fan. Likewise, the media publicize hockey for fans. After a game, whether you feel like answering questions or not, asking them is their job, so be courteous.

In other social situations you might encounter, a good technique for figuring out how best to handle them is to put yourself in the shoes of the other person involved. Ask yourself what, from their perspective, might you do that could encourage them to respond the way you hope?

Remember that your skills are developed through skill-building projects, as described in Chapter 9. Each year, you will have new skill-related objectives and projects through which you can progressively develop your skills to keep up with higher levels of hockey. To help you identify suitable practice drills and other skill-building suggestions for your Social Skills project, check our website.

Social Skills might not seem like hockey skills, but they are an important part of the puzzle of making it.

EXPERTS' RECAP

Remember . . .

· You may not think of Social Skills as hockey skills, but they are very important in hockey as in most other things.
· Advancement in hockey depends on the subjective judgment of other people.
· Make a good impression on others, using the skills from this chapter.
· Master the skills for striving for favourable outcomes in dealing with people.
· Hockey puts you in various social contexts which call for their own specialized skills.

safety skills—preventing and dealing with injuries

CHAPTER 13

> **SCOUTS' PREVIEW**
> In this chapter . . .
> · What Safety Skills are, and why they're important for hockey
> · Safety Skills for injury prevention and minimization
> · Safety Skills for handling injuries when they do happen
> · Tips to avoid getting sick

What Are Safety Skills?

In a rigorous and demanding physical sport like hockey, the potential for injury exists. Even minor injuries—"bumps and bruises" or muscle strains, for instance—can hinder performance, or cause you to miss an important game. There is also a chance of more serious injuries. Ligament or bone injuries, severe sprains, or concussions, for example, could sideline your progress for months or leave you with some long-term limitations.

As a result, it's critical to develop skills that can help you minimize your risk of injury, and deal as effectively as possible with injuries you do experience. This way, you can preserve your health and maximize your career potential and longevity.

Safety Skills for Injury Prevention and Minimization

You have probably heard the medical expression, *"An ounce of prevention is worth a pound of cure."* Once an injury occurs, only so much can be done. But if there's a way to prevent an injury occurring in the first place, then that is the perfect prescription. While nothing can eliminate the risk of injury from hockey, or anything else for that matter, you can learn how to minimize your risk.

In Section 3, you learned some important things you can do to prevent injury: a foundation of strong basic health makes you safer and more injury-resistant, steering clear of pitfalls avoids the injury risk associated with many of them, and selecting proper equipment allows your body the freedom to move to avoid injury, plus cushions it from impacts that might cause injury.

In Section 5, you will learn about fitness training, which makes your body stronger, more durable, more agile, and thus more injury-resistant. Part of Fitness Training is allowing sufficient rest when your body has been strained. Whether it is the strain of training, of competition, of illness, or of a bodily nuisance that isn't quite an injury, that rest is essential for you to avoid getting worn down until you suffer actual injury.

There are also some specific skills you can learn and utilize just for the very purpose of avoiding injury. These include:

WARM-UP BEFORE EXERCISING: Prior to any game, practice, or other exercise session, it is important to warm-up. This eases your body into the upcoming exercise, so that it is not suddenly under intense strain, which increases the risk of injury. Warm-ups start with easy, low-level exercise, and gradually raise their intensity level to that of the upcoming exercise session. Try to involve most of the body parts you'll be using in the actual session. For example, prior to practice, you may want to jog slowly on the spot, gradually speeding up over a few minutes. Then you might do some dynamic movement exercises like hip rolls and jumping jacks. Your warm-up might conclude with exercises that get you thinking and reacting like carioca or juggling a hacky sack with a few teammates.

COOL DOWN AFTER EXERCISING: Just like you don't want to start intense exercise suddenly, you don't want to stop suddenly. After any type of exercise session, do a cool-down routine. Like the warm-up, this starts with several minutes of a low-level basic exercise such as a light ride of a stationary bike. Then you can do stretching exercises. This will help prevent your muscles from stiffening up too much after exercise, and will relax them so you can recover for the next time you play.

---

ask the AUTHOR-ity

What about flexibility?

An appropriate level of flexibility is important in injury prevention. If your muscles are stiff and inflexible, and they get stretched beyond their "comfort zone" while playing, you can pull or tear a muscle. On the other hand, you don't want to take flexibility to the extreme. A bit of resistance in the muscles can stop a violent movement so that the stress doesn't end up borne by a joint instead, causing a severe joint injury.

There are some common misconceptions about flexibility. We asked athletic therapist and trainer Doug Stacey of Hockey Canada to give us the latest scientific consensus on the best use of stretching exercises: "The big view now is that stretching in terms of studies has shown no effectiveness at reducing injury prior to activity. Stretching is still important for increasing range of motion, but it's actually better not to do it just before you play. If you're stretching beforehand, you're lengthening your muscles statically, whereas it should be done as part of a more dynamic movement (as in the warm-up exercises above). After playing is actually a good time for passive stretching, because you're all nice and warm and you're going to get a good stretch."

ICE SURFACE AWARENESS: Whenever you are on the ice in a competitive situation, it is crucial to be aware of your surroundings. Know where you are on the ice in relation to the boards, nets, and so forth. Be alert to where other players are, the directions they're headed, and what they seem to be doing. In practice, watch for any teammates who like to be pranksters, or—particularly if you are a goalie—for players who shoot pucks outside planned drills. In games, watch the play, but at the same time learn to use your *peripheral vision* to monitor your changing location on the ice and the movements of nearby opponents. If any of them have a reputation for injuring other players, keep an extra eye on them. Keep your head up at all times, including when you have the puck, where you must use peripheral vision to see the puck. This is crucial to avoiding injuries.

POSITIONING AND MOVEMENT TO AVOID INJURY: Keep your knees well-bent at all times. Don't turn your back to the play. When standing near the boards, face them on an angle, as opposed to directly, so that if you are bumped or checked, you will not go faceward into the boards. For the same reason, when retrieving a puck from the boards with opponents chasing you, do not skate directly toward the puck, but take an angled approach. Keep some weight on both feet so that if a stick ends up sliding under one of your skate blades, you can balance on the other foot instead of falling. In any case where you might be knocked down or into the boards, be ready to extend your arms to break your fall. On offence, don't stand still near the boards or goalposts; move around so you are more difficult to check. On defence, if you miss a check on an opponent, don't stick out a limb at the last second to try to get a piece of them, as this could injure both of you (and result in a penalty for your team).

PROTECTING YOURSELF: In Chapter 10, you learned skills to help you avoid injury from bodychecks. And above you learned to try to be aware of possible cheap shots within the play. If you see someone who appears to be coming at you in a different suspicious manner, try to face them and keep your arms and stick up in order to protect yourself until the officials arrive.

---

the inside story

Your safety is important to your health and career, so be considerate of other players by respecting theirs as well, and not playing dirty. Think about it: If everyone plays that way, everyone is less safe. Playing cheap is poor sportsmanship and hurts your character. Read the rules of hockey (www.hockeycanada.ca), and discover what all the fouls are, as well as exactly what a legal bodycheck is and isn't.

RECOGNIZING HIGH-RISK OFF-ICE SITUATIONS: There are lots of ways you could get injured outside of hockey, and end up being sidelined. Some of these possibilities can't realistically be avoided. But you can always take steps to minimize the risk. For example, if you can't avoid riding in a car to get to games, you can at least minimize the risk of being injured in a car accident by always wearing a seatbelt, riding in a safe vehicle, and driving safely. Never ride in a car driven by someone who has been drinking alcohol.

As you learned in Chapter 6, playing other sports can be good for you. But make sure you are properly prepared, equipped, and use good judgment. You don't want to, for example, turn an ankle playing pickup basketball and miss a heavily scouted upcoming hockey tournament. Take extra caution with potential activities such as football, boxing, martial arts, alpine bike racing, or motor sports (motorbikes, ATVs, snowmobiles, etc.) that carry significant injury risks. Use common sense: Know the water you are diving into. Avoid precarious building structures, heights where there is a chance to fall, slippery walkways and steps, unruly crowds, and other situations of obvious potential danger. Stay away from fights, even if you have been wronged, and find a way of dealing with the offense that doesn't involve risking an injury that could hurt your career. If you are at a party, bar, or other place where people are drunk or acting unpredictably, take note if it looks like trouble might be brewing, and leave before it starts. You don't want get caught up in it and get hurt.

the inside story

My (standard NHL player) contract with the Pittsburgh Penguins stipulated, "The Player and the Club recognize that the Player's participation in other sports may impair or destroy his ability and skill as a hockey player. Accordingly the Player agrees that he will not during the period of this Contract . . . engage or participate in football, baseball, softball, hockey, lacrosse, boxing, wrestling or other athletic sport without the written consent of the Club . . ."

Handling Injuries When They Do Happen

Despite your best efforts to avoid them, injuries can still happen. You want to deal with them in the best way, to recover as completely and quickly as possible. You also want to manage the time you are out and any physical limitations you have when you first come back, to play the best you can.

What you read in Section 3 is again a starting point for how to handle injuries: The general principles you learned for managing your health will help your body heal the best it can. While being sidelined can leave you isolated and down, you've learned not to compound problems by letting them lead you to fall prey to a pitfall. And if you heal to the point that your doctors say you can play even though you're not yet 100 per cent, the right equipment will be important in protecting you from re-aggravating the injury.

Aside from the elements of your foundation, there are some specific skills you can learn and use to help handle your injuries. These include:

DAMAGE ASSESSMENT: The first thing to do immediately once you realize you've been hurt is a damage assessment. If you have a team trainer on hand, have them check you out right away. If you don't, you may have to do it yourself, with the help of a parent or coach if possible. Hockey Canada trainer Doug Stacey advises, "Usually there's three things I look at in terms of your ability to continue or how serious it is. Number one, do you have full active range of motion? Number two, do you have full strength without pain? Number three, do you have function (the ability to control your motion through your range)? If you don't have those three, the risk is much greater for causing further damage to whatever's going on or putting stress on something else, because you aren't able to protect it." The bottom line is, if you think your injury could be significant enough that you're putting yourself at risk if you keep playing, then you shouldn't continue until you've had it evaluated by a medical professional. If it's an injury to your head, and you're not sure whether it might be a concussion, adhere to the adage "If in doubt, sit out."

PRO-file

Dr. Jim DeMarco

Dr. Jim DeMarco is a specialist in Sports Medicine who lives and works in Whistler, B.C. He has covered a variety of sporting events in Canada and abroad including hockey, mountain biking, skiing, and snowboarding. Dr. DeMarco has worked with Alpine Canada for twenty

years. He was a member of the 2006 Canadian Olympic medical team in Torino, Italy. And he worked with Hockey Canada at the 2007 Under-18 World Junior Hockey Championships in Finland.

In terms of the medical process for dealing with acute injuries, we sought expert advice from Dr. Jim DeMarco, my uncle and an emergency room physician and sports medicine specialist who has worked with both Hockey Canada and the Canadian National Ski Team.

MEDICAL EVALUATION: According to Dr. DeMarco: "It's very important for every team to establish a clear chain of command for the evaluation of an injury reported by a player. And if the injury is deemed anything more significant than a bruise or minor strain, you should see a doctor." Some of the things you should learn from the medical evaluation of an injury are:

- Expected *lost time*. Will the injury:
  - Allow you to continue playing and is it *safe to* play with?
  - Keep you out *short to medium term* (up to two months)?
  - Keep you sidelined *long term* (over two months)?
- Expected *prognosis*. As a result of the injury, will you have:
  - No limitations or effects to deal with?
  - Some temporary limitations and effects?
  - Permanent limitations and effects?

CARE REGIMEN: According to Dr. DeMarco: "Different injuries will have very different treatment guidelines, which your doctor will go over with you. Another thing is, if you're not confident you're getting proper treatment or care, there is no reason not to seek a second medical opinion. Your health is just too important." Aside from the doctor's care recommendations, which will form the main part of your medical treatment regimen for the injury, here are some additional things that can sometimes help:

- Dr. DeMarco says, "For virtually any musculoskeletal and soft-tissue injuries, in the acute phase (two to three days following injury) follow the *'RICE IT'* prescription: rest, ice, compression, and elevation."
- Longer term, sometimes it can help to talk to someone who's had the same injury and knows what you're experiencing. They may even have some advice for you on what helped them get through it.

RETURN TO PLAY DECISION: According to Dr. DeMarco: "If you've had an injury that's kept you out, a medical person should be involved in your return to sport. Typically, there are progressive return protocols where you follow a series of steps in coming back from the injury, although the process varies depending on the injury. When you are medically cleared by your doctor, and capable, then you can return. Sometimes even though medically cleared, a player doesn't feel ready. Injuries don't just have a physical component, but also a mental impact, and if a player's not emotionally ready to return yet, it's important to acknowledge that. A player shouldn't be forced to play under any circumstances. And if there's any question of not being ready, don't take a chance."

As a hockey player, here are some other things to consider in timing your return:

- Hockey is a tough and demanding sport. You can't just be healed, you also need to have regained the strength to not immediately get reinjured, as well as regained the fitness level you need to play effectively.
- At higher levels, you also want to consider what level you will be able to perform at if you come back at that time. You don't want to stay out longer than necessary and hurt your team or give rivals a chance to seize the opportunity of your absence. But you also don't want to return when you're not able to perform at a strong level, because this won't help your team either, and could worry scouts and coaches about whether you can be the same player you were before the injury.

PLAYING THROUGH INJURIES: Playing through injuries is often part of hockey. According to Doug Stacey: "It's the whole idea of hurt versus harm. So sometimes you're going to play, and it's going to hurt a bit, but as long as it's not going to cause further problems, we'll let athletes do it." The skill of being able to play effectively despite not feeling 100 per cent is important for a hockey player. Here are some further details on playing through injuries:

- Dr. DeMarco: "For less serious injuries, the athletic therapist might wrap the injury with a tensor bandage or tape to provide some support and minimize the effects of the injury. And you can ice between periods or even shifts to reduce the amount of pain and swelling."
- Doug Stacey: "With more serious injuries, we'll pad it, brace it, and tape it to protect it. A brace stabilizes a joint, but often doesn't actually touch the area of the injury. So the tape helps, because it goes right on the skin."
- Your doctor or trainer can advise you about safe and appropriate medications or over-the-counter aids to minimize pain, stiffness, and inflammation.
- You may need to make adjustments in your game to work around the pain or limitations of the injury, until it fully recovers.

MENTALLY COPING WITH BEING OUT: Another important skill to learn is how to mentally cope with being sidelined. Of course you want to play, but that is out of your control for the time being, so you must accept that. At the same time, you can still be eager to return. You also want to be optimistic and determined to make the fullest recovery you can, both in terms of your health and game.

- For short-term and medium-term injuries, you may want to:
  - Continue to be around your team for games and other functions.
  - Participate as a team member in other ways, whether just encouraging teammates, or helping the coaching staff with game notes or stats.
- For long-term injuries, you may want to:
  - Focus on your rehab. Don't feel pressure from yourself to be around the team constantly if that makes it mentally harder on you because you won't be able to return soon.
  - Don't think about the injury as time lost from hockey. Below, you will learn how to use the time as a chance to pursue other positive activities you couldn't pursue if you were busy playing. Doing that can help you feel refreshed when you come back.

MAKING USE OF TIME OUT: For short-term and medium-term injuries, you may want to:

- Stay as ready as possible for your return: physically, mentally, and in every way. This will enable you to "hit the ground running" and play as well as you can when you get back.
- Find constructive things to do while out, so you are not just losing time. At your team's games, move around and watch from different spots in the arena, such as up close and bird's-eye view, to get new perspectives on the game you can use when you come back. Study video of your own prior games or professional games and see what insights you can pick up. If your injury is such that you are not to exert yourself mentally, maybe it's a good time to just reconnect with your feelings of how much you enjoy the game and what a privilege it is to play. Then when you return, you will be reinvigorated.
- For long-term injuries, you may want to:
  - Do everything you can that's medically recommended to return as fast as possible. But don't waste too much time trying to preserve elements of game-readiness. It serves little purpose to work on that until you are closer to being able to return.

◦ Find a positive preoccupation to apply yourself to while you are out. Consider it like a "sabbatical" where you may be able to learn new ideas from this other preoccupation, which you can take back to hockey and apply when you return.

Tips to Avoid Getting Sick

What about illness? A lot of what you read above with respect to injuries can apply similarly to illness. Make sure to consult a doctor about your illness, how to treat it, and what strategies (including any of those above) are safe and appropriate for you to use in dealing with it.

Here are some good common-sense pieces of advice from Dr. DeMarco for young hockey players to help reduce their risk of getting ill:

- "Properly air out your equipment, and cleanse it regularly according to the equipment care guidelines. Clean undergarments are essential."
- "Proper hygiene is important, including washing your hands with soap after wearing hockey gloves, especially before eating."
- "Make sure you dry off properly afterward. Don't go out wet into cold weather."
- "When possible, have your own water bottle. This is absolutely critical if there is any question of an illness going around. It's also important to use it properly: Don't put your mouth right on it, squirt the water. You see NHL players squirt water away before they drink, to rinse anything on the nozzle. Proper care of bottles means don't leave water in them for days, and wash them between uses."
- "Get adequate rest, sleep, nutrition, and fluids so that you don't get worn down. A body that's tired or malnourished is way more likely to get sick or injured."
- "Parents and coaches have a role to play in reinforcing all this. Also, it's their responsibility that if a player has the flu or another communicable disease, they shouldn't be playing or be in contact with the team until they're better. Otherwise you're putting the whole team at risk of getting sick."

EXPERTS' RECAP

Remember . . .

· Safety skills are important for avoiding and handling injuries, which are part of sports.
· Try to avoid injuries with the help of proper warm-ups, cool-downs, special on-ice skills, and managing high-risk off-ice situations.
· Deal with injuries as best you can through proper medical evaluation and care, smart decisions about returning to play, constructive use of time out, and learning to play through pain when deemed medically safe.
· Follow simple steps to minimize how often you get sick and miss time from hockey.

skills of the stars

CHAPTER **14**

THIS LAST CHAPTER ON SKILLS IS A BONUS SECTION COVERING SPECIAL SKILLS OF THE STARS.

These are unique skills that superstar players have developed, or regular skills they have found a way to raise to a unique level.

The reason such skills are worthy of attention is because studying those who have already reached the highest levels helps you succeed. If you watch star players, you will notice that they are proficient at the game's physical skills (in fact, all high-level players are, not just stars) and stars usually have highly developed mental skills that give them an edge over their peers. But many stars also possess one or more special or unique skills that help set them apart. These skills may not be obvious to every observer, but an expert can discern these skills, and what they do for the players employing them. Often, these special skills are a key secret to a star's extraordinary success. The best part is, once you identify the secret Skills of Stars, in many cases you can learn and acquire them too.

Sometimes, one unique skill makes a pro out of a player who otherwise might not make it, or a superstar out of an otherwise ordinary player. So just imagine what it could do for your game to systematically study and copy the signature skills of *several* of the world's greatest hockey stars!

In this book, there isn't space to cover all the world's top hockey stars and their special skills, but in the pages that follow you will find a few examples, to give you a taste of the impact of these skills.

You can find more Skills of the Stars on my website.

PRO-file

Mats Sundin—"The Reach-By"
Mats Sundin led the Toronto Maple Leafs in scoring twelve of his thirteen years with the team. He is the franchise all-time leader in goals and points. Sundin is the longest-serving NHL team captain of European origin in history. In 2006, he was captain of the Swedish team that won Olympic Gold, setting up the game-winning-goal in the third period.

For a decade, **MATS SUNDIN** was the Toronto Maple Leafs' big scoring threat. As a result, opponents would guard him closely, forcing Sundin to find innovative ways to get free and continue to score. Sundin found a way to turn close-guarding against his opponents: He would let them draw close, and then push and muscle himself around them onto the offensive side of the play. I call it "The Reach-By," because Sundin often dropped his bottom hand off his stick in order to reach that arm in front of the defender and push himself by. If Sundin already had the puck, he would continue fending off the defender with that free arm until he got close enough to score. Then he would put that hand back on his stick, and quickly get a shot off before the defender could check him, or the goalie could get ready. When he didn't yet have the puck, Sundin would wait until a teammate was almost ready to make a pass to him, and then use the same reach-by technique to get on the offensive side of the player checking him. That way, when he received the pass, the defender was already stuck behind him, and he could score before the defender got back in front.

PRO-file

Brett Hull—"Hide and Seek"
Brett Hull has the third most goals of any player in NHL history. In 1999, he scored the goal that won the Dallas Stars their first and only Stanley Cup. He later won a second Stanley Cup with Detroit. It was Hull that scored a late tying-goal against Canada, as Team USA won the first World Cup of Hockey, one of the greatest feats in U.S. hockey history.

BRETT HULL had an incredible shot, just like his father Bobby. But Brett was never the great skater his father, "the Golden Jet," was; nor did Brett have the all-around raw physical talent Bobby turned into superior Physical Skills in his day. However, Brett was one of the smartest players of his era—a master of the Mental Skills of hockey. His greatest skill was his ability to get away from checkers, and get to a spot where he would be both open for a pass and able to score. When the puck got into the offensive end, the first thing Brett would do is "hide." He would drift out of the play, where no checker would be concerned about watching him. That way, he shook off defenders guarding him. Next, he would read the play and anticipate what might happen. Based on that, he would figure out the right spot to go, and the right time to be there, where with no one watching him, he could "seek" a pass and quickly score before the defensive team could react.

PRO-file

Sidney Crosby—"Opposite Edges"

Sidney Crosby is one of the top hockey players in the world today. After setting numerous Junior records, Crosby took the NHL by storm, scoring over 100 points in his first season. In just his second season, Crosby won the NHL's Hart Trophy for MVP. And in his third and fourth seasons, he led the Pittsburgh Penguins team that had only recently missed the playoffs for several years to the finals in 2008 and the Stanley Cup in 2009. Crosby has a very bright future.

SIDNEY CROSBY is not the NHL's biggest player, fastest skater, smoothest stickhandler, nor does he have the league's hardest shot. But he has the greatest Mental Skills in hockey, perhaps ever. And he has developed several unique skills as well. One of the unique skills introduced into high-level hockey by Crosby is his use of "opposite edges." When Crosby gets close to a defender or finds himself in a high-traffic area, he stops skating on parallel edges, and shifts onto opposite edges. Anticipating possible physical contact, he does this to give himself extra stability and maneuverability. If an opponent gets a piece of him, he can lift the leg on that side off the ground, turn sideways, and glide-and-slide by the opponent on the other foot, instead of being stopped or knocked down. Crosby is able to use this skill both on the rush and in the corners. From the opposite-edge stance, Crosby will also pump one foot at a time in a C-motion. This allows him to maintain speed instead of just gliding and losing speed as he approaches the defender. And it also allows him to meander unpredictably side-to-side, making it difficult for the defender to get the right handle or angle on him. All in all, this makes Crosby very difficult to stop, as he can use his skill to squirm out of most attempted checks or pins. You can learn this unique skill and use it to your advantage as well.

PRO-file

Pavel Kubina—"Shot? I Think Not"

Pavel Kubina has been referred to by Czech teammates as the country's defensive version of Jaromir Jagr. Big, strong, and difficult to stop when he's determined, Kubina was a star for the Tampa Bay Lightning in their surprise 2004 Stanley Cup victory. He won an Olympic Bronze Medal with the Czech Republic in 2006.

Great defencemen help their goalie by minimizing the number of opposing shots on net. One player who is exceptional at this is PAVEL KUBINA. When doing this, at first it may not even look like Kubina is doing anything at all, much less exhibiting a skill. But by having a keen sense of where his net is, and keeping himself positioned between it and the prospective shooter, Kubina often deters the player from even taking a shot. If the player *is* going to shoot, the least dangerous shot is one that ends up nowhere near the net. So, during the time the shooter is winding up, Kubina uses his reach to lunge his stickblade toward the puck, as in a poke-check. He may not be close enough to poke the puck away before the shot, but he is close enough to neutralize the shot at impact and deflect it backward, or catch it just after impact and deflect it forward high over the glass. In some games, I have counted as many as ten shots Kubina has diffused away from his goal. In trying this, make sure to angle your stickblade so that the puck will be deflected away from *you* as well as your net. After all, the best kind of shot-block is the one you execute without the puck ever even striking your body.

PRO-file

Rob Blake—"The Butt-Check"

Rob Blake is one of the greatest all-around defence-man in the modern NHL. He has consistently been among the league-leaders in ice time. Blake won a Stanley Cup with the Colorado Avalanche in 2001, and made it to the Finals with the Los Angeles Kings in 1993. He also won a Gold Medal with Canada at the 2002 Salt Lake City Olympics. And he has won the Norris Trophy for best defenceman in the NHL.

Playing good defence means playing the body. For a guy that plays a lot, that means dishing out a lot of bodychecks. This can be hard on your hands and shoulders. Plus an occasional opponent's stick, hand, or forearm can accidentally catch you in the face. On the ice for nearly half of each game he plays, ROB BLAKE probably figured he had to do something. So he invented what we can call "The Butt-Check." Blake first uses body position to force his opponent to go a certain way. Next, he uses his angling skills to approach the opponent for the bodycheck. Then he uses his special skill: At the last second, he leans forward, accelerates straight at the opponent, and then spins completely backward to check his opponent butt-first. With its built-in padding, the butt isn't something that often gets hurt. So which way do you spin? Having the proper angle, Blake can take away the opponent's cut-back option by accelerating toward the opponent just before spinning. That leaves the opponent only the other way to get by. So Blake spins into them that way, such that if they try to speed up to sneak by, they only end up striking his hip instead, before he finishes spinning all the way around. And a hip-check is the last thing a forward wants to get hit by. Even worse than a butt-check!

PRO-file

Martin Brodeur—"Pinpuck"
Martin Brodeur has won three Stanley Cups with New Jersey, a Gold Medal in the 2002 Olympics for Canada, and Gold in the 2004 World Cup. He has won the Vezina Trophy for top goalie four times, and is first among NHL goalies in all-time wins. His puck-handling ability is reflected in being one of only two goalies ever to score a goal in both the regular season and the playoffs.

Over the course of **MARTIN BRODEUR**'s career, his New Jersey Devils have employed a strategy of clogging up the neutral zone with defenders, forcing the offensive team to dump the puck in and chase after it to get it back. But against Brodeur, playing Dump 'n' Chase means a lot of chasing and not a lot of catching up to the puck. That's because Brodeur handles the puck better than any goalie in history. Just before the puck is dumped in, Brodeur uses the advance glance skill to survey the ice, see where the other players on both teams are, and figure out what play to make. Then while the puck makes its way in on the dump, Brodeur goes to where it's headed, to intercept it. As the puck comes around the boards to him, Brodeur leans slightly toward the boards to trap the puck along the boards right where it hits him. All of this gives him time to make a good pass to a teammate to start a breakout, or to shoot the puck out of his end himself. If the other team can't get control of the puck in his end, it's awfully tough for them to score! And seldom does the opposition retrieve a puck they have dumped in on Brodeur. He turns Dump 'n' Chase into a game of pinball—or "Pinpuck" we should say—where opponents dump the puck in, but Brodeur immediately clears it right back out.

PRO-file

Angela Ruggiero—"Complete Leadership"

My friend Angela Ruggiero is one of the world's top female hockey players, and perhaps the best defender in women's hockey history. She has "a complete set of Olympic medals" (Gold 1998, Silver 2002, and Bronze 2006). In 2004, she won the award for top collegiate hockey player. She scored the shootout game-winning goal as Team USA defeated Canada to win its first World Championship in 2005, and won the tourney again in 2008. A trailblazer since the beginning, her Olympic Gold was won while she was still in high school. Later, she became the first female skater to play a men's pro hockey game, recording an assist and being +3 for the Central Hockey League's Tulsa Oilers. Off the ice, Ruggiero authored a book called *Breaking the Ice*. Also, from a fan con-

test during the Torino Olympics, Ruggiero was chosen to appear on the television show *The Apprentice*. Although eventually eliminated from the TV competition, host Donald Trump was so impressed with Ruggiero's team values that he offered her a job despite having "fired" her on TV.

ANGELA RUGGIERO has been referred to as the Mark Messier of women's hockey: an intense, strong, able, and exceptional leader. Leadership, unlike the other types of skills above, isn't a skill you can always see as a spectator watching. The people best placed to appreciate it are a player's teammates. According to teammate Nicole Corriero (an NCAA star herself), "Angela just had a presence about her—in the locker room, on the ice, off the ice, everywhere. You had an automatic respect for her not only for her hockey skills, but also from how she carried herself as a person. She had great self-respect. And she held herself to a high standard in practice and in games, which helped raise everybody else up as well." Leadership can take many forms—instruction, inspiration, encouragement, or example. Ruggiero displayed all of them. "I like to empower others and help them reach their potential, because that's how the group does best," Ruggiero says. According to Corriero, Ruggiero could also take matters into her own hands. "If Angela was fed up with the score of the game, or how we were playing, or an opposing team putting players out to hound her and take liberties against her all game, we would see her face change and she would get the puck with a determination about her that she would be unstoppable." Leaders don't wait for others, and leaders don't just talk, because talk alone is cheap. "She wasn't the type of person who would chew out teammates or scream on the bench," Corriero explains, "but whenever she did say something, people would listen, and they knew she would follow it up. She would lead by example. And her example provided a spark for the team. She would show us, 'This is how it's done,' and that would inspire us to take our game to the next level." Leaders make other players play better and become better. Jennifer Botterill, another former College teammate of Ruggiero and now an opponent of hers with Team Canada, says, "You can tell even when you play against her on Team USA that she's always trying to bring up people around her. She brings that focus, and strength, and fire and intensity. And that's something that's contagious. The others feed off that." But leadership doesn't just occur during games. Corriero explains, "She was wonderful to all her teammates, she was caring, she was friendly, and even though she was a leader, she hung out with all of us and was a real leader in encouraging team bonding." According to Ruggiero, this was part of her philosophy on leadership: "Chemistry can completely break a team or empower a team. Part of the role of a leader is to make the team come together as a collective, even as each player draws on their individual strengths." As captain for Harvard in 2002–03 and 2003–04, Ruggiero led her team to its first two appearances in the NCAA Championship Game. In recent years, Ruggiero has been assistant captain for the U.S. National Team, and may be the captain for the Olympics in 2010. Recently, Ruggiero passed up an invitation to play Men's Pro Hockey in Finland to stay and train with her Team USA teammates, in order to show the leadership she knows her team needs as they gear up for what will be her fourth and final Olympics—where she's determined to once more win gold.

Remember that your skills are developed through skill-building projects, as described in Chapter 9. As you strive to emulate Skills of the Stars, realize that you likely will not achieve their level of proficiency in the skills right away. It may be that a series of skill-building projects over several years allows you to make gradual improvement in these skills toward the level of the stars you are copying. It takes patience, but it can be a great benefit if you dream of someday becoming a star yourself.

EXPERTS' RECAP
Remember . . .
· Studying top players can help you learn what might make you a better player.
· Stars often have a signature skill—which you can learn too, if you identify it and practice.

5

Russians have always been renowned for their training for hockey. Evgeni Malkin was well-trained indeed to succeed in the NHL. He set a modern NHL record by scoring a goal in each of his first six games in the NHL.

TRAINING
performance
superpowers

THIS SECTION TEACHES YOU WHAT AN ASPIRING PLAYER SHOULD KNOW ABOUT TRAINING FOR HOCKEY.

" Train hard, fighting easy ...
Train easy, fighting hard. "
ALEXANDER SUVOROV, LAST GENERALISSIMO OF RUSSIA

the purpose and the power of training

SCOUTS' PREVIEW
In this chapter . . .
· The difference between skills and training
· What training is, and why it's important
· Being a "competitor" when it comes to sports

CHAPTER 15

BEING AN ATHLETE IS ALL ABOUT COMPETITION.

Every sport in the world—from running to rhythm gymnastics, from polo to pool, from bocce to baseball, from horseshoes to hockey—is a competition at heart.

Great athletes are ones who thrive in competitive situations.

As a hockey player, the two main competitive situations you face are games and tryouts. In every tryout drill, your goal is to measure up well versus the other players. In games, during every shift you are battling against opposing players for control of the puck, fighting to maneuver your team into scoring position and the other team away from it.

Each step up the scale—from beginner to pro—go only to those hockey players who stood out in competitions before: past seasons and playoffs, present tryouts and exhibitions.

The Difference between Skills and Training

In Section 4 of this book, you learned that to advance as a hockey player, you need skills. Indeed, these skills *enable you* to be a great hockey player.

But by themselves skills aren't enough to *make you* even a good hockey player. You need something more in order to help deal with the fact that your skills will be used—not in isolation, or in just any ordinary environment—but in a competition.

To get an idea of what more is needed, let's imagine a boxer named Raw. Raw has been taught all the skills of boxing—the stance, the hand positions, movement, all the different kinds of punches and fakes, dodges and blocks— and other skills that are similar to those you learned for hockey in Section 4. He has perfected them all. Now, without doing anything else, he steps into the ring for a match. What will happen?

Well, even before the bout starts, his opponent, a veteran boxer named Steel, stares Raw down and says menacing things to intimidate him. Raw's skills don't help with this, so it affects him mentally: He is distracted and defensive when the fight starts—hesitant with his punches and slow reacting to Steel's. There are people watching, crowds screaming, bright lights shining in Raw's eyes. None of this was going on while working on his skills with his teacher at his gym! In this wild and unfamiliar environment, Raw is having trouble concentrating in order to execute his skills. After missing with several punches and taking a few punches from Steel, Raw is weak, tired, and in pain—another unfamiliar circumstance. He has no power left in his punches, and he can't hold his arms up to protect himself or move his legs to get out of the way of incoming punches any longer. Steel sees this and pounces, attacking Raw, and knocking him against the ropes. Even though Steel is considerably smaller and less skilled, Raw is struggling to fight back. Before the bell tolls to end the first round, Raw is down for the count. The match is over.

So what did Raw do wrong? Even though he did learn and perfect all the *skills* of boxing, what Raw hadn't done was *train*.

What Is Training and Why Is it Important?

According to the dictionary, to train is "to make fit, qualified, or proficient by exercise for a test of skill." In other words, training is doing a series of activities that will condition you to succeed in competition. Raw had the skills, but they had not been seasoned so as to be ready for testing in competition.

Raw should have trained by doing regular strenuous physical exercise so that he would be in top physical shape and not quickly get tired or weakened during a bout. He also ought to have trained by sparring (simulated fights) with other boxers. Doing so would have helped make him immune to intimidation attempts. It would also have given him the opportunity to try his skills in a match-like situation and execute them in spite of pain. By going to watch other matches before his, Raw could have noted the bright lights and the screaming crowds, while picturing himself in the ring. This would have helped train him not to be thrown off his game when he got in the ring for real.

Just as each of these exercises would have helped Raw prepare for competition in boxing, similar kinds of exercises can help you train to succeed in hockey.

Being a Competitor When it Comes to Sports

While skills allow you to be a *player,* training makes you a *competitor.*

When my brothers and I were teenagers, the best player on the Toronto Maple Leafs—and maybe the best all-around player in the NHL at the time—was Doug Gilmour. Doug wasn't the fastest skater or the smoothest stickhandler out there. Nor did he have the most punishing bodychecks or the hardest shot. When people looked at his skills, it was hard to understand what it was that made him such an awesome player.

That's because focusing on his skills was looking in the wrong place. Doug Gilmour wasn't the highest skilled player in the NHL or even on his own team. But he was the ultimate competitor. In fact, teammates gave Doug the nickname "Killer" because of his "killer instinct," a sports expression for the fierce competitiveness necessary to be great.

PRO-file

Doug Gilmour
After having won a Stanley Cup with Calgary in 1989, Doug Gilmour came to the Toronto Maple Leafs and led a team that had struggled for over a decade into the playoffs and back-to-back final four appearances. In 1993 while scoring 127 points, he simultaneously won the NHL's award for best defensive player. He holds the Toronto Maple Leaf record for most points in a season.

---

the inside story

Years before Gilmour, Rocket Richard was a legendary competitor. And today, Sidney Crosby shares the same reputation. In fact, being a great competitor is key in virtually any sport.

Some of my favourite examples are basketball superstar Michael Jordan, former NBA Champion and MVP; football wide receiver Hines Ward, Superbowl winner and MVP; soccer defender Fabio Cannavaro, World Cup champion and winner of the Golden Boot; tennis star Jimmy Connors, winner of eight Grand Slam titles and former World No 1.

What do these athletes have in common? They all reached the pinnacle of very different sports, and they are all ultimate competitors.

Of course, not everyone can be the world's *ultimate* competitor, but to make it to any high level of hockey, you do need to be a *great* one. Every high-level player in a sport as popular as hockey today is a great competitor.

You may have heard sports commentators refer to an athlete's competitiveness by saying "that's something you just can't teach." It's a line that sounds good on TV, but don't let it discourage you: With hard work and shrewd guidance, any athlete can become a great competitor.

It's true that some people are more competitive by nature than others. But make no mistake, being competitive in life is not the same as being a competitor in sports. Some "competitive people" get into a sports competition, have trouble controlling their emotions, lose their cool, and don't perform up to their potential. Others are constantly competing, and don't spend enough time on the "groundwork" of their game that will enable them to be successful down the road. There are competitive people, however, as well as plenty of less competitive people, that do learn to compete and excel in their sport. It's not about personality, it's about training. In sports, competitors are not born, they are made one day, one exercise, at a time.

Personality isn't what you use to play sports, skills are. As was the case with Raw the boxer, sports contests don't come down to who has the greater skills, but to who uses their skills more effectively in competition. And this is a matter of conditioning yourself—by training—to master executing your skills to their maximum in competition.

---

the inside story

What the commentator said may in fact be true. Many commentators are former coaches, and they may have found that competitiveness wasn't something they could themselves teach players. However, players can learn it on their own, through training, as you will discover in Chapter 19.

Whatever your level of hockey, you probably know players who are highly talented and skilled, but when it comes to games, they are only average players. You probably also know players with more limited talent and skills who continually stand out in games. A complete set of skills, and even the ability to do rare or fancy moves on the ice, won't matter much if you are not a first-rate competitor once the puck is dropped and the game begins. Of course the more skills you have, the better. But just having them is not the same as applying them in competition. And in sports, competition is what counts. Luckily, you can learn to thrive in competition.

While skills probably receive more attention, training is just as important to success in sports. Training transforms your skills into superpowers designed to bring you incredible game results. The better trained you are compared to your opponents, the greater your edge. Anyone whose dream is to make it in hockey should make it their policy to always try to out-train their rivals.

The rest of this section outlines the optimal training for hockey. Following this training can help you translate your athletic potential into powerful performances that catch the attention of scouts.

ask the AUTHOR-ity

What about practice? Is it the same as training?
Practice and training are not the same thing. Practicing your shot in your garage is skill development, not training. Hockey team practices, for the most part, are training—but they are team training. Team training is designed to condition the team as a combined unit to win games. This is different from the individual training you need to improve and achieve your future goals in hockey. Every hockey player needs to do some team training in order to learn how to play within a team system and strategy. However, this can usually be done in a limited amount of practice time. Many team-training drills do have some carry-over benefit for individual training. For example, a team breakout drill against forecheckers helps train you to make passes in game situations and through traffic. A team, however, will

probably practice breakouts very frequently in order to have its group of players on the same page—far past the point where the drills are having a worthwhile added benefit to the player's individual ability to make passes in traffic. The carry-over individual training benefit "maxes" out in much less time than competitive teams spend practicing. The time spent can be justified for its benefit only to team training, not to individual training.

Team practices are a critical part of training and participating in hockey. They just aren't in themselves a major tool for individual training. To reach your goals and dream as an individual player, you will have to take the initiative to train yourself—through a range of exercises designed specifically to make you the complete competitor any elite hockey player must be.

ask the AUTHOR-ity

How does one conduct individual training?
Unlike team training where you rely on scheduled team practices, for individual training, you must take the initiative to organize and do the exercises you need to progress. At the same time, you can still get help from trainers, coaches, and parents. And just

because it's called individual training doesn't mean you must always do it alone. When appropriate, training with a friend or teammate can give you someone to compete against and make training more fun. When I was growing up, I included my brothers Steve and Dominic in many parts of my training.

heads up!

EXPERTS' RECAP
Remember . . .
· In sports, competition is what counts.
· Training prepares you for competition.
· To be a great athlete, you must be a great competitor.
· Make it your goal to always out-train your opponents.

While team practices are not what you rely on for individual training, it doesn't mean you should skip them. It is true that some youth teams practice far too much, which takes precious time away from other necessary aspects of good individual athletic development as well as other life commitments and obligations. But unless you have an alternative team you can play for instead, or make prior arrangements with the coach that you will not attend certain practices, it is generally not a good idea to just skip them. It may create conflict with the coaches or resentment by teammates, which will undermine the competitive experience you are pursuing as part of the team. It is also worth considering that good teams often attract more attention from scouts at higher levels.

the optimal training program for hockey

SCOUTS' PREVIEW
In this chapter . . .
· The key categories of training for hockey
· Training exercises, sessions, and programs

IN THE LAST CHAPTER, YOU LEARNED ABOUT THE POWER OF TRAINING TO HELP YOU EXCEL IN HOCKEY.

Types of Training

In a sport as complex as hockey, there are several areas your training should cover in conditioning you to succeed in competition. As you reach higher levels, these training needs become more extensive and sophisticated. To help organize hockey training and ensure each key area gets taken care of, we group the different aspects of training into three major categories: (1) *Fitness Training*, (2) Psychological or *"Psych" Training*, and (3) Competitive or *"Comp" Training*.

FITNESS TRAINING consists of conditioning your body to be fit and tuned to the physical demands of your sport. Effective fitness training allows you to meet these demands in competition, and hopefully establish a fitness advantage over opponents and rivals.

PSYCH TRAINING conditions your psychology or state of mind during competition. This includes your thoughts and attitude, your emotions and mental arousal level, and your focus and connectedness with the competition taking place. Psych Training is necessary to fully utilize all of your talents and abilities and perform your best in competition.

COMP TRAINING conditions you for the act of competing, as well as for specific details and scenarios that may be part of competition in your sport. Successful Comp Training allows you to thrive in a competitive environment, and master doing what competition calls for without thinking or hesitating.

Training in these three areas makes you seasoned and ready for competition, unlike Raw, the boxer from the last chapter.

Each training category includes elements that are key to performance, and therefore to advancing up the ranks in hockey. So your life's routine should allow time to be devoted on a regular basis to each category of training. Don't neglect one while working solely on the others. In fact, sometimes one area of training is affected by another. For instance, neglecting your Fitness Training and ending up overtired during a game will hurt your ability to mentally concentrate, a key part of your Psych Training.

Training Exercises

Training is done is through *exercises* designed to target and improve a specific ability. For example, your Fitness Training might include jogging as an exercise to enhance your physical endurance. Sometimes, exercises have overflow benefits for other aspects of your training. So if your jog took the form of a race against a friend, it would have a Comp Training benefit as well. But typically, exercises are designed to isolate and train a very specific ability among the many you must master in order to thrive in hockey competition.

Training Sessions

Similar to team training practices, a group of individual training exercises within one category are often done together in succession as part of a *training session*. How to structure your sessions, what to include in them, and when to do them depends on your personal needs, preferences, and schedule. Consulting with someone who is both knowledgeable about hockey training and familiar with your personal situation can help you identify what kind of sessions you should do, and when.

Unfortunately, there is no space in this book to provide all our knowledge about hockey training. For example, we will not be able to provide a complete list of training exercises, instructions, and specs. Whole books exist, filled with just the single topic of Fitness Training, or the single topic of Sports Psychology Training. And, even those would not take into account all the different ages, maturity levels, life circumstances, and schedules that apply to the various readers of this book and affect their recommended training. What we can provide is a summary of key aspects of training we have found to be effective in hockey. Some elements we learned by reading books like those referenced above. Other important aspects were learned by actually training for hockey and observing from personal experience which elements improved performance and allowed for progress up the ladder of making it—and which didn't.

Training Programs

In the following chapters, you will find training breakdowns and overviews, phases and scheduling suggestions, exercise recommendations and details, and suggested ways of tracking your progress. Together, all of this forms what is called a training *program*. Training smart means following a good program that is based on a keen understanding of the abilities you need in your sport, and that provides an intelligent plan for training them. The program here is designed specifically for making it in hockey, from first-hand knowledge and expert experience of what it takes and what works best.

In sports' early days, such sophisticated training may not have been necessary to make it. But over time, the science of training has advanced, more top athletes have shared their experiences, and so training methods have dramatically improved. The program here is the most sophisticated, effective, and practical tool this section of the book can provide to aid you in your training.

EXPERTS' RECAP

Remember . . .

· A range of exercises can help your individual training.

· Individual training is most effective with a specific program designed by experts.

fitness training—"survival of the fittest"

CHAPTER 17

SCOUTS' PREVIEW

In this chapter . . .
· What Fitness Training is and why it's important
· The seven fitness requirements of hockey
· Methods of Fitness Training
· Fitness Training program for hockey
· The importance of rest, water, and nutrition
· Differences in Fitness Training for goalies

MOST SPORTS DEMAND EXCELLENT PHYSICAL CONDITIONING. THIS CONDITIONING IS CALLED PHYSICAL FITNESS.

The Importance of Fitness Training

In Chapter 15, Raw the boxer became so tired he had no more power in his arms and couldn't move to protect himself. Fitness Training could have helped him avoid that. Hockey players have fitness needs too. By becoming as fit as possible, a hockey player can meet the physical demands of their sport, and establish a competitive advantage over rivals.

Besides getting a player in shape for games and tournaments, at high levels, Fitness Training can be important in its own right. For example, most College hockey and NHL teams start the Training Camp where they pick their team with mandatory fitness testing. Players who test poorly put themselves behind the eight ball from day one. Evaluators may question their commitment and work ethic, and scrutinize their play for flaws that could exist from being out of shape. On the other hand, a player who tests exceptionally well can seize the attention and admiration of the evaluators before skating one stride.

The way to perform well in fitness testing, games, tournaments, and try-outs, is to be in top physical condition, through following a comprehensive and well-designed Fitness Training Program designed for hockey. This is what you will find outlined in this chapter.

Below are the key physical attributes required of skaters in hockey, which their Fitness Training should be geared toward. For goalies, some of the training objectives and principles are the same, and some are different. A segment at the end of this chapter will detail some differences in the Fitness Training needs of goalies.

The Seven Fitness Requirements for Hockey

1. **STRENGTH:** Strength is the capacity to exert physical force.
   - Examples of what strength can help you do in hockey:
     - win puck-battles;
     - resist being knocked off the puck by an opponent's check or push; and
     - move an opposing player out of your crease so the goalie can see.
   - Some players who've thrived on exceptional strength:
     - Rod Brind'Amour, Alexei Kovalev, Angela Ruggiero

2. **SPEED:** Speed is the ability to move fast.
   - Speed can help you to:
     - skate by defenders;
     - chase down an opposing player on the back-check; and
     - stickhandle the puck into position and make a nice pass before a nearby defender closes in.
   - Some players who've thrived on exceptional speed:
     - Paul Kariya, Mike Modano, Paul Coffey

3. **ACCELERATION:** Acceleration is the ability to quickly go from a standstill or moving slowly to moving at maximum speed.
   - Acceleration can help you to:
     - have the *quickness* to win a race to a puck that springs loose only a short distance away from both you and an opponent;
     - have the *power* to launch yourself forcefully into a bodycheck;

- ◦ have a rapid arm-whip, to shoot the puck hard with a quick release, and beat the goalie; and
- ◦ for a goalie: explode laterally across the net to make a save on the far side.
- • Some players who've thrived on exceptional acceleration:
  - ◦ Teemu Selanne, Saku Koivu, Marc-André Fleury

4. **ENDURANCE:** Endurance is the ability to last as long as possible before tiring.
- • Endurance can help you to:
  - ◦ continue competing at the end of a long shift, when you are stuck in your end, and can't yet get off for a change;
  - ◦ beat your opponents in the third period and overtime, when they are more tired than you; and
  - ◦ be consistent over a long season or through the playoff grind, and not have your performance gradually tail off after a strong start.
- • Some players who've thrived on exceptional endurance:
  - ◦ Henrik Zetterberg, Daniel Alfredsson, Martin Brodeur

5. **BALANCE:** Balance is being able to maintain correct and stable physical posture, whatever you are doing on the ice.
- • Balance can help you to:
  - ◦ fend off defenders, and maintain control of the puck;
  - ◦ hold your ground in front of the net; and
  - ◦ shoot off the rush while moving fast, usually by balancing on one foot.
- • Some players who've thrived on exceptional balance:
  - ◦ Sidney Crosby, Denis Potvin, Roberto Luongo

6. **COORDINATION:** Coordination is being able to execute a difficult movement with exceptional precision.
- • Coordination can help you to:
  - ◦ execute difficult stickhandling moves or dekes;
  - ◦ shoot the puck through a tiny opening, when that is the only part of the net not covered by the goalie;
  - ◦ make pinpoint passes to teammates, while skating full stride; and
  - ◦ for a goalie: flash their catching glove to grab a blazing shot out of mid-air.
- • Some players who've thrived on exceptional coordination:
  - ◦ Mario Lemieux, Evgeni Malkin, Martin St. Louis

7. **AGILITY:** Agility involves being "light on your feet" in order to change directions sharply but smoothly.

- Agility can help you to:
  - weave through heavy traffic, carrying the puck, on a rush;
  - change directions in close quarters along the boards in order to escape a pursuer, and emerge into a scoring area;
  - dodge a potential check, to get off a good shot or pass; and
  - for a goalie: change body position several times quickly, in order to make a rapid series of saves.
- Some players who've thrived on exceptional agility:
  - Denis Savard, Tomas Kaberle, Dominik Hasek

The aim of Fitness Training is to meet the above physical demands of the game and exceed your rivals' levels.

Methods of Fitness Training

There are three areas of Fitness Training:

1. **CARDIOVASCULAR CONDITIONING ("CARDIO"):** Cardio exercises train your heart to deliver oxygen efficiently to your muscles. Your muscles need that oxygen in order to move and exert force. This applies to every muscle and every action. The heart is the most important muscle in your body, and cardio is the most important part of your Fitness Training Program. In training for hockey, here are four kinds of cardio exercises that can be helpful:

a. STEADY-STATE: These exercises involve sustaining a steady level of exertion for a long period of time (usually at least thirty minutes) to develop endurance.

b. INTERVALS: These exercises consist of alternating several times between periods of a few minutes duration at a moderately high level of exertion, and periods of a few minutes duration at a moderately low level of exertion.

c. LONG SPRINTS: These exercises involve a series of sprints of approximately thirty seconds to a minute in length, at the highest speed you can maintain constant over the full course of the sprint, with slow-speed rest periods in between.

d. SHORT SPRINTS: These exercises involve a series of full-speed short sprints of approximately ten to twenty seconds in length, with slow-speed rest periods in between.

Some popular methods of cardio training include running outside or on a treadmill, riding a stationary bike, swimming, running up and down hills (for intervals), and skating.

2. **RESISTANCE TRAINING ("RT")**: RT exercises involve moving your body's muscles against resistance several times in a row, followed by a break. Each exercise is targeted to a particular few muscles, and will help you strengthen just those muscles. In doing RT, often a series of exercises work on a group of muscles in one session. Sessions could focus on upper body or lower body muscles. Or they could be even more focused, for example, on just upper-body exercises that involve pushing against resistance, or just ones that involve pulling against resistance. The more focused a session is, the more exercises you do for the group of muscles in question. Three kinds of RT exercises can be beneficial for hockey:

   a. STRENGTH: These exercises are designed to build muscular strength, and involve a medium number of repetitions and a moderate level of resistance.

   b. ENDURANCE: These exercises are designed to build muscular endurance, and involve more repetitions but a lower level of resistance.

   c. POWER: These exercises are designed to help build muscular acceleration, and involve fewer repetitions but a higher level of resistance.

Some popular methods to do RT include exercises that use your own bodyweight (with gravity) as resistance, exercises using external weights, or exercises against tension such as special elastic bands or cords.

3. **NEUROMUSCULAR CONDITIONING ("MOTOR")**: Motor exercises train your brain (which controls your deliberate movements) to communicate better with your muscles (which execute the movements). Specifically, motor training conditions your muscles to execute more exactly and consistently what your brain intends them to do. Different kinds of motor training exercises for hockey are designed to help with:

   a. agility
   b. balance
   c. coordination
   d. explosiveness/acceleration

Popular methods of agility and coordination training include foot exercises using agility ladders or lines painted on the ground or ice, and hand exercises such as catching a tennis ball thrown or bounced from close range. Popular exercises for balance and explosiveness might include balance boards and hops or plyometrics.

Certain methods of training are not appropriate for kids of younger ages. In addition, the overall benefit of Fitness Training before puberty is limited, compared to after. So for younger children, a very watered down program might make better use of their time and avoid them getting discouraged. In general, as a person progresses through puberty, it might make sense to increase their Fitness Training in step. But each individual case is different. Before embarking on a Fitness Training Program, every athlete should get a full physical examination from their doctor, and consult the doctor about what's safe for them to do. They should also consult with a fitness expert who can assess them individually and advise what precise training is appropriate given their stage of development, current fitness level, and experience. Training itself should be done under the supervision and monitoring of adults, and preferably fitness experts—for example, the staff in a gym, or a certified trainer. Whenever possible, it can also help to train with a friend.

Fitness Training Program for Hockey

The Fitness Training Program below follows a specified schedule intended to maximize your training benefits. The training exercises are organized in groups as part of *workouts*, which have an overall focus or particular set of training aims they are designed to achieve. The workouts are organized by day into a *weekly cycle*, which repeats. The weekly cycles are part of longer-term *phases* of your program. The phases are ordered to allow you to build each new phase upon what you have accomplished through the training in the prior phase. Each phase is geared toward your training needs at different times in relation to your sport's competitive season, as part of the overall desire to be at peak fitness during your sport's season of competition.

The days within the weekly cycle are numbered in order to indicate the intended order and spacing of the week's training. You could start with Day 1 being Monday, Day 2 being Tuesday and so on. But we chose to give you numbers rather than days of the week, so that you can start Day 1 on whatever day of the week best suits your personal schedule and other commitments.

Before you train, be sure to read the training guidelines in Chapter 20.

For more on specific exercises and specifications see my website.

Fitness Training Program, Phase A: BASE (4–6 Weeks)

This first phase of the program is designed to build a base of fitness in the physical attributes needed for hockey. Without a proper base, it will be difficult later on to develop more finely tuned fitness levels effectively and safely. It is best to start your Base Fitness phase a few weeks after the end of your previous sport season. The Base phase should take four to six weeks, depending on your fitness startpoint, how fast you progress in developing the base you need, and how much time you have before the start of your next season.

> Weekly Cycle:
> *Day 1:* Cardio (Steady-State), RT (Lower Body—Endurance)
> *Day 2:* Cardio (Steady-State), RT (Upper Body—Endurance)
> *Day 3:* Motor (Agility & Coordination)
> *Day 4:* Cardio (Steady-State), RT (Lower Body—Endurance)
> *Day 5:* Motor (Balance & Explosiveness)
> *Day 6:* Cardio (Intervals), RT (Upper Body—Endurance)
> *Day 7:* Day Off—No Fitness Training

Fitness Training Program, Phase B: GROWTH (8–10 Weeks)

This second phase of the Program starts immediately following the end of the last week of the prior phase. The objective of this Growth phase is to increase your fitness levels as much as you can within the time allotted for the phase.

> Weekly Cycle:
> *Day 1:* Cardio (Steady-State), RT (Upper Body Pushing—Strength)
> *Day 2:* Cardio (Short Sprints), RT (Lower Body & Upper Body Pulling—Strength)
> *Day 3:* Motor (Agility & Coordination)
> *Day 4:* Cardio (Steady-State & Intervals), RT (Upper Body Pushing—Strength)
> *Day 5:* Motor (Balance & Explosiveness)
> *Day 6:* Cardio (Long Sprints), RT (Lower Body & Upper Body Pulling—Strength)
> *Day 7:* Day Off—No Fitness Training

Fitness Training, Phase C: PEAK (2–4 Weeks)

The third phase of the Fitness Program, which starts immediately following the end of the second phase, is the Peak phase. The purpose of this phase is to help you "peak for performance" with your upcoming sport season set to immediately follow this phase. Here, you reduce the total volume of training exercises you are doing. You also put more focus on motor training, which can help transform the enhanced fitness potential you developed in Phase B into precise fitness-related abilities you will use playing hockey.

> Weekly Cycle:
> *Day 1:* Cardio (Steady-State, Intervals), RT (Upper Body—Power), Motor (Agility & Coordination)
> *Day 2:* Cardio (Short Sprints), RT (Lower Body—Power), Motor (Balance & Explosiveness)
> *Day 3:* Day Off—No Fitness Training
> *Day 4:* Cardio (Steady-State, Long Sprints), RT (Upper Body—Power), Motor (Agility & Coordination)
> *Day 5:* Day Off—No Fitness Training
> *Day 6:* Cardio (Short Sprints), RT (Lower Body—Power), Motor (Balance & Explosiveness)
> *Day 7:* Day Off—No Fitness Training

Fitness Training, Phase D: MAINTENANCE (during your season of sport competition)

The Peak phase ends with a few days break before your new hockey season or tryouts begin. Then, during tryouts and the competitive season, your Fitness Program is very different than in the off-season. Whereas the off-season is the ideal time to raise your fitness level, your aim throughout the competitive season is just to maintain your current fitness level as best you can. Games and practices will soak up a lot of time and energy. Plus, you want to play well, and need to play well in order to advance to higher levels. So you definitely don't want to tire yourself out for games and cause your performance to suffer by being too aggressive in your Fitness Training.

> Weekly Cycle:
> *Game Days:* Cardio (Steady-State), after-game only; never before game.
> *Days Before a Game:* Cardio (Short Sprints)

All Other Days: Cardio (Steady-State *or* Intervals *or* Long Sprints), RT (Upper Body *or* Lower Body), Motor (Agility & Coordination *or* Balance & Explosiveness). Each time you train, alternate between the above choices for each of the three training areas.

Following the end of your sport competitive season, take a few weeks off to give your body and mind a chance to rest, recover, and refresh. Then you will repeat the same sequence of phases above, starting again at Phase A. Don't think you're going backward in returning to a phase you've done before. Each time you complete the sequence of phases, you raise your fitness level, and are beginning at a higher start point when you go back to Phase A. Your fitness level is built up in layers, with each new layer created by going through the sequence of phases again.

In doing your training, if you are going to work very closely with a fitness trainer, and not just rely on them for clarification and supervision, try to find one with expert understanding and preferably first-hand experience with hockey and its physical demands. In the past, I found I sometimes lost time or achieved counterproductive results doing training recommended by fitness experts who were not experts on hockey. I've also seen other athletes incur injuries while doing training that wasn't necessary or suitable for hockey. As you reach higher levels, it becomes increasingly important that your training be guided by someone with high-level understanding or first-hand knowledge of what is needed in hockey. The hockey program here draws upon elements of training that I've become aware of through my and my brothers' experience with aspects of training from Harvard and from a combined ten NHL organizations.[5]

In Fitness Training, exercises place strain on your body. When you are finished exercising, your body is wired to automatically respond to the strain that was put on it by trying to increase its fitness level, so it won't so easily be strained again in the future. In the case of muscles, this means rebuilding the muscles with greater strength or endurance or speed or power. In the case of the communication between your brain and muscles, it means refining the precision, speed, and familiarity of the messages travelling back and forth between the two, to provide better balance, agility, coordination, and explosiveness. Each time your body rebuilds and refines between exercise sessions, you become better trained to meet the physical demands of your sport. So you actually do not become more fit while exercising, but rather during the time in between.

The Importance of Rest, Water, and Nutrition

In order to rebuild and refine itself your body requires rest and fuel.

Time to rest between training sessions, as well as getting sufficient sleep at night, are essential. Pay attention to messages your body gives you about how much sleep and rest you need, and also consult with your doctor. Typically, the more physical exercise you are doing, the more rest and sleep you will need. Try to choose activities between workouts that are physically restful, not ones which place strain on your body. As far as sleep goes, the body is usually good about telling you how much sleep you need. The key is not to ignore what it's telling you such that you cut into the sleep you need by staying up watching TV, going out with friends, or simply trying to squeeze more hours into your day. This short-changes you the benefit of all the hours you spent training.

In terms of fuel, adequate and proper hydration (water intake) and nutrition are the basics. Generally, sometime prior to training, you will want to consume extra energy food for your body to store and use while training. And after workouts, you will want to provide it with extra recovery and growth foods. However, don't go overboard, thinking that if some is good, more is better. The human body is complicated and it depends and thrives on proper nutritional balance. Also, certain foods, like junk food and alcohol, can counteract the results you are trying to achieve through your Fitness Training. As well, be careful with substances billed to enhance the benefit of training. Remember what you learned in Chapter 7 about the dangers of performance-enhancing substances, and don't feel pressure to use them even if others might be. Consult your doctor or appropriate licensed health and nutrition expert about any training supplements you are considering.

Differences in Fitness Training for Goalies

As mentioned, there are some differences in the Fitness Training recommended for goalies versus other players. Here, again, are professional goalie coach Sudarshan Maharaj's thoughts on what the focus should be in a goalie's Fitness Training Program:

> "Foot-speed is important, as is agility. Any kind of nimbleness with your feet is hugely important for goalies. For these, goalies can do a lot of the same footwork exercises as skaters.

"Balance is also absolutely crucial. Goalies should do core strength exercises, as well as training their glute (butt) muscles, because of the demands of their stance. They also need to develop good overall physical strength, because goalies do get bumped and pushed. At the same time, they shouldn't be doing the 'beach body' workout. They can't afford to get bogged down and slowed by too much mass; they need to be limber. From a very young age, goalies should work on their flexibility through stretching exercises.

"Goalies also need to have a lot of explosiveness on pushes and in closing down the five hole and things like that. So a lot of plyometrics is a big part of Fitness Training for goalies.

"Coordination and hand speed are also important. Goalies can improve this by trying to catch tennis balls or superballs hit off a wall. There are also high-tech light boards where they tap on a light that is lit up, and their reaction speed is timed.

"In terms of cardio, the goalie position is one that requires action that is like a sprint in a lot of ways. For ten to twelve seconds, a goalie is exploding and diving and pushing, and then there might be forty-five seconds before they are called on again. So anaerobic sprint training is hugely valuable. But as with skaters, this needs to be built on top of a good aerobic base."

EXPERTS' RECAP

Remember . . .

· Fitness Training allows you to meet and thrive against the physical demands of your sport.

· Hockey requires strength, speed, endurance, acceleration, agility, balance, and coordination.

· Fitness Training must only be done with medical approval and under expert supervision.

· Training involves cardio, RT, and motor exercises, with rest and refueling in between.

· Exercises must be chosen that are appropriate for a player's stage of physical maturation.

· Training is guided by a strategic program, and is usually focused on the off-season.

psych training—mastering "the mental game"

CHAPTER 18

SCOUTS' PREVIEW

In this chapter . . .

· What Psych Training is, and how it works
· Controlling your thoughts and emotions, and creating your "approach"
· The four components of the ideal mental state for competition
· Psych Training Program for hockey
· Minding the other factors that can influence your emotions

NOT THAT LONG AGO, THE VALUE OF ALL TYPES OF TRAINING WAS UNDERAPPRECIATED, AND THE FOCUS IN HOCKEY WAS PRIMARILY ON SKILLS.

In recent years, Fitness Training has garnered significant attention from a good number of hockey players, parents, and coaches. Yet there are still two other major categories of training whose importance is often underestimated. The first is Psychological Training, or Psych Training for short.

What Is Psych Training?

It's easy to understand why the importance of Fitness Training would be more readily recognized and acted upon than Psych Training. Think of Fitness Training as physical training, and Psych Training as mental training. You see physical things and therefore appreciate them, whereas you cannot see mental things. Also, it is straightforward (although still hard work) to do physical training, whereas mental training can be confusing and frustrating. After all, your mind must direct the training exercises, but at the same time is the very thing being exercised!

However, as mind-bending as it may seem, Psych Training is essential. While many players and their tutors may neglect it, those who have made it are keenly aware of its significance and have achieved a notable level of mastery of it.

Psych Training conditions the *psychology* of your mind, the state of your thoughts and emotions. Thoughts and emotions dictate your behaviour—which, when you are playing a sport, includes influencing your performance.

Psych Training simply conditions you to take control of the thoughts and emotions you carry into competition so that they have a positive effect on your play.

How does this work? Think of a computer: There is both the hardware (the computer itself and all its parts and what they can do) and the software (the programs that run on the computer). You need to have the right software and run the right programs to control the hardware properly and have it do everything you might want it to do. In the same way, your talents, skills, fitness level, and all your other abilities together are like the hardware of a computer. And your psychology is like the software running on the computer. There is an optimal psychology for competition consisting of a certain set of thoughts and emotions. If you have that psychology "running" in your mind during competition, you can use all your abilities to perform your best. On the other hand, just as software bugs or the wrong software can prevent your desired use of your computer's hardware, faulty psychology in your mind or the wrong set of thoughts and emotions during competition will interfere with you using your hockey abilities to perform the way you want and can.

Let me tell you a story from back when I was ten. I had just joined an older age team, which had an upcoming tournament in Lake Placid, site of the *Miracle on Ice*. One player from each team would get to participate in a shootout supervised by the legendary Mr. Hockey®: Gordie Howe. Our coach decided to hold a shootout in practice, with whomever won getting the chance to represent our team in the real shootout. I was inspired to get a chance to be on the ice with Gordie Howe, and felt no pressure because I had just joined this older age team, and nobody expected me to win. I easily won our team's shootout! A few weeks later, with my whole team, the coach, and all the parents watching from the stands, my turn came, and I stepped off the bench onto the surface of the *Miracle on Ice*, and skated to centre ice

---

the inside story

It's not quite as simple as Fitness Training = Physical, and Psych Training = Mental. For example, Fitness Training's motor conditioning involves mental signals being sent to your body, telling it what to do. Likewise, you will see in this chapter that you can use your body to send signals to your mind to guide your psychology.

where Gordie Howe was waiting for me with three pucks. What ensued was far from miraculous. In this environment and with Gordie Howe watching over my shoulder, I was so nervous that I skated in, fell down, and didn't even get a shot on goal, as the puck slid into the corner of the rink! On my second shot, I was so embarrassed I did the exact same thing *again*! Before my third and final shot, Gordie said to me, "Just relax, son; remember the reason we're out here is for fun." I went down and scored, making such a good deke, the goalie ended up sliding into the corner! From the practice competition to the competition in Lake Placid, and from my first two shots there to my third, there was no difference in my skills that produced these dramatically opposite results, the only difference was in the emotions running through my mind.

Since thoughts and emotions have such a profound impact on performance, and since performing well is how you advance in hockey, you can't leave your game frame of mind to chance. You want to cultivate the right performance psychology, and condition yourself to consistently run that psychology in competition.

Controlling Your Thoughts and Emotions, and Creating Your Approach

Sports psychology has two key components.

The first aspect you want to control is the mental *approach* you bring into competition. Your approach consists of two different levels of thoughts: One is the conscious thoughts actively going through your mind during competition. Examples could be, "How can I stop this opposing rush?" or, "I want to score a goal." The second level of thoughts are called *beliefs*, and are present in a deeper area of your mind which you are not aware of unless you draw your attention to them. Beliefs are a more ongoing kind of thought, and can stay in your mind indefinitely. Even if they are present in an unconscious area of your mind, you still operate on the basis of them, including during competition. Examples could be, "I'm a good player" or, "As long as I try my best, I deserve to be proud."

The other aspect of sports psychology you want to control is your *emotions*. Unlike the way you learned to control your emotions in Chapter 4, in the midst of competition you often don't notice what emotions are present in your mind, and can't take a "time out" to get control of them. Luckily, your emotions are heavily influenced by your thoughts. So by properly controlling your approach, including the two levels of thoughts that go into it, you automatically also exert strong control over your emotions. That control isn't 100 per cent. Other factors such as sleep, nutrition, and the body's natural chemical-level fluctuations can affect your emotions as well. So additional actions can help you manage these other factors, as you will learn about later in this chapter.

The Four Components of the Ideal Mental State for Competition

Your Psych Training should condition you to have the following elements during competition:

POSITIVE THINKING: Countless thoughts are present in your mind during competition. This includes those conscious thoughts where you are effectively "talking to yourself" in your head, plus those deeper underlying beliefs silently there without you noticing. Thoughts that are positive create useful emotions that help you perform better in competition. Thoughts that are negative create detrimental emotions that hurt your ability to perform well.

Examples of Positive Beliefs	Examples of Negative Beliefs
· "I am able, ready, and deserve to succeed"	· "I am not good enough, not ready, or don't deserve to succeed"
· Confidence that you will do what it takes to succeed	· Doubt that you will do what you need to succeed
· Optimism that things will go your way, will work out well	· Pessimism that things won't go your way, will turn out badly
· "I am here to have fun"	· "This is not the time or place for fun"
· "Competition is a challenge, and I enjoy a challenge"	· "Competition is everything, if I fail, all is lost"
· "Regardless of hockey, I have value in being a good person"	· "Hockey is everything, if I fail, I am a worthless loser"
· "Mistakes and failures are opportunities to learn"	· "Mistakes and failures are catastrophes"
· "Special adversity provides a special chance to exceed expectations"	· "Adversity is increased danger"

Examples of Positive Thoughts	Examples of Negative Thoughts
· "If I do my best, I can be proud of myself, no matter the outcome"	· "The only thing that matters is the outcome—win or loss, success or failure"
· "I can do this"	· "I can't do this"
· "Something good is going to happen"	· "Something bad is going to happen"
· "I am determined to succeed"	· "I'm afraid I won't succeed"
· "I am impatient to succeed"	· "How long can I avoid screwing up?"
· "I shall make something good happen right now!"	· "Just try not to make any mistakes the whole game!"

AROUSAL: Your arousal level is how activated and excited your brain and therefore your body are during the competition. Being in a frenzy is one extreme, while being half-asleep is the opposite. The ideal level of arousal for competition is in between, and differs somewhat for each person. Being in your ideal state of arousal allows you to make the best use of all your abilities.

Features of ideal arousal level

· Perceiving a challenge at hand, and relishing it
· Motivated with positive anticipation
· Emotionally excited but mentally calm and relaxed
· Feeling of fun
· Feeling some pressure, but not feeling stressed

Features of undesirable arousal levels

· Apathetic, bored, disinterested, unengaged
· Feeling of life-and-death importance
· Mentally hyper or out of control
· Anxious in a negative way, or panicked
· Not feeling any fun
· Feeling stressed out or overwhelming pressure

FOCUS: Focus refers to how well you are concentrating, and whether you are concentrating on the right things, during competition. The more powerfully you focus on what is at hand during competition, the better you will perform. The weaker your focus in a game or the more your focus is drained or distracted by outside things, the more your performance will be hurt.

Examples of successful focus

· Completely focused and concentrated
· Disciplined in your focus, resistant to temptations and distractions
· Always focused on the present moment
· Focused in following and anticipating the play

· Focused on what you need to do as a result (e.g., get the puck, get open, cover your man, stop a rush, etc.)

· Focused on what you are striving to do (e.g., score, prevent goals, win your shift, win the game, etc.)
· Ignoring extraneous matters, outside life events, etc.

Examples of unsuccessful focus

· Unfocused, mind wandering
· Focused to begin with, but easily distracted when tempted
· Focused on the past or the future
· Distracted by fans, scoreboard, or other attention-diversions within the competitive environment
· Focused on aspects of the competition outside your control, such as how much ice-time you are getting, referee calls, etc.
· Focused on what others should be doing

· Distracted by outside life events

FLOW: Athletes' most incredible performances occur when they "get into the flow" of the game, and feel connected to it. Flow is feeling like you are engrossed in the play, or have actually become a part of it. Sometimes people refer to it as "being in the zone," or in the case of a goalie, "standing on their head." In this state, you seem to be able to predict every play before it happens, the puck seems to follow you around, and you do things that amaze others and even yourself. But flow isn't something you can orchestrate, all you can do is put yourself in position to give it a chance to happen on its own.

Ways of helping to put yourself in position to get into the flow	Ways of preventing yourself from falling into the flow
· Trusting your instincts and relying on them	· Thinking about anything other than the play
· Not self-consciously trying to think of what to do on the ice	· Talking to yourself
· Not self-consciously trying to control your mind	· Being self-conscious
· Not thinking about yourself at all	· Mind wandering, unfocused
· Being focused (as you learned above)	· Preoccupied with trying to control your mind
· Taking the play as it comes	· Trying to make yourself get into the flow
· Letting flow happen if it happens	· Trying to make yourself do anything

the inside story

A lot of times, when you read about sports psychology, the importance of confidence is mentioned. But how do you become confident in competition? Part of it comes from carrying your positive beliefs into competition. And the rest comes from focusing with 100 per cent intensity on realizing your objective within the competition. Such focus leaves no room in your mind for doubt about what you are trying to do. Without this type of interference, you play to the best of your abilities. This helps you get into the flow of the competition; you notice yourself playing well, and confidence automatically follows, allowing you to play that much better still. Confidence, then, as important as it is, comes as a by-product of the four factors above.

You may hear other people talk of different elements of sports psychology than those above. Sometimes they may be referring to one of the same things, but under a different name or in a different way. In other cases, they may be referring to a characteristic of the right psychology for competition, where that characteristic in fact comes from a combination of the components described above.

For example, you may have heard the term *Mental Toughness*. Mental Toughness means performing well consistently, particularly in especially difficult circumstances such as high-stakes pressure, feeling unwell or hurt, or facing a strong threat of distraction or intimidation. But consistent performance comes from consistently being properly aroused and focused in competition. And the way you deal with adverse circumstances is through an attitude of positive thinking. So Mental Toughness results from mastering the components above.

There are countless characteristics people can identify of the right psychology for sports. But, the way to have the ideal psychology for sports, with all its characteristics, is by training yourself in the four components above: positive thinking, arousal, focus, and flow.

Psych Training Program for Hockey

Below is the Psych Training Program and schedule. Psych Training should be done over the course of the entire year. The key period (opposite to Fitness Training) is *during* your sport's competitive season. Psych Training actually ties into your schedule of competition in games and practices, as follows:

There are three different types of days within the schedule—Game-Competition Days (days when you have a game), Practice-Competition Days (days when you have an official practice), and Non-Competition Days (days when you have neither). On each type of day, you will do a different group of exercises. This is because different aspects of Psych Training are best worked on at different times in relation to your sport's competitive schedule. For example, the farther away you are from a competition, the better when it comes to working on ingraining positive beliefs into the unconscious part of your mind, or building your raw potential for focusing. The closer you are to a competition, the more your Psych Training must be geared to whisking you out of the state of mind used in regular life and into the special state of mind used for sports performance. For a similar reason, Game-Competition Days are additionally broken down into groups of exercises needed Pre-Competition (before a game), In-Competition (during the game), and Post-Competition (after the game). For each day, we don't expect you to do all the exercises listed below. These are examples of some of the types of exercises you might consider doing on those types of days.

Be sure to read the principles of effective training in Chapter 20 before embarking on your Psych Training Program.

Find more information, examples, and illustrations of how to do the exercises on my website.

Non-Competition Days

SUCCESS MODELLING: Success modelling is similar to the skill modelling you learned in Chapter 9. Pick successful players (it doesn't need to be the same player each time), and notice the way they act in and around competition. Anything you observe that they do to help create and maintain their excellent mental state for performance can be useful to your Psych Training. Some clues could be: the way they carry themselves leading up to and during games, what their facial expression tells you about their frame of mind and emotions, or any comments they make in interviews relating to what their mindset was.

SELF-HYPNOSIS: Self-hypnosis is just a concentrated method of focusing. It can be used to strengthen your ability to focus and can also help condition your mind and behaviour through a process called positive suggestion. This involves repeating statements under self-hypnosis such as, "I am a good player," or, "In my next game, I will be focused and on fire." To reinforce those suggestions, while under self-hypnosis, you plant what are called anchors. These anchors then cue you, when you are not under self-hypnosis, to think or do what you suggested. Examples of anchors could be: "When I hear my alarm clock and get straight up in the morning, I will remember that I am mentally tough," or "When I set foot on the ice, I will know I am ready to play." Self-hypnosis is a technique that requires instruction and careful use. To learn self-hypnosis to help you in hockey, contact a reputable sports psychologist.

VISUALIZATION EXERCISES: In Chapter 1, you learned what a visualization exercise was, and did one to enhance the power of your dream. Visualization exercises can be used for many purposes. Find a quiet place. Then repeat the same process as in the exercise in Chapter 1, except the focus this time will not be on realizing your dream. For Psych Training purposes, the focus of the exercise could be any or all of the following: you executing skills and plays in competition, you experiencing successful outcomes from competition, or you realizing achievements after a series of competitions.

HOCKEY DIARY: Many athletes find it helpful to have a diary for their sport, in which they can record personal notes, and review previous notes on a regular basis. This allows them to chronicle their progress, reflect upon experiences, and refer back to lessons they learned from past successes, mistakes, and outside observations. Diary entries could be based on a training session, a competition, watching a high-level game, or any hockey-related experience or thought that comes to mind. It isn't necessary to make entries every day or every game. Entries can be made simply whenever you're inclined. And likewise, you can review notes from your diary whenever you're inclined.

Practice-Competition Days

CLEARING YOUR MIND: Prior to a game or practice competition, it is good to clear your mind of all the thoughts and emotions carrying over from whatever you were doing beforehand. This will allow you to be better focused for the upcoming competition. Again, find a quiet place to do this. One method of clearing your mind is *compartmentalization*. This involves imagining your mind as a filing cabinet, with separate drawers containing your thoughts and emotions about each area of your life: school, obligations, family life, social life, hockey, etc. When it is time for each, you imagine yourself opening that drawer, and closing the others—along with all the thoughts and emotions held in each. So prior to a hockey game or practice, you would close all the other drawers, and open the hockey drawer. An alternate method of clearing your mind is *meditation*. Meditation means bringing your mind to a point of stillness. From there, you can then focus, free from any distracting carry-over of thoughts or emotions, on whatever new topic you choose. There are many types of meditation, each with a different object to focus on to clear your mind. Some common methods include focusing on your breathing, focusing on a single point in the distance, or focusing on repeating a string of meaningless, made-up words over and over in your mind. You continue this over and over, noticing and letting go of any thoughts or emotions that enter your mind and refocusing on your object of meditation, until no more thoughts and emotions enter. Then your mind is still, the exercise is over, and you are free to focus fully on hockey.

VISUALIZATION EXERCISES: See earlier.

COMPETITION ROUTINE AND RITUALS: Leading up to competition, successful athletes typically use a set routine to get ready. Examples of parts of a routine could be eating a pre-competition meal a certain time in advance, wearing a team or self-imposed dress code to the rink, arriving at the arena a certain time prior to the competition, sitting in a certain spot in the dressing room, and putting equipment on in a certain order. Always using the same routine cues your mind, at each step within it, that it's time to move itself into competition mode. Set rituals can also help in the very same way. Rituals are like elements of a routine, only they don't need to occur in a precise order. Rituals could include re-taping and prepping your sticks, checking over your equipment, filling your drink bottle, and doing your personal pre-ice warm-up.

Game-Competition Days

PRE-COMPETITION:

CLEARING YOUR MIND: See earlier.

VISUALIZATION EXERCISES: See earlier.

PASSIVE VIDEO: Passively watching a video of mixed hockey highlights or of players successfully executing different plays can help get your mind closer to being in the flow, even before you get to the rink. This isn't the same as the video analysis you learned about earlier—don't watch video of yourself, and don't think about what you're watching, just passively watch and follow the plays.

RECALLING PAST SUCCESSES: Spending a bit of time recalling or reliving in your mind a past success can help put you into the right psychology for competition, through a process called association. In recalling the past success, the unconscious part of your mind automatically remembers the frame of mind and emotions you were in at the time, which allowed you to have that success. With that frame of mind and emotions present again, you may play well again.

COMPETITION ROUTINE AND RITUALS: See earlier. For games, there will also usually be a set of team rituals as well. These may include a certain music playlist in the dressing room, doing a team cheer or tapping the team logo with your stick before heading out to the ice, pre-ice dressing room talks by the coach, and walking in a certain order when your team heads out and comes back from the ice.

PSYCH-UP: Prior to a game, athletes often do a series of actions to get "psyched up" and attain the proper arousal level. These may include listening to a certain song on your headphones; repeatedly cycling your attention through a few key positive suggestions, anchors, visualization images, and motivations; and warming up vigorously when you get on the ice.

BEHAVIOURAL CONDITIONING: Believe it or not, acting can help you perform better in competition. Acting and behaving as though you are confident, positive, focused, and aroused can cue your mind to actually become those things. The way you carry yourself and your facial expressions are body language that can subtly tell your mind the frame you want it to be in. Likewise, if you included as anchors any behaviours, these can help even more. For example, if you planted the anchor, "When I put my helmet on, it is game-time and I am primed and focused to play," then when you put your helmet on to go out to the ice, this act will send a cue to your mind to arouse it and get it focused to play.

IN-COMPETITION

Earlier in this chapter, you learned the proper elements of Psych Training during competition. However, if you are in the midst of competition and find yourself struggling to get in the right competition mindset, try the following potential corrective actions:

* Take an aggressive, enthusiastic focus on the game or a personal goal you have for the game.
* Focus on the present and take one shift at a time.
* Act as though you are in the right mindset, to send behavioural cues to your mind.
* Follow the play from the bench as though you are part of the play.
* Don't think about whether you are in the right mindset, because self-conscious attention directs your mind in the opposite direction than the one you want.

POST-COMPETITION

HOCKEY DIARY: See earlier. After a game, reflect briefly on your performance, and make brief notes on how you did, a few things you did well, and a few things you want to try to improve in the future.

POST-COMPETITION ROUTINE AND RITUALS: Similar to how they help cue you to prepare for competition, a different set of routines and rituals once the game is over can help cue your mind to turn the page, mentally. Examples could include a warm-down in the dressing room, changing out of your dress code when you get home, a routine post-game meal, or listening to the radio on the way home or watching non-hockey TV or reading a non-hockey magazine or book after you get home.

Other Factors that Can Affect Your Emotions

All of the exercises above are either directed at controlling the thought portion of good sports psychology, or they rely on the link between thought and emotion to control emotion. But remember that other factors, including sleep, nutrition, body chemical levels, and outside life events and issues can also affect your emotions. Here are some guidelines for managing these:

- Get a good night's sleep.
- Get enough additional rest as suggested in Chapter 17.
- Ensure proper nutrition as described in Chapter 17.
- Keep a balance of activities, as described in Chapter 6.
- Get regular check-ups with your doctor, and inform your doctor that you play sports competitively and have sports aspirations. This helps the doctor properly monitor your health and health needs in terms of hockey.
- Use the compartmentalization technique you learned earlier to prevent strong emotions caused by events within your sport pursuit from carrying over into your life and disrupting your sleep, life routine, or general emotional balance.

Together, the above guidelines and exercises can help you become a master of the psychology for sports performance. This Psych Training Program will allow you to avoid the common problems of mental interference and self-sabotage, and make the best use of your abilities in competition, which is where you make your case for making it.

EXPERTS' RECAP
Remember . . .
- Psych Training conditions you to master the ideal psychology for performance.
- Your psychology consists of your thoughts, emotions, and approach to competition.
- The ideal psychology consists of positive thinking, focus, proper arousal, and flow.
- Training is guided by a strategic program which varies with your competitive schedule.
- A number of specific exercises condition you in the various aspects of Psych Training.

comp training—consistently coming out on top

SCOUTS' PREVIEW
In this chapter . . .
· What Comp Training is, and why it's important
· A smart approach to Comp Training
· The four layers of Comp Training
· Comp Training Program for hockey

ANOTHER CATEGORY OF TRAINING THAT'S NOT WELL UNDERSTOOD IS WHAT I REFER TO AS COMPETI-TIVE TRAINING, OR COMP TRAINING FOR SHORT.

Most aspiring athletes and coaches have probably never heard of Comp Training. It is certainly the least studied and appreciated of the three most important types of training for sports. And yet, I doubt a single athlete has ever made it in any sport that has not been through a massive amount of Comp Training.

How could that be?

Well, most elite athletes probably completed this Comp Training without knowing that's what they were doing. Several of the exercises that were part of their training were likely activities they did for other reasons. Other times, they may have done some hockey related activity for fun, and not thought about how it could help their training. And in still other cases, their instincts may have told them they ought to do a certain exercise for hockey, even though they may not have understood precisely how it fit into the picture of all their training needs. But these exercises were all part of the category of Comp Training. In personally knowing many great athletes, and having studied the biographies of top stars, I have noticed a clear pattern: they have all done a tremendous amount of Comp Training.

Through this chapter, you will have the opportunity to pursue Comp Training systematically, rather than leaving to it to chance. This "smart" approach to Comp Training should allow you to train in this aspect of your game better than any athletes who have gone before. Today, virtually every sport is more specialized than ever, and the top athletes in these sports are reaching higher performance levels than ever. Optimal Comp Training is one of the best secrets for keeping up and gaining an advantage in this new sports world.

What Is Comp Training?

Comp Training is training yourself in the very act of *competing*. Sports involve skills, physical fitness, and trained psych abilities, but every sport is fundamentally a competition. Successful athletes must be able to deal with and thrive in competition. So training targeted to the very abilities of performing, of outperforming others, and of winning, is very beneficial.

Some young athletes accomplish a bit of this, likely without knowing, through card games and video games, just as some older athletes do through golf. Since these are competitive activities, they do have a Comp Training benefit. However, these choices also have drawbacks: Card games can lead to the pitfall of gambling, video games can be addictive and jeopardize your time management, and golf is very time consuming as a way to obtain a little Comp Training benefit. They are also not the best choices because they are all fairly passive activities, compared to the vigorous sport of hockey.

This brings us to our next point. Competition can take many different forms. The best kind of Comp Training includes components that take into account the specialized nature of competition in your sport. The Comp Training you will learn in this chapter will train you for the precise nature of competition in hockey: games, the smaller game situations that occur within games, and the surrounding environment in which games are played.

Recalling the story in Chapter 15, Raw the boxer did not do this: He didn't train for matches by sparring, or for the match situation where he would be affected by being struck by an opponent, or for the bright lights and screaming crowds of the match environment. A negative outcome was thus predictable. By training the corresponding elements of competition in hockey, you can avoid an outcome like Raw's.

The Four Layers of Comp Training

The different elements of Comp Training for hockey are like a series of increasingly specialized layers that help you prepare for the nature of competition in hockey. Starting with the most general, these layers include training for:

1. **COMPETITION ITSELF**: This layer of Comp Training is devoted to training the basic ideas and acts of competition itself.

Examples of what training for competition conditions you for

- Thriving in contention and competitive situations
- Not being fazed by competition's uncertain outcome, and competing your best to be the one who wins
- Sustaining evenly-matched competition for long periods, while looking for an edge, to master being one of those competitors that consistently comes out on top in close competitions
- In competitions where you are just not at your best, or your usual strategies aren't working, still "finding a way to win"
- Playing with a determination and expectation to win
- Being at your best in competition, wherever and whenever it's on
- Throwing others off their game (through fair and appropriate means)
- "Imposing your will" on a competition, or "setting a tone" that places the competition on terms that are to your advantage
- Exhibiting the "killer instinct" of a champion to finish off victories

Examples of potential results of failing to train for competition

- Being off-balance in a competitive setting
- Being uncomfortable with the uncertainty of a competition's outcome, and not being able to put your best foot forward to win
- "Folding," or "losing it," and going over the top emotionally in tight contests

- Consistently losing whenever you are having a bad day or your usual strengths or strategies are being foiled
- Playing without a determination and expectation to win, and thus being predisposed to lose
- Being inconsistent or a "practice superstar" who can't replicate good results in games
- Doing nothing to challenge others, and allowing them to be at their best against you
- Allowing others to set the tone of a competition on their terms

- "Choking" or allowing victories within your grasp to slip away

2. **GAMES (AS A WHOLE)**: Games are the fundamental units of competition in hockey. And in Chapter 20, you will learn that a key principle of good training is that it be game-specific. This layer of Comp Training, which focuses on games themselves, is the most game-specific training you can ever do.

Examples of what training for games conditions you for

- Competing in the format of a hockey game—with all its specific details that define it versus other kinds of competition
- Playing hard for three periods, every shift, without lulls

Examples of potential results of failing to train for games

- Not being comfortable with the format of a hockey game, with all its specific details, and therefore not performing as well as you could
- Inconsistent play over the course of a game, including poor stretches continued >

Examples of what training for games conditions you for (continued)	Examples of potential results of failing to train for games (continued)
· Managing the back-and-forth of a game, staying in it, and consistently giving yourself a chance to win	· Failing to handle the back-and-forth of a game well, causing you to fall out of contention in all cases except those where everything goes your way from start to finish
· Mastering different means of winning hockey games	· Not mastering the different means of winning hockey games, and thus being at a disadvantage against opponents who have
· Executing your Mental Skills faster and faster in games, as you will need to do to succeed at higher levels, where the play moves faster	· Not improving the speed with which you can execute your Mental Skills in games, so that you end up unable to keep pace at higher levels where the play moves faster

3. **GAME SITUATIONS:** As you learned in Chapter 11, there are many different competitive situations within a game, and specific Mental Skills for each of them. This layer of Comp Training conditions you to perform your Mental Skills to the best of your potential in game situations, and to prevail in each of these smaller sub-units of game competition.

Examples of what training for game situations conditions you for	Examples of potential results of failing to train for game situations
· Winning races and battles for loose pucks	· Losing races and battles for loose pucks
· Winning one-on-one battles with opponents	· Losing one-on-one battles with opponents
· Generating good offence off the rush or in the zone	· Failing to generate good offence off the rush or in the zone
· Scoring when you have chances to	· Missing too many scoring chances
· Controlling the area in front of the nets	· Losing control of the net front areas to opponents
· Successfully getting into and staying in position on defence	· Failing to get into, or falling out of, proper defensive position
· Stopping opposing rushes or scoring chances in your end	· Failing to block opposing rushes or scoring chances in your end
· For goalies: Picking and executing the right save for the situation	· For goalies: Not employing or executing the right save, and letting opponents score a goal you could have saved

4. **THE COMPETITIVE ENVIRONMENT:** Games take place within a physical environment that includes other players, coaches, spectators, referees, the arena itself, and sometimes much more. There is also an intangible environment that includes the rules, people's attitudes, and the game's inclusion in an official league or tournament series of competitions. This layer of Comp Training conditions you to perform well and not to be thrown off by any element of this environment surrounding games.

Examples of what training for the competitive environment readies you for

- Executing your Social Skills in a game environment
- Being able to perform well with spectators or crowds present
- Being comfortable with the arena setting, and not being thrown off by any aspect of it, including signs or scoreboard distractions
- Respecting the presence of referees, and the potential for calls you perceive to be unfair, without being thrown off
- Being familiar with the league rules, playing by them, and making good use of them

- Not allowing others' attitudes around games to throw you off your mental approach from Chapter 18
- Respecting how this one game fits into a league season, playoff series, or tournament

Examples of potential results of failing to train for the competitive environment

- Failing to execute your Social Skills in a game environment
- Underperforming when spectators or crowds are present
- Being uncomfortable with the arena setting, including being distracted by signs or scoreboard images and sounds
- Not respecting the presence of referees, and being thrown off by calls you perceive to be unfair
- Being unfamiliar with the league rules, and running afoul of them, or not employing the right strategies for taking advantage of them
- Allowing others' attitudes around games to throw you off your mental approach (from Chapter 18)
- Not respecting how this one game fits into a league season, playoff series, or tournament

The Comp Training Program

In the pages that follow is the Comp Training Program and schedule. Comp Training should be done over the course of the entire year. Like Psych Training, the key period for Comp Training is during your sport's competitive season, as Comp Training ties into your schedule of competition in games and practices, as follows: There are three different types of days within your Comp Training schedule—Game-Competition Days (days when you have a game), Practice-Competition Days (days when you have an official practice), and Free Days (days when you have neither). On each type of day, you will have a different regimen of training exercises. This is because different aspects of your training are best worked on at different times in relation to your sport's competitive schedule. For example, days when you have an official game are obviously an ideal time to work on the Game layer of your Comp Training. Free Days, where you aren't at the rink, are a good time to do exercises that involve watching hockey video, as well as cross-training (exercises involving other sports). For each day, we don't expect you to do all the exercises listed under them. These are just examples of some of the types of exercises you might consider doing on those types of days.

Find more information, examples, and illustrations of how to do the exercises on my website.

As you will see below, one fortunate thing about Comp Training versus other types of training is that activities you are already doing or might consider doing for non-training reasons can also be put to use as Comp Training exercises. This includes some frequent activities such as your own team games and practices, plus watching professional hockey on TV, and participating in other sports. If you incorporate these activities into your Comp Training, it can save you time for other hockey-related or outside activities.

Before applying yourself to your Comp Training Program, familiarize yourself with the principles of effective training in Chapter 20.

---

the inside story

In general, I recommend time off from competitive hockey in the off-season, rather than participating in summer hockey leagues. The off-season provides a needed mental break so that you are fresh each competitive season, and don't get mentally burnt out or run down. In addition, you need a period when you can work on improving skills, and other aspects of training, without upcoming competitions getting in the way. All sports have off-seasons for a reason. If you want to keep playing in the off-season, I recommend the no-pressure informal game-like competitions you will read about further along.

Game-Competition Days

OFFICIAL GAME COMPETITION: Participating in actual games is a natural and necessary element of training yourself to get better at performing in future games. So while you're busy playing, having fun and doing your best, you can actually be training at the same time. To get the most Comp Training benefit out of your games, focus on some of the issues mentioned above under Training for Games (see page 231).

Practice-Competition Days

PRACTICE DRILL COMPETITIONS: On their own, team practices are mostly geared to training teams to compete better, not to your individual training needs. However, there are many ways you can turn practices and specific drills into very useful exercises in Comp Training for Game Situations. Some examples might be:

- You decide that in today's practice you will work on backhand passing in game situations. Throughout the practice, you employ a backhand pass instead of a forehand pass, at every sensible opportunity.
- You decide that in today's practice, you will work on shooting to the top right corner of the net (one of the key scoring spots) in the game situations offered by the practice. In all your shots throughout the practice, you aim for that spot—focusing only on how your aim was, and ignoring completely whether, after a while, the goalie knew you were shooting there and saved the shots or not.
- You are a forward: For the next month, in all your practices, you will work on your finish in game situations. You will try to score as many goals as you can in however many shots you get, and keep track each practice to see if your percentage is improving over the month.
- You are a defender: For the next month, in all your one-on-one drills, you will work on a different aspect of defending one-on-one's during each practice. Today it will be using the hipcheck, next practice it will be keeping a close gap with the forward, the following practice it will be angling, etc.
- You are a goalie: In today's practice, you will work on being as smartly aggressive as you can to the shooter, in game situations.

There are unlimited ways to use practices for Comp Training. Look for ideas within the areas listed under Game Situations previously, and be creative but intelligent in figuring out how you can get a Comp Training benefit from all your practice time.

VIDEO TRAINING: There are several types of video training you can do. Simply watching a game and rooting for a team trains you for Competition itself and for the game as a whole. To get the most out of watching a pro or high-level game, take it a step further by focusing on one top player on the ice. Feel as though you are in that player's body, and notice what plays the player makes in each situation. This can be excellent training for Game Situations. Studying pre-recorded video of your opponents can also help train you for games and game situations, by making you familiar with their tendencies, and conditioning you to know what to do when you encounter them in a live game.

GAME-LIKE COMPETITIONS: A number of game-like competitions can train you for Competition, for Games as a whole, and for certain Game Situations. Examples include *shinny* or pick-up hockey, *ball hockey* outside (on foot or on in-line skates). Another great one is the game of *keepaway*, in which each player or team of players tries to keep control of the puck (or ball if not on the ice) and not let the others get it. *One-net games* are also good, where each player who gets the puck (or ball if not on the ice) must clear a specified line a distance from the goal, and then come back inside it, before they can score. The one-net game *hog*, where each player is their own team, and there can be several teams playing in one game, is a good one, because each player is engaged at all times and must participate in all facets of offence and defence.

SIMULATIONS: Simulations are training exercises that mimic some of the conditions of real situations you will face, but in a controlled environment conducive to training. They are excellent training for game situations and for the Competitive Environment. Simulations can take many forms, and can be an opportunity for you to use some creativity in creating a good simulation for a particular purpose. A few examples include:

- training with a friend, and having the friend mimic the tendencies of a key opponent you will be up against in an upcoming competition;
- doing training exercises with a friend designed to help each of you improve your bodychecking ability in various specific game situations. To avoid the risk of injury in the simulation, you don't follow through all the way on the checks the way you would in a real game;
- while working on your shot at home, having a friend or parent simultaneously drop a tennis ball and call what spot in the net is open. You have to get the shot to that spot before the tennis ball hits the ground; and
- having a parent or friend "referee" one of the above game-like competitions.

When I was playing College hockey for Harvard, one of the toughest road arenas to play in was at Clarkson University. They had loud crowds, standing-room only; with lots of raucous students and a giant bell they would sound directly over our net whenever they scored. To ready us for this intimidating situation, during practice the week leading up to playing Clarkson, our coach would bring huge speakers out on the ice during practice and have a recording played on them full-blast of the unpredictable sound of a radio station with reception cutting in and out. Every now and then, the recording would cut to a loud bell sounding, and then go back again. Clarkson was still a tough arena to play in, but only because they had good players like future NHLers Todd White, Willie Mitchell, Erik Cole, Chris Clark, and Kent Huskins, not because of the crowd and the bell.

When I was playing in the Pittsburgh Penguins organization, one of my coaches was former Toronto Maple Leaf coach John Brophy. Besides Scotty Bowman, Brophy is the only hockey coach with over one thousand professional wins.

One of the reasons for his success and longevity was his creativity in finding ways to communicate messages to players. One day after practice, Brophy wanted us defencemen to improve our ability to pin forwards to the boards in our end. So to simulate that game-like situation, Brophy had a boxing heavy-bag brought out on the ice, which is heavy like a player, and slippery like a crafty player because of its round shape and leather covering. We took turns having to lift and pin the bag to the boards in the corner, then let it go, navigate it with our legs one pane of glass over, and repeat this process once for each pane of glass in the corner. Sure enough, when we got back in a real game, we had a much easier time pinning forwards to the boards!

CROSS-TRAINING: Cross-training means playing a sport other than hockey. Cross-training trains you for Competition itself, and sometimes, depending on the sport you choose and the format in which you participate, it can train you for Games as a whole and the Competitive Environment. Cross-training in a variety of other sports is good, as it conditions in you a broad base of athletic ability and adaptability, which can pay off in hockey. Because cross-training does not feel like a hockey activity, even though it is hockey training, it also helps keep you mentally fresh for hockey. Examples of cross-training sports you might consider include soccer, lacrosse, table tennis, swimming, basketball, squash, or any other sport you can think of that's safe to play and which you're able to play or can learn in a reasonably short time.

Free Days

CROSS-TRAINING: See earlier.

VIDEO TRAINING: See earlier.

GAME-LIKE COMPETITIONS: See earlier.

SIMULATIONS: See earlier.

The above Comp Training Program will help you master the art of competing in hockey. It will help you maximize your skills and abilities in competition, like the boxer Steel in the story in Chapter 15, who surprised and defeated Raw—the better boxer "on paper." More than any other form of training, Comp Training transforms your talents, skills, and abilities into superpowers come competition time. Successful Comp Training will give you a great edge in striving to make it.

EXPERTS' RECAP

Remember . . .

· Comp Training conditions you to compete optimally, in the particular mode of your sport.

· While others leave Comp Training to chance, we have created a strategically designed, comprehensive, planned approach that offers you a tremendous advantage.

· Your Comp Training must address different layers (competition itself, games, game situations, and the competitive environment).

· Comp Training occurs most during your competitive season.

· A number of specific exercises can help you cover the key aspects of Comp Training.

the secrets of successful training

SCOUTS' PREVIEW
In this chapter . . .
· Twelve keys to effective training

BEFORE YOU GET STARTED WITH THE TRAINING YOU LEARNED THUS FAR, THERE ARE SOME IMPORTANT PRINCIPLES YOU SHOULD KNOW THAT APPLY TO ALL TYPES OF TRAINING. THE SECRETS OF SUCCESSFUL TRAINING YOU WILL LEARN HERE CAN GUIDE YOU TO GREAT RESULTS WHICH WILL GIVE YOU AN ADVANTAGE OVER RIVALS AND HELP YOU ADVANCE CLOSER TO YOUR DREAM.

In addition to allowing you to get the most out of your training, knowing these principles can help you modify your Training Program if required. You will understand what should be present in any training regimen for it to work.

The Twelve Keys to Effective Training

1. **REPETITION:** You know the saying about skills that "Practice makes perfect"? Well, a similar one applies to training: "Training makes tried and true." Remember that training is conditioning. You must do it over and over before it sticks. Plus, the more you exercise an ability in training, the stronger it will hold up when you need it in competition. This applies to all types of training: conditioning your muscles to exert force; conditioning your mind to preserve positive beliefs; conditioning yourself to apply the killer instinct and not let opponents come back. Repeating training exercises conditions you by habit to execute your abilities successfully in competition.

2. **QUALITY OVER QUANTITY:** While you need to repeat training exercises, quality is more important than quantity. Poor quality training just trains you to compete poorly! Some people become "compulsive trainers" and think: "If I do more than the expert program says, I will improve faster." But it's not always true that if some is good, more is better. Rest periods are just as important to training as exercises. So the phrase "Go hard or go home," isn't pointless trash-talk, it's actually sound advice when it comes to training. Follow a sensible program, and do every exercise as well as you can.

3. **ROUTINE:** In Chapter 18, you learned a bit about routines. Routines are useful not only for competition but also for training. A routine helps you avoid wasting time wondering where to start or what to do next. Routines also keep you focused so you train better. Training routines can involve having a certain location and time for your different exercises, or doing a series of exercises in a set order. For Fitness Training, you may have a regular outfit that you wear, a particular music playlist you listen to, or a water bottle you drink from between exercises.

4. **ADAPTABILITY:** While routines are helpful, some adaptability is also good. Don't forget that training is for competition, where unpredictable events often occur. Since you can't predict these events, you can't train for them—*except* by dealing with any unpredictable events that occur during your training! Suppose, for example, one day a piece of equipment you normally use is broken. Rather than not training at all, or being foolishly rigid and trying to use the broken equipment, why not see if you can find a similar exercise you can do to train the same ability? Now if a game comes where a usual article of your equipment has been forgotten at home or breaks, your training has made it easier for you to use a substitute article and still perform. Also, sometimes sports themselves evolve, and for you to keep pace your training must evolve with them.

5. **CYCLICAL:** As you read in Chapter 17, training works by a cycle of exercise (strain), followed by rest and recovery (R&R). For all types of training as well as competition and practice, you need R&R time in between. That R&R time is just as essential to your training as the exercises, so make sure the R&R is just as high quality as the exercises. There is also another cyclical aspect to training. Since training is conditioning, abilities you haven't recently exercised will slowly fade, so you have to take turns training each of them, to keep each in shape.

6. **PURPOSE***:* As you are training, remember that every exercise has a purpose in conditioning one of the abilities you need to make it. None of the exercises are "random," and you never train just for the sake of training. Being mindful of this helps you stay motivated and train better. Knowing the purpose of a given exercise can also enable you to pick up new things or little refinements that over time provide an extra edge to you personally. Understanding the purpose of exercises is also critical if you need to modify them for your own situation.

7. **PROGRESSIVE:** In order to make it, you must keep improving as a player, which means your training must keep pushing you to higher levels of performance. Through training, you want to continually get physically stronger, mentally tougher, and better as a competitor. "Raising the bar" by progressively pushing yourself to do each exercise a little harder, faster or better each time you train is what makes you perform harder, faster, and better in games. Training is progressive in a different way as well. Advanced training is *periodic*, which means it has a sequence of phases that build upon the ones before, and then the whole cycle repeats. Your Fitness Training had four phases. Psych and Comp Training had in-season and off-season phases. All of this also helps prepare you for sports competition, which is also periodic, progressing from off-season to training camp to regular season to championships.

8. **FUN:** Training is not always the most naturally fun part of sports, but there are ways to find enjoyment in it, and this makes for better training. When training is drudgery, it becomes an ordeal, and eventually you start to cut sessions or cut corners within sessions, causing your training to suffer. So look for sensible ways to make training fun, such as:
- train with a friend, whenever possible
- train in a place that you enjoy being
- listen to music during training
- make little games or competitions with yourself out of your training, such as trying to do better than you did last time; establishing a new "personal best;" imagining you are training for a World Championship, going for an Olympic record, or competing against your idol
- anything else you think of that makes training fun yet still effective

9. **VARIETY:** One way to add some fun to your training is to include a little variety in your regimen. This will help keep you fresh, focused, and energetic. Remember, since training never completely mimics competition, some variety in your training will make that training broader, and enable you to condition yourself for more potential aspects of competition. So every few training sessions, pick a few things to do differently. For example, train in a different location, or at a different time, or use a different variation of an exercise. When you really need a complete break, replace your whole training program for the day with an extended fun cross-training activity.

10. **GAME-SPECIFIC:** Variety is an important element of training, but overall, you want your training to be geared as much as possible to your sport. In fact, we included exercises in your Comp Training Program that don't train one specific ability, but are very valuable precisely because of how closely they mimic game conditions or game situations. Of course it's true that the reason you train and don't just play games is that often isolating and training a particular ability can only reasonably be done through a non-game-like exercise. But sometimes, you can still tailor that exercise to fit your sport. For example, jumps are a common training exercise. A basketball player would want to do jump-ups, because their sport involves leaping up for shots, blocks, and rebounds. A football player would want to do forward jumps, because their sport involves leaping forward from the line of scrimmage. And a hockey player would want to do diagonal jumps, because skating is a diagonal motion of the legs. So, if you see an opportunity to do a training exercise in a more game-specific manner without detracting from the purpose of the exercise, go for it.

11. **INDIVIDUAL-SPECIFIC:** Anybody who says that every player should train the exact same way is ignoring a key fact: Not every person is the same and different things work best for different people. So training should be tailored to some degree to be individual-specific. For example, many of my friends liked to Fitness Train first thing in the morning to get it out of the way and get on with the rest of their day. But I didn't have the energy to train as hard as I needed in the morning, whereas later in the day, I did. So I trained much more effectively in the afternoon or evening. As you train and compete, notice patterns in what works for you and doesn't so you can adjust your training accordingly. Also, everyone has limited time and resources, so set priorities for your training and decide what will get the most time and attention. Usually, you'll want to choose these priorities based on what you think are the *limiting factors* most holding you back from improving or reaching your goal. Customizing your training accordingly can help you make rapid strides in limited time.

12. **FEEDBACK:** As with every other aspect of making it, you want to monitor the results of your efforts. This allows you to appreciate your improvements and decide if any changes are required to make faster progress toward your goal. Many players find it enjoyable and beneficial to track their training with the aid of a sport diary. Recording in the diary what

they just did in a training session immediately provides them "something to show" for those efforts, and a black-and-white confirmation that they've accomplished a task. It then can serve as a benchmark to measure future progress, and feel good about improvements made over time that otherwise can be hard to notice because they happen gradually. And it provides a space to make notes-to-self about your feelings, lessons learned, and questions to be answered.

EXPERTS' RECAP
Remember . . .
· Follow the set of principles in this chapter to get optimal results from your training.

6

STRATEGIES game plans for getting results

"Hockey's favourite parent," Walter Gretzky guided his famous son through tricky situations and immense pressure, and did it while keeping a smile on his face.

THIS SECTION TEACHES YOU ABOUT THE CHALLENGES YOU WILL FACE AND THE PLANS YOU SHOULD MAKE.

Chapter 21: the world of youth hockey

Chapter 22: the road to the pros

Chapter 23: plotting your career

"A man who does not plan well-ahead will find trouble right at his door."
CONFUCIUS, FATHER OF CHINESE PHILOSOPHY

the world of youth hockey

SCOUTS' PREVIEW
In this chapter . . .
- The benefit of having a plan—right from the beginning
- Issues to plan for in the world of youth hockey

IN TODAY'S COMPLEX SPORTS WORLD, IT'S IMPORTANT FOR ATHLETES WITH AMBITIONS TO DO MORE THAN JUST WORK ON THEIR GAME. IT CAN BE A BUMPY JOURNEY TO REACH THEIR DREAM. THERE ARE ISSUES TO SETTLE, DECISIONS TO MAKE, PITFALLS TO AVOID, AND PROBLEMS TO SOLVE, ALL OF WHICH CAN AFFECT THEIR CAREER OUTCOME. PLAYERS AND THEIR FAMILIES OR SUPPORT PEOPLE ARE WISE TO DEVELOP A PLAN FOR DEALING WITH THESE.

In this section, you'll have the opportunity to learn from the experience of players who have already been through the journey. With this, much of what you should plan for can be anticipated, and you can develop specific strategies in advance.

Issues to Plan for in the World of Youth Hockey

The journey to making it begins as soon as a child is old enough to dream. And the time when it becomes important to start planning is usually not far behind.

This chapter will cover the first phase of that journey: the world of youth hockey. Here you will learn to develop a plan and strategies to successfully manage that phase. Below are some important matters to consider.

1. Don't Lose Sight of Your Overall Purpose

Fun and enjoyment are big reasons you chose hockey as your dream, so it doesn't make sense to sacrifice them as part of a misguided attempt to reach your dream.

If you want to make it to the pros or a high level of hockey, you must make sure to always remember that youth hockey isn't it. Anyone in youth hockey who treats it like it's the pros is almost assuring themselves of never reaching the pros. That's because the things you do when you are at your destination are different than the things you must do to get to your destination.

The journey from youth hockey to high-level hockey is a marathon, not a sprint. Don't be overly positively or negatively concerned with how you stack up each day or each year in youth hockey. If your aim is to reach high-level hockey, what matters more is how you stack up at the *end* of youth hockey, when selections for the next level are made. This means your choices should reflect what will benefit you in the long run, not just the short run. For example, it may not be the best decision to play for the best youth team you can, if it means you are going to sit on the bench all season and not get ice time and experience to develop your game.

Besides fun and enjoyment, your focus while in youth hockey should be on developing your hockey abilities. Success and prestige in youth hockey are not that significant in the big picture. The aim is to maximize your abilities for when youth hockey ends—either to help you make it to higher levels, or just to enjoy being able to play well at recreational levels over the rest of your life. So sometimes you may want to let your game suffer temporarily in youth hockey while you break down and rebuild improved versions of your skills.

In youth hockey, unlike professional hockey, the priority should be on the needs of all the individual children rather than on the desire for the team to win. That includes each player's fun and enjoyment, and their development as players, team members, and people. Athletes must learn that sports are about competing to win, and that they should always do their best and be good team players. But decisions in youth hockey should not be made in the interests of teams winning at the expense of fun, enjoyment, or development.

These aspects of keeping sight of your overall purpose will also come into play within other issues you encounter, as you will see below.

2. Deciding Where to Play

The location you play hockey in, if you have any choice in the matter, is one factor you may want to consider. Big hockey-crazy cities have the advantage of more development resources (ice, expert instructors, and challenging opponents). At the same time, they can sometimes also have the drawback of getting overheated to the point of jealousies, politics, and more of the "dark side" of youth hockey you will read about later in this chapter. In smaller towns and places where hockey is not as big, you might generally expect the opposite on both counts. So wherever you play, be aware of these factors, prepare for them, and try to manage them as best you can.

In some places, girls have a choice of whether to play on a girl's team or a boy's team. In that case, unless a girl is unusually advanced compared to her female peers, girls' hockey is typically the best choice. For advanced girls, playing in a boys' league can allow them to push themselves to improve more, as long as they are safe, competitive, and comfortable at that level and in that environment. At a certain age, as boys get much bigger and stronger, the body contact permitted in boys' hockey but not girls' hockey will likely induce girls to want to switch back to girls' hockey. Social dynamics are another factor. Girls who have been through it report that some boys' teams are simply not welcoming to girls, while some girls' teams are not welcoming to a girl who is much more advanced than the others.

Most children play in organized youth leagues which offer the basic experience of formal hockey. Sometimes, for different reasons, certain children want a one or two year break from it. In those cases, more informal summer leagues, friendly recreational adult leagues, or local shinny hockey can provide a competitive experience while the player works on their game while taking a break from formal competition. Some areas also have a choice between organized club leagues and school leagues. The nature of these differ from league to league, so there is no general rule that can be given. Sometimes children can play in both simultaneously, as long as league rules permit and the coaches consent.

There are a succession of levels to choose from. Although these may vary in different areas, club team levels typically range from House League (recreational) to Select to A to AA and in boys' hockey, to AAA (most advanced). School programs vary widely as well, but are not so generally and easily classified. With club teams, usually the calibre of competition, the seriousness of the approach, the ice time, travel time commitments, and associated costs increase with each higher level.

Some areas may offer a choice among different youth organizations. These can vary drastically in their expertise and approach, as well. For each organization you are considering, talk to the executives running the organization, and talk to the team coach. If possible, also talk to people who recently played for that organization or coach, to find out about their experience.

Advanced players sometimes have the opportunity to play in a higher age group. The factors to consider in deciding whether to do so are similar to those above in the discussion of an advanced girl considering a boys' team. Also consider any other factors particular to your circumstance before deciding what makes the most sense. Don't make a decision solely based on whether the player is good enough.

3. Your Development Strategy

While you are young, development is everything. You need to continually build up your game to be able to reach your ultimate ambition. Yet organized play is typically not geared for development. It is geared to participation, and to the experience of being part of a formal competitive sports structure with teams, leagues, games, practices, and rules. As you learned in Section 5, some important development does happen through the process of practicing and playing. The most valuable part of this occurs in earlier age groups, where players first learn the basics of how their sport works. But, as you also learned in Section 5, there is a limit to the individual development you get from formal participation, and you will want to do much more to build up your game to reach your ambition. As a result, as a totally separate matter, it's crucial to have a complete strategy for development.

This book is an excellent start. From it you are able to learn what areas of your game are important to develop, the ways in which these can help you, and some key guidelines and special tips for how to develop them. But development requires more than knowledge and understanding, it requires action. For each area of your game that you'd like to develop, you must take the appropriate action. Examples include the goal-setting exercises, character-building exercises, time-management methods, skills projects, and training programs.

Many of these areas of development you can work on alone or with the help of parents, friends, or teammates. But in other cases, outside hockey development programs are important in helping you acquire or improve the abilities in question. Some programs can help with areas of skills, areas of training, and even character building and other items.

Hockey development programs come in many forms. Some have a wide focus that in theory allow you to work on many aspects of your game. Others are more focused on specific aspects. Both can be useful, depending on your needs.

Hockey programs also come in different types. Examples include week-long camps, regularly spaced clinics, private lessons, personal coaching or mentoring, and others. Consider your schedule, budget, and preferred learning environment in choosing the right one for the purpose at hand.

Sometimes non-hockey programs can also help with development. For example, courses, camps, or tutoring might help with things like goal setting, time management, character building, and your maintaining personal health and balance of activities.

One of the most important factors in choosing programs is considering the provider. In selecting programs, the hockey expertise and personal character of the instructional staff is crucial. There is also a matter of personality fit between you and the program staff. Make your development choices carefully.

Typically, development strategies change over time, as your development needs and priorities change, and as you learn what works best for you. One beginner player might perhaps benefit most from just spending lots of time on the ice, getting a feel for things without too much direction. When that player later becomes an advanced prospect, they might benefit most from reviewing game video off the ice with a hockey expert. Your development plans will likely need some modification at least once a year, to go along with setting your new annual goal and objectives for each year.

Development providers and programs are not all equal—far from it! A lot of time and money can be wasted on poor-quality programs that provide little development benefit, while sometimes even a few minutes with an insightful and attentive top expert can make a major difference.

heads up!

4. Choosing a Position

Typically, young children naturally gravitate to the way they prefer to shoot. Shooting left or right does not need to correspond to whether they are left-handed or right-handed. Nor is one better than the other. I believe it is best that a child go with what they prefer. In my family, although everyone is right-handed, my father and brother Dominic shoot left, while Steve and I shoot right. Among the top pros, Wayne Gretzky shot left, Mario Lemieux shot right. Sidney Crosby is a left shot; Alexander Ovechkin is a right shot. There's no right or wrong, only right or left. If the child does not seem to have a preference, and continues switching back and forth, it is best for parents or coaches to decide the matter one way or the other without waiting too long.

The choice of a position takes more consideration. At the top levels, defencemen are typically bigger and stronger, while forwards are usually smaller and faster. There are certainly exceptions, but the type of physical attributes you are likely to have as an adult may be a factor worth considering. Another factor is personality. People who like to attack and score usually play forward. People who like to defend and get the game under control usually play defence. It is good to experiment at younger age groups, in order to get a broad base of skills and hockey sense, and see where your natural abilities and tendencies lean. The nature of goaltending is so different that trying it is the *only* way to tell whether that is the right choice.

5. Managing Key Relationships

One key relationship is between the player and their parents or support persons. As you learned in Chapter 8, it's crucial for everyone to be on the same page. Yet sometimes friction can develop if the parent or support person feels the child should be at a certain level, but the child isn't. Expectations must be realistic and manageable. Not every child has the same ability, progresses at the same rate, or blossoms at the same time. Sometimes youngsters go through a phase where their play suffers, for whatever reason. If a parent overreacts, that can compound the problem. On the other hand, through our hockey schools I have often met parents who describe their surprise at a recent surge in their child's ability—long after the parent gave up on the idea that the child might ever reach such a level.

Another key relationship is between the coach, on one hand, and the player and parents or support person, on the other. Properly managing these interactions is crucial to avoiding misunderstandings, lost time, negative experiences for a child, or conflict between parents and coach. Before you join a team, it is a good idea for you and your family to talk with the coach and be clear on how things will work. Each team should also have a proper set of rules which cover interactions between parents and the coach. Generally, parents should avoid interfering with a coach's proper interaction with a player, and coaches must not overstep or abuse their authority in dealings with players.

additional help

For guidelines on appropriate team rules, visit Hockey Canada's website at www.hockeycanada.ca.

6. Dealing with the Dark Side of Youth Sports

Everything has a downside. The trick is not to let it take you down or get you down. Sports are competitive by nature. And for those who dream of making it, there is an even higher level of intensity. From there springs the "dark side" of youth hockey.

Chances are, during your time in youth hockey, you will encounter jealousy, arrogance, and selfishness. You will witness bad attitudes such as cheating or resorting to violence, in order to win at all costs. There will be "politics" where someone will try to use their personal influence to engineer an outcome that isn't merited, and "corruption" where money is used in the same way. You will feel a natural pressure to do what others are doing. The answer is to stay poised, don't panic about what others are doing, and stay focused on your game plan. Also, don't compromise your character by trying to win at all costs, as nothing can guarantee success, and even if it could, it wouldn't be worth that price.

You will experience friction and sometimes even conflict with others. Emotions run high. Nothing excites a child like pursuing a dream, and nothing excites a parent like looking out for their child. Bear this in mind, and you may be able to diffuse situations before they progress into true problems. Sometimes you will need to protect yourself, just don't overreact in a destructive way. And try your best not to let the dark side of youth sports spoil your enjoyment or weaken your resolve to pursue your dream.

7. Creating a Positive, Nurturing Side for Your Sport

To counteract the negative side of youth sports, it helps to foster a positive, nurturing side. Elements of this could include:

FRIENDS: Often, doing things with friends is more enjoyable than doing things without them. Developing friendships you can maintain over your youth hockey career can be enjoyable, rewarding, and helpful toward your goal of making it. In my case, I was lucky enough to have two great friends who shared the same personal values and hockey dreams as me: my two brothers. We were able to talk to each other about hockey issues, share fun experiences, play shinny or ball hockey together, and give each other tips from our respective experiences.

MENTORS: It always helps to have someone to turn to who knows what you are going through, and can offer practical assistance in addition to moral support. Former high-level players and caring, insightful coaches can make good mentors. Although it was after youth hockey, I had a coach who was particularly helpful because he not only knew my ability, but also understood my personality, and thus how to help me achieve my goals.

ROLE MODELS: As you learned in Chapter 5, a role model is a person who you look up to and aspire to be like. Having a hockey role model can be a very positive experience because you can feel a connection to someone already living your dream. Every time you see them play, it is motivating and thrilling for you. And you can have fun following their career and rooting for them. You can also learn from how they play, what they say, and how experts or books describe them—and be excited about your progress as you follow in their footsteps.

8. Keeping Your Efforts Sustainable

Because your hockey journey is a marathon, it's important to do whatever you can to keep your efforts sustainable over the long haul.

Remember that it's the long run that counts; don't emotionally live and die with each success or failure. Athletes who have made it generally keep an even keel, and don't make their career into an exhausting "emotional roller coaster."

---

the inside story

As a teenager, I had some rough times in hockey where I was trying my best to persevere to make it to the pros, but there were challenges, obstacles, and injustices and I wasn't sure how I would get through them. One thing that helped me was to see the unflappable confidence of my hockey role model, Mario Lemieux. Lemieux was a superstar, yet he faced plenty of adversity: He had opponents shadowing him and trying to rough him up. He was unfairly criticized as not being the "ambassador for the game" that Wayne Gretzky was said to be, just because Lemieux was shy and occasionally spoke frankly about issues in the game he hoped to see improved. And most of all, he had constant health trouble including ongoing severe back problems, a broken wrist, and then cancer! Yet, nothing could stop him, and he always had a look of calm assurance that things would work out. I made it through the difficulties of my teen years, and the next year, I was drafted by none other than the Pittsburgh Penguins with their new owner—Mario Lemieux.

Use the character you developed in Section 2 to respond the best way you can to inevitable challenges. The rest is outside your control, and there is no point distracting yourself by worrying about it. Focus always on what you *can* do.

Keep hockey fun and enjoyable so that you don't suffer burnout and quit, thereby depriving yourself of your chance to make it.

Try to find a team whose time commitment for games, travel, and practices provide what you need for hockey without consuming an excessive proportion of your personal schedule.

When considering teams, development programs, and equipment, get a firm idea of what you'll be getting for the cost. Sometimes, foregoing one needless expensive item can save you enough for several good inexpensive items. Other times, one expensive item can provide an incredible benefit, while numerous inexpensive items provide next to none.

9. Coping with the Different Phases of the Youth Progression

Youth hockey extends through several different stages of children's personal growth and maturation. Each brings new changes and challenges. Here is a little bit about what to expect, what to focus on, and what to guard against:

YOUNG KIDS (AGES 9 AND UNDER): Having fun and developing passion for the game is the first priority. Passion and fun will also come in handy when it comes to the challenge of keeping children attentive, in order to learn and develop strong fundamental skills. This is also a time to start developing character.

THE "GOLDEN AGE" (AGES 10-12): In this stage, motivation is usually strong, and attention is easier to maintain. Broadening hockey skills continues to be a priority. But for those with ambitions, pursuing hockey should start to become more sophisticated, gradually incorporating more of the elements of making it described in this book.

THE "ROCKY ROAD" (AGES 13-16): At this age, some kids start to have serious attitude problems that interfere with their continued development. Parents and support persons thus play a key role in helping their child be one of those who stay on track. This stage can then end up presenting a great opportunity to gain ground over the many rivals who get sidetracked. With tantalizing Junior, prep school, and College hockey opportunities for their children now close at hand, it can also be a challenge for parents or support persons to stay grounded during this stage. Some get carried away with overbearing schemes for their kids, or overzealous dealings with coaches and scouts which are detrimental. Others, by receiving attention from high-level hockey people such as scouts and agents for the first time, develop an over-inflated perception of their knowledge and accomplishments to date, which gets in the way of further learning, development, and greater accomplishments. Again, for those who can stay grounded, the result is a great opportunity to get a leg up on rivals who didn't. With the higher levels of hockey quickly approaching, this is the time to start expanding efforts into as many of the areas described in this book as are appropriate for you. While there are plenty of players who will bloom even later than this age, this is a pivotal stage for many in terms of determining whether they will make it.

the inside story

Don't get discouraged if you are not where you'd like to be or think you need to be by this age. Be patient and persistent.

My brothers and I were all late bloomers. In our Major Junior draft years, none of us was even drafted.

Yet, as the best example of how quickly things can change for the better, less than two years after not even being on the radar of any Junior team, my brother Steve was rated in the 1st round by NHL Central Scouting in their Entry Draft Rankings.

EXPERTS' RECAP

Remember . . .
· Youth hockey involves a number of issues.
· The best way to deal with them is by having a game plan in advance.

the road to the pros

CHAPTER 22

SCOUTS' PREVIEW

In this chapter . . .

· How the Road to the Pros differs from the world of youth hockey
· Lessons to learn if you want to make a career out of hockey
· Planning your path
· Major Junior versus College hockey
· Surviving and thriving on the Road to the Pros
· Differences for girls' hockey

THOSE WHO SUCCESSFULLY MAKE IT BEYOND THE WORLD OF YOUTH HOCKEY GRADUATE TO THE NEXT PHASE: THE ROAD TO THE PROS.

How Does the Road to the Pros Differ from Youth Hockey?

The Road to the Pros consists of all the levels between youth hockey and the very highest levels of the men's and women's game (roughly speaking, "the pros"). The higher the level you reach along the Road to the Pros, the fewer teams, and the fewer player spots. Not everyone can make the pros, so this sequence of levels helps scouts at each level separate from the pack those players they feel are good enough to advance another step.

Like youth hockey, the Road to the Pros involves processes to navigate, decisions to make, and issues to address. But the Road to the Pros has some significant differences from youth hockey, and calls for new advance planning and strategies.

The nature of hockey on the Road to the Pros is different than in youth hockey. The people involved have all excelled at lower levels, and are striving for the top. These levels are within reach of the pros, so ambitions are very real, and the competition is serious. Indeed, if you make it to even the first level of the Road to the Pros, you can feel proud that you have made it to a *serious level* of hockey, because a serious level is a notably high level. The fact that it is a serious level doesn't mean that hockey is no longer fun; always keep hockey fun because fun is a key part of your dream.

Lessons to Learn If You Want to Make a Career Out of Hockey

In order to survive and thrive in this new world of hockey, players must adapt. They must learn that high-level hockey is about:

WINNING, NOT JUST PLAYING: While youth hockey is meant to be about pure play, high-level hockey sees winning as a clear and serious goal. Coaching at these levels is a job, and the job is getting their team to win. For players, playing is not enough. The scouts watching are working for higher-level teams that also need to win. They are looking for players who do the things that help teams win.

PERFORMANCE, NOT JUST PARTICIPATION: While the focus in youth hockey should be on participation, at this stage the focus is on performance. The reason a player made it to the Road to the Pros is because it is anticipated that they will perform well. And if they want to advance further, performance, not just participation, is what matters—and what scouts assess.

PROFESSIONALISM: Players typically no longer have to pay to play here as they did in youth hockey. Teams pay all the costs, and in return players are expected to perform and do what the coaches ask. They must understand that they've been engaged to do a "job" for the team, in the way they play to help the team win. Teams will try to instill the ethic of doing a job well and doing it consistently. Professionalism means being able to be counted on to follow instructions and fulfill duties.

ACCOUNTABILITY BEYOND YOURSELF: As a youth player, your accountability is to yourself, because you are playing for your own enjoyment. However, in this phase, players are also accountable to coaches, teammates, and even to the team's fans, for how they perform in helping the team win. They are still accountable to themselves first and foremost, but are now accountable to a larger entity as well.

CONSEQUENCES: Because youth hockey involves children and is designed for fun and learning, you don't always experience consequences from poor performance as you would in adult life. However, in this phase, players learn the reality of consequences. If they play well, they can expect acclaim, rewards, and enhanced opportunities. If they play poorly, they can expect to be benched, demoted, traded, or cut.

These lessons of the Road the Pros can be a shock, coming out of the very different world of youth hockey. However, they are not meant to be harsh or cruel. For those seeking to make a career in hockey, these lessons prepare you for that career. And your success in applying them is how scouts know that you are ready for such a career. Some athletes may decide they don't want to continue pursuing hockey in this form. They may prefer to keep playing hockey purely for fun through juvenile and adult recreational leagues, while pursuing a different career. This is a perfectly reasonable decision. However, it should be pointed out that the same lessons as above must be learned in order to prepare for and succeed in the world of jobs and adult life outside hockey.

The Roads to the Pros in Canada and the United States

Below are maps of the Road to the Pros for men's and women's hockey in Canada and the United States:

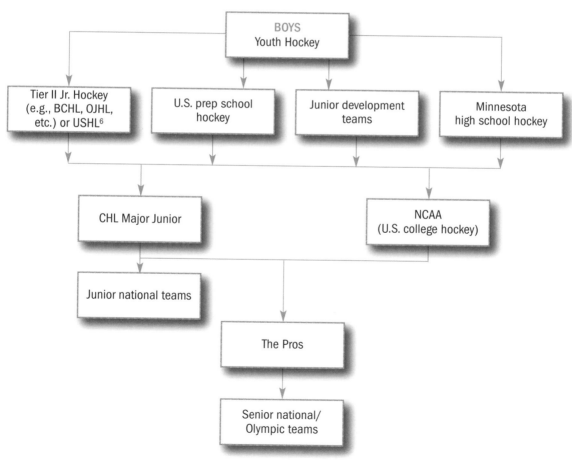

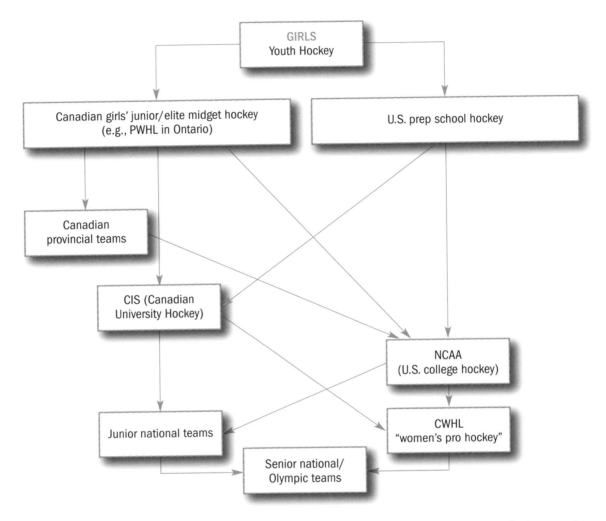

Different players have different dreams. Some may dream of playing in the Olympics. Some may dream of being an NHL player or a player in the equivalent female league, the Canadian Women's Hockey League. Some may dream of playing College hockey, or Major Junior. And some may realize their dream just in making it out of youth hockey onto the Road to the Pros. A dream is a personal matter, and no dream is better than another. Not everyone aspires to make it to the very highest level. The chart is just meant to clarify the hierarchy of levels in this phase where levels don't simply correspond to player age, as they do in youth hockey.

Note that the charts represent the typical paths, but not necessarily the *only* paths, to reaching a given level. For example, some players have gone on from Canadian university hockey to the NHL. And that may be what a particular player prefers to try to do. However, you should know that this path is rare. A player who aspires to make the NHL should not mistake this for a typical course to that goal.

Be aware that there are also regional differences in what is typical. Take, for instance, boys trying to make U.S. College hockey: In Minnesota, a player may be recruited directly out of high school hockey into college. In New England, a player might play prep school hockey after high school and before College. Elsewhere in the United States and Canada, a player may go from youth club hockey to Tier II Junior in the USHL or one of the Canadian leagues, and from there to College.

The Road to the Pros also involves some important decisions.

Major Junior versus College Hockey?

One very significant decision for boys is the choice between playing Major Junior or College hockey, the two major paths to the pros in North America. It's a decision that concerns not only hockey, but also education and non-hockey career prospects, as well as meaningful personal factors.

Deciding between these two options is a personal matter for each individual player and their parents or support persons. Key factors to consider can include your personal aspirations, your level of hockey ability, the style of game you are best suited to, your academic potential and interest, your family resources, your stage of physical and mental maturity, and your comfort level with what's involved in each choice. Coaches of teams you are considering and player agents can give you additional useful information in making your decision. But be aware that they have their own interests at stake in your decision. It's your life. And your own judgment, and the judgment of those who have cared for you over the course of your life, is what you should base your decision upon.

To some people, it may seem like there are not two options. Major Junior drafts and recruits players starting at age sixteen, while they are still a couple of years or more away from being able to play College or be seriously recruited by Colleges. Yet it is important to think ahead, because if a player goes for the "bird in the hand," and things don't work out, they can't change their mind and play in the NCAA. If they're able to keep up their academics and have the resources, they could still get an education at a Canadian university. But Canadian Inter-University Sport is not a typical route to the NHL.

The lowdown on Major Junior hockey

· Playing Major Junior cancels your eligibility to play NCAA College hockey
· Roughly same number of teams and player spots available as College hockey
· For players within the ages sixteen to twenty-one years old
· Typically leave home at younger age, stay with a billet family
· Typically do not pick where you play—teams get rights to players through draft
· Can be traded to another team in another city

· Schedule has more games than College, less practice and training
· Smaller ice surface than College, which tends to produce more physical contact and boardplay

· Players wear half-visors
· Rules do not ban fighting (five-minute penalty)
· According to a recent study, approximately 50 per cent of NHL players come from the CHL, and a CHL player's chances of making the NHL are about 4 per cent[7]

· Offer tuition toward Canadian universities, but with important limitations
· Less than 20 per cent of players receive a university degree
  · Average salary in Canada with less than college diploma: $30,116[8]
  · Average salary in U.S. with less than high school diploma: $19,169[9]
  · Average salary in U.S. with high school diploma but not university: $28,645[9]
· From a typical CHL roster of 25 players, 1 player makes the NHL, 4 obtain a university degree and 21 do not obtain a university degree[10]

The lowdown on NCAA College hockey

· Can switch from NCAA College hockey to Major Junior, age permitting
· Roughly same number of teams and player spots available as Major Junior
· For players within the ages seventeen to twenty-four years old
· Leave home after graduating from high school, stay in housing for college students
· Have the opportunity to choose where you play from among interested schools
· Cannot be traded to another team, but also restrictions on transferring yourself

· Schedule has fewer games than Junior, more practice and training
· Larger ice-surface than Junior, which tends to produce less physical contact and more open-ice skating

· Players wear full-visors or face-shields
· Rules ban fighting (ejection, suspensions)
· According to a recent study, approximately 25 per cent of NHL players come from the NCAA, and an NCAA player's chances of making the NHL are about 2 per cent (it might be noted these figures have been progressively rising)[7]

· Education included (and mandatory) as part of hockey participation
· Over 80 per cent of players receive a university degree
  · Average salary in Canada with university degree: $58,767[8]
  · Average salary in U.S. with university degree: $51,554[9]
  · Average salary in U.S. with university post-graduate degree: $78,093[9]
· From a typical NCAA roster of 28 players, 0.5 players make it to the NHL, 23.5 graduate from university, and 4.5 do not graduate from university[10]

In other cases, players may truthfully not have two options. Many players are late bloomers, and are not on the radar of Junior teams at sixteen, but develop later, in time to attract interest from Colleges. This possibility is a good reason to always do as well as you can in school, and not to give up on hockey if you don't happen to be drafted at sixteen.

Once you have identified your preferred route, how do you make it happen?

Sean McCann is a veteran former pro hockey player, and the assistant coach and chief recruiter at Harvard. His uncle is also an NHLPA certified player-agent. Below you will find some of Sean's thoughts.

If your plan is to go the College route, contact the NCAA and specific schools you aspire to play for. Find out their academic requirements, and strive to meet or exceed these. The charts on pages 257 and 258 show which hockey sources Colleges typically recruit their players from. As McCann explains, there are some special events that are particularly important: "Most Tier II leagues including the USHL and the Canadian leagues have showcase tournaments that bring all the teams and kids together for the recruiters to go and watch. In the summer, there are also the Canadian prospects tournaments, the U.S. festivals for fifteen-, sixteen-, and seventeen-year-olds, and the USHL tryouts which are all very heavily scouted." Some people also choose to employ companies that will promote players. According to McCann, "They can give players some initial exposure by gathering and providing recruiters with information such as basic hockey facts, test scores, transcripts, resumés, references, contact information, and sometimes DVDs. From that, the recruiters can see if it's worthwhile connecting with the player or going to see them in

PRO-file

Sean McCann
My friend Sean McCann was captain of Harvard, an All-American defenceman, and a finalist for the top player in College hockey. In 1994, he was the first pick overall in the NHL Supplemental Draft, by the Florida Panthers. He played seven seasons and more than five hundred games of professional hockey in the IHL and AHL. He was IHL Rookie of the Year in 1995, and during his career won both the IHL and AHL's ironman awards.

person. On the other hand, people can also do this themselves." If recruiters are interested in a player, they will follow up with calls and visits. If a player has more than one actual offer, it becomes a matter of deciding which to choose. In the next chapter, you will learn about making that decision.

For those who plan to go the Major Junior route, it typically starts with being drafted while in youth hockey (or Tier II Junior) by a CHL team in their priority selection. From Training Camps, a player may make the team, or be assigned to the CHL team's Tier II affiliate at first. Otherwise, if a player is undrafted, they would themselves choose a Tier II team to play for, and try to attract the attention of a Major Junior team through their play. As you will learn in the next chapter, a player agent may be helpful in getting some exposure and other advice including contract negotiation for a player who chooses this route.

Surviving and Thriving on the Road to the Pros

Whichever route one chooses, the most important thing is what they make of it. In order to thrive in Major Junior or College, players should prepare for what the game is like at those levels. A good career there is critical if the dream is to continue on to the pros.

At the College level, according to McCann, things to prepare for include: "the speed, the size, and the quickness of everything, especially decision-making. A big challenge is the physical development, the strength." The players already at that level are older, and have been playing fewer games while doing extensive physical training.

Players going the Major Junior route need to prepare for the pro-type schedule with a long season and many games. They will also have to get used to playing without a full facemask, and prepare for the presence of fighting. Junior players will face fierce competition and physical challenges, and must prove they won't be intimidated into performing less than their best.

To thrive in College or Major Junior, goalies will have to prepare for a faster game and the fact that virtually every player at these levels is a skilled shooter. As a result, goalies will need to improve their positional play, as the ability to make reaction saves or recover to make saves after being out of position will be diminished.

Besides preparing for the game itself, players will want to prepare for what life will be like in Major Junior or College. This may include:

BEING AWAY FROM HOME AND FAMILY: Most often, playing at this level will take a player away from living at home and with family. Being in a foreign place or even country can be difficult, especially at first. One must prepare for this, both mentally and practically. This might include developing a plan for staying in touch with family and friends from home, and a plan for developing new friends and getting to know your new home.

PROCESS OF MATURING TO ADULTHOOD: Being away from home and not under the daily supervision of parents or adult guardians requires new responsibility. Players will need to be able to develop the ability to, in a sense, "be their own parent," and look at situations from a parental kind of outside perspective. They will need to take charge of making decisions, setting directions, getting done what needs to be done, and looking out for their best interests and welfare. Gradually assuming more responsibilities even before moving out is a good way to prepare, although it will likely still be a challenge when it happens. It is, however, a necessary step in maturing and being ready to take control of one's life, future, and fate.

PRESENCE OF PITFALLS AND DISTRACTIONS: Late adolescence and early adulthood is an age that can present many distractions and potential pitfalls including drugs, alcohol, and reckless ideas of fun and entertainment outside hockey. The "star status," attention, and adulation given to College and Junior players can increase these exposures. It's important to stay focused on your dreams, goals, values, and character to guide you. Along with the tips you learned in Chapter 7, this will help you avoid getting caught up in diversions that can sidetrack or terminate progress toward your aspirations.

TIME ISSUES: Junior and College players both face time-related challenges. As McCann explains: "You have the issues of the abundance of time in Major Junior, and the lack of time in College." Junior involves frequent long bus trips where potential activities are limited. Also, for those players no longer in school, there's suddenly much more unscheduled time than they've had in their life to this point. In Chapter 29 you will find tips to help prepare for this in advance. Aspiring College players, meanwhile, must progressively improve their time-management skills as outlined in Chapter 7, so they are ready to handle the dual needs of higher education and a serious hockey schedule.

How Are Things Different for Girls' Hockey?

Some of the same things apply as in boys' hockey during the Road to the Pros phase. This includes the nature of the game in this phase, and the lessons that must be learned to thrive in this phase. It also includes the challenges that even higher levels will pose on and off the ice, and what kind of preparation can help.

However, there are some important differences between girls' hockey and boys' hockey in the Road to the Pros phase. For starters, girls don't currently have their own truly professional league, in the sense of being paid to play. The closest equivalent to the NHL for girls is the Canadian Women's Hockey League or CWHL—an elite league for adult players. Players in this league typically have other jobs to provide themselves income. Aside from Olympic and National Teams, this is the highest level of Women's Hockey.

For girls aspiring to make the CWHL or to make their country's National or Olympic teams (where some players receive stipends as income in lieu of a job), the road to get there is a little bit more straightforward than for boys. There is no Major Junior option, unlike boys, so NCAA College is the primary option for girls aspiring to make the top levels, with Canadian university being a secondary option.

According to Jennifer Botterill, "Playing NCAA College hockey is a great situation. For many girls, I think it is the highlight of their lives as an athlete. For me and most of the people I've talked to, it provided a great opportunity to really improve both as a hockey player and as a person. It's a great environment in which to have balance in your life, to receive a great education, and play incredible hockey all at the same time. It's a very competitive environment and a very well-run league."

Girls are recruited to Colleges from a number of places. In Canada, scouts closely watch the Junior level (equivalent to boys' Tier II Junior) or highest level of youth organizations. In the United States, top high schools and prep school hockey are the main recruiting grounds. In Canada, there are also Provincial Teams featuring the top players from each province at different age groups. These teams compete in national tournaments that are very heavily scouted. In both Canada and the U.S., there are also Junior National Teams at various age groups. Girls who make these teams stand a very good chance of attracting attention not only from colleges but also from their country's all-ages National and Olympic teams. Girls who are advanced can sometimes even go straight from those programs into the Senior National Team programs or the CWHL. However, because there is no paid professional league in girls hockey, the value of a college education is even greater in terms of what a player can receive as a result of her hockey prowess. So even if a girl could make it to the top without going to college, it may very well still be beneficial to play College hockey.

Another difference for girls is that there are no player agents. There are, however, placement companies that try to help girls gain exposure for scholarship purposes, as there are for boys. Again, it is the choice of the girl and her family if they would like to use one.

Here are some tips from Jennifer Botterill:

"I think that being proactive is very important in making sure that girls and their families are contacting a lot of schools. Beyond that, they should make sure they are focusing on their own play and performance, as opposed to worrying about scouts that may be in the stands. Focus on your own game, and the outcome will hopefully take care of itself. Also, don't feel that there is only one set path for how you can be successful or make a national team down the road. Every person is going to be a little bit different in what they need in order to become a better hockey player or just as a person. A lot of people took different paths to get there."

> **EXPERTS' RECAP**
> Remember . . .
> · This stage has a new set of issues that calls for a new set of plans.
> · The nature of hockey at this stage is different than earlier, reflecting the transition from "hockey for fun" to "hockey as a career," and from childhood to adulthood.
> · Those aspiring to reach the top must choose a route in advance (for boys, this includes deciding between College hockey and Major Junior).

plotting your career

SCOUTS' PREVIEW
In this chapter . . .
· The importance of having a strategy
· Approaching hockey as a career

FROM THE TIME YOU HAVE COMMITTED TO CHASING YOUR DREAM, AND MADE A REASONABLE AMOUNT OF PROGRESS TOWARD IT, THINK AHEAD ABOUT YOUR CAREER IN BROADER TERMS AND STRATEGIES: PLOT YOUR CAREER.

Approaching Hockey as a Career

If your intention is to make your sport your career, it's important to approach it in a business-like way.

Businesses divide tasks into different "functional areas." Each functional area serves a different purpose for the business. For example, the building of the business' product at the plant is covered by an area called "Operations." Figuring out what customers want and how to supply that to the customer is part of "Marketing." Engaging potential customers, and trying to connect with people who would like to buy their product, falls under "Sales." The decision making that takes place in the head office is included under "Management." When all of these functional areas are being taken care of properly, the business profits.

As a hockey player, you can think about your career in similar terms.

"OPERATIONS" = YOUR GAME

In hockey, the Operations category applies to your game. This includes all the things you have learned about earlier in this book—your sense of purpose and motivation, your character, skills, training, and strategies for dealing with various challenges. All these things together comprise your game. The game you possess and the way you perform fall under the area of your athletic career we'll call Operations.

This area is the most fundamental, because if you don't have the game to make a career out of, then nothing else can compensate. It would be as if our imaginary business had a product that didn't work. It would be nearly impossible to get anywhere even with the most ingenious Marketing, Sales, and Management work. The business simply could not succeed without sound Operations.

This is precisely why your game has been covered so comprehensively in this book. Indeed, from Section 1 on, the entire book up until now has been devoted to your game. So you've already learned much about the Operations aspect of your career. As you continually strive to move up the ladder in your sport, keep a couple more general Operational points in mind:

- Continual self-improvement is the only way to keep pace with better and better competition at higher and higher levels. In every area of your game, you must strive to do better tomorrow than you did today, and better this year than last year. High-level hockey scouts often try to assess where they think a player is on the "trajectory" of their career. They assume the shape of that trajectory is an arc, where a player improves for a time, reaches a peak, and then gradually declines—all relative to their competition. For some players, the peak may be at age twelve. For other players, it may be at age fourteen, sixteen, twenty, thirty-three, thirty-seven, etc. These scouts are most interested in players who are still on the upswing, and who will be better in the future than they are now. This is yet another reason to focus on continually striving to improve every aspect of your game.

- Maintaining keen self-awareness is very important. An overinflated view of your abilities will prevent you from seeing needed areas of improvement. At the same time, an underinflated view of your abilities can leave you feeling hopeless and unmotivated. You need an accurate view to help you identify the weaknesses in your game at each point in time, and make them a priority in your efforts to improve. Repeatedly shoring up your biggest weakness will allow you to improve rapidly. A keen view of yourself also helps you know what your strengths are. These are the "tickets" that got you to where you are. You will want to make sure to keep exhibiting those strengths to stay where you are and have a chance to move up.

"MARKETING" = IDENTIFYING WHAT TEAMS WANT AND HOW YOU CAN HELP THEM

Using our business analogy, the area of your career we'll call Marketing refers to making yourself aware of what teams are looking for in players, and figuring out how you can fulfill their needs.

What do hockey teams want? There are some things every hockey team wants in every player. Put yourself in the shoes of the people picking the team:

1. At all levels, scouts look for players capable of succeeding at the level they are scouting for. They want to endorse players who definitely have the game. You've built your game through Operations, but you must ensure that your play is consistent. Don't count on a scout overlooking a bad game because you were sick, tired, hurt, or eased up against a weak opponent. They might decide not to take a chance of hurting their reputation by endorsing a player they feel is a risky choice.

2. If there are standards or expectations of how players at a certain level are to look and behave, be aware of them. For example, high-level teams often expect players to dress professionally (shirt and tie or female equivalent) coming and going from games. Also, high-level teams won't tolerate negative body language from players when being called off the ice as a youth team might. Behave appropriately.

3. Coaches at high levels want players with excellent character and attitude. They can take players with those attributes, put them together, and build a team that jells and stays strong through the tough times in any game, season, or playoff series. Such players are coachable, will listen, and are eager to improve. So when you communicate with team representatives off the ice, make sure you demonstrate the right qualities: respect, commitment, enthusiasm, competitiveness yet a team player, confidence yet humility, and a positive outlook.

4. Managers want players with desire. Desire signals to them that the player is eager to be part of their team. Desire provides them reassurance that when they are in the emotional heat of competition, that player will be by their side, always competing their hardest to help the team win. Desire is the mark of a player who won't be satisfied just "being there," but will strive to excel. To play with desire means maximum effort in hustling and battling for loose pucks, backchecking, and bearing down in front of the net. It means doing everything you do on the ice with an intensity and fire that has nothing to do with playing rough or violent. Sidney Crosby is a great example of a player with desire.

Teams don't look for all the same things in every player. The obvious case is their need to fill different player positions: centres, wingers, defence, and goalies. But it goes beyond that, to the idea of specialized player *roles*. Each role corresponds to a particular set of on-ice responsibilities. Some teams want players who can fulfill different roles, and they slot players into these roles to create what they consider a complete, versatile team. At lower levels, this is less common and teams often just choose the best overall players they can at each position. It is best for you not to specialize at this early stage and to keep developing your overall skills anyway. This will help you gain a better idea later of what role is best for you to pursue when you reach higher levels, where roles are expected. Here are some of the common roles that many teams look for:

Offensive Playmaker: Sets up scoring chances, earns lots of assists (e.g., Joe Thornton)

Sniper: Converts scoring chances, scores lots of goals (e.g., Mike Bossy)

Power Forward: A physical player and an offensive-producer (e.g., Cam Neely)

The Complete Forward: Great in all aspects (e.g., Peter Forsberg)

Checking Forward: Guard opposing star, keep them scoreless (e.g., Sammy Pahlsson)

Two-Way Forward: Solid offensive and defensive contributor (e.g., Ron Francis)

Energy Forward: Fast or physical, forechecks and creates momentum (e.g., Marty Gelinas)

Offensive Defender: Defenceman who specializes in creating offence (e.g., Mike Green)

Shutdown Defender: Unbeatable defensively, even by opposing stars (e.g., Zdeno Chara)

Physical Defender: A physical defender who hits hard (e.g., Scott Stevens)

Complete Defender or Horse: Great offensively and defensively (e.g., Nicklas Lidstrom)

Keep-it-Simple Defender: Steady defensively, gets the puck out (e.g., Craig Ludwig)

In the words of every high-level coach I've ever had, any **Goaltender**'s role is simple: Stop the puck!

Is there a role or two in particular you think you might be able to fulfill? What do other people who know your game, abilities, and potential think? Sometimes it can be frustrating if you think you don't match up well with any role, or if there are several roles you think you could fill. As the game evolves over time, the strategies teams use change as well, and roles can too. It's also true that sometimes a player comes along and makes a splash playing in a new way that causes teams to re-think the roles they use. But for a young player aspiring to make it, the odds are far better "playing by the roles" than trying to change them. Once you gain a foothold, you may have a better chance to show new dimensions of your game, and have them appreciated. Until then, choosing a typical role can be a smart strategy. You must then tailor which skills you prioritize developing, and how you play, to fit the role you have chosen. Check with knowledgeable people whom you trust whether they think your choice makes sense and your progress looks good. Sometimes you may need to adjust methods, or even change the role you target.

Also bear in mind that people can't see your game in an objective, scientific sense. The way they see it is subjective, with a perspective based on their experience. Sports scouts, in assessing your game and how you might help their team, often naturally think in terms of comparisons to players they are very familiar with. This includes current or former players of theirs, players from elsewhere in their league, or any well-known players. They may think of you as "a player in the mold of [the comparable player they know]." As you reach higher levels, sometimes it can be helpful to choose a successful player to pattern yourself after. You can consider this your *game model*, because it is their game that you want to emulate and create potential comparisons to. Your game model should fit with the role you choose (see the players in the table on page 269, for example). Try to pick a game model who suggests a natural comparison, not one who is far-fetched. It's even fine to frankly admit that you appreciate this player's game, and are aspiring to pattern yours after theirs. But the most important thing is to develop the skills associated with that player and any role they play.

Remember that not all teams think alike. Some have different-than-usual conceptions of the roles they want. Some may not think in terms of roles at all. For any teams you are considering, it can be helpful to talk to a representative (manager, coach, or scout) and find out what they are looking for. Likewise, it can be helpful to talk to people who are not part of the management of the team, but are familiar with them, to get their insights into that same question.

All of this Marketing helps you match what teams want with what you are able to offer.

"SALES" = SECURING TEAMS' INTEREST IN YOU

In our business analogy, the Sales area of your career refers to securing teams' tangible interest in you, and doing what you can to "close the deal."

the inside story

Sometimes you have to be patient to get your chance. During my freshman season in College I didn't get a chance to play my normal position of defence until late in the season. Our number two defenceman broke his foot in a game, so the next game the coach was forced to insert me in the lineup. A few minutes in, our number one defenceman and captain was ejected. All of a sudden, players that didn't normally play much were going to get their chance. I ended up playing more than half the game, and in a 6–3 loss, was +3. When we got back home in the middle of the night after a long bus trip, the coach told the team that despite the loss, he was pleased because he had found a great new defenceman he never knew he had: me. A short while later, we needed to win our last game of the season in order to get home-ice in the first round of the playoffs. The game was against top-ranked University of Vermont, and our coach called me in before the game and told me that I was his most reliable defenceman and so he was going to match me up against "St. Louis" and wanted me to shut him down. I didn't know who "St. Louis" was, but I went out and successfully did as the coach asked. We upset Vermont and got our home-ice advantage. After the game, our famed Athletic Director Bill Cleary, who had coached Harvard to a national championship in hockey in 1989 and had won a gold medal as a player with the U.S. hockey team in the 1960 Olympics, came into the dressing room to see me. He was beaming with pride at the victory, and he grabbed my hand and slapped me on the back and said: "Helluva job, kid. One helluva job!"

PRO-file

Martin St. Louis

The player they were all so afraid of was a 5'7" forward named Martin St. Louis. He was a finalist for College Player of the Year, yet despite posting incredible numbers of points in college, he was undrafted by any NHL team because scouts thought he was too small to succeed in the NHL. For three seasons, he had to play in the minor leagues. The next two seasons, he was in the NHL, but didn't see much ice, even on a team miles out of playoff contention. Finally, he got his chance. Within two seasons, St. Louis was the leading scorer in the NHL, won the MVP trophy, the Stanley Cup, and the World Cup with Team Canada. St. Louis is one of my favourite players in the NHL, and not just because he's so exciting to watch. He is an inspiring example for aspiring players written off for being too small or any number of other reasons. And he is a great example in that he had to persevere just to make it, yet later was recognized as the top player in the world.

The first step of the process is to identify particular teams that there may be a chance of joining. Sometimes, teams will come to you and express their interest. Other times, you may need to contact teams to gauge or engage their interest. The aim is just to identify teams where there is a reasonable possibility from their perspective, and yours, of joining.

When you interact with potentially interested teams, there are several things that can help in trying to secure those teams' interest in you:

- Express the interest you have in playing for them. Prove that your interest is genuine by explaining some of your reasons that show your knowledge about their team, or the team's situation.

- If there is someone who knows you and whose opinion carries credibility with the team, and that person puts in a good word for you, this can sometimes help. This could be someone involved with the team, a prior coach of yours, or another hockey expert, for example. Sometimes teams will specifically ask you to provide references. Here, the character and social skills you learned earlier may come in handy, because people will typically only be willing to help you if they truly respect and like you as a person, not just your hockey ability.

"MANAGEMENT" = IMPORTANT CAREER-GUIDING DECISIONS

In our business analogy, the Management area of your career refers to making important career-guiding choices, including deciding on a team.

Certain decisions can have a profound impact on the direction of your career and your ultimate chances of making it. As a result, it is important to have a strategic approach to the management of your career.

Making smart decisions starts with a smart decision-making process.

If you look back at the way we approached the College versus Major Junior decision in Chapter 22, you can see several features that can help in making important decisions. These include:

- looking at things from all angles (hockey, educational, and personal aspects; best-case and worst-case scenarios; present, short-term, long-term, future, etc.);

- writing your thoughts on paper, where you can look at them critically;

- summarizing key points in a form that helps you easily compare and contrast the options being weighed (including facts and figures, pros and cons); and

- relying on your own judgment and that of people you trust.

For this last point, as you move up in hockey, try to develop a *personal network* of advisors and confidants. This network might include parents and family or the people who care for you most. It might include a close friend or teammate that is knowledgeable and trustworthy. It might include a personal mentor, or a trusted coach or teacher, past or present, who has expertise. This network can help give you outside feedback, consider different aspects of decisions, and talk through issues. But at the end of the day, your life and your dream are your responsibility. So for decisions you can make, don't leave others to decide matters that apply most to you.

The word Management also brings to mind career management companies (player agencies). Indeed, for players at higher levels who may have agents, one of the primary purposes of the agent is to help guide shrewd decisions. Reputable agents should know the industry and the people in charge of teams, and have other useful contacts. They should be experienced at communicating with teams and guiding career decisions through their own personal experience or prior clients. At the same time, there is a limit to what agents can do. Since the agent is working for you, teams will obviously view the agent's opinion as somewhat biased, and not rely on it as they would an impartial source. Most agents have several clients, and can spend only a fraction of their time on your case. They can provide you with good general advice about the nature of opportunities, but they can't know everything about you and your situation, and what is best in every case. The bottom line is, they can help, but you cannot rely exclusively on them, nor would any reputable agent advise or expect you to.

---

ask the AUTHOR-ity

When should you get an agent?
The point at which you truly need an agent is when you are negotiating a hockey contract. Before that, an agent can provide valuable career guidance and promotion.

Typically, a good rule of thumb might be that you don't want to commit to an agent before you reach a point where you are important enough to the agent that the agent will commit significant and sustained time and attention to you.

How do you choose the right agent?
Factors to consider may include the agency's reputation, clientele, experience, track record, the number of clients they must look after besides you, and the staff and resources they have at their disposal. Ultimately, your choice of agent is a personal decision, and should also depend a lot on your rapport and trust of the agent as an individual. Typically, agents require certification, and so agency contracts should be bound by relatively similar terms.

One of the key types of Management decisions for your career is choosing what team to play for (or try out for, or attend Training Camp for), especially at certain pivotal points. There is no simple formula for making these decisions. Consult your network above. Consult your agent, if you have one. Perhaps most importantly, communicate directly with the teams you are considering (through their recruiters, scouts, coaching staff, or management). Try to find out as clearly as you can what playing opportunity you will likely get. Assess your level of trust and rapport with the team management. If you can, visit in person, and judge your comfort level with them and the players, the organization, the city or campus and location. Consider the prestige, reputation and track record of the team in producing the outcome you want. You will have weighed several different factors to come to a final decision, so once you make a decision, don't look back. The most important part of any decision is what you do after you make the decision. Do everything you can to make your decision turn out to be the right one.

---

the inside story

Sometimes you may not have a choice of team. For example, where there are drafts (Major Junior, NHL) or in the case of a National/Olympic Team.

Taking care of the four areas above will help you take care of your career in a business-like way. And using smart strategies to do so will give you the best chance of succeeding and getting your chance to make it.

EXPERTS' RECAP
Remember . . .
There are four key areas of your career to keep in mind and take care of
· Operations = Developing your game.
· Marketing = Knowing what teams want, and fulfilling one of their needs.
· Sales = Generating tangible interest in you.
· Management = Making important career decisions.

7

MAKE IT!
meeting
the ultimate
challenge

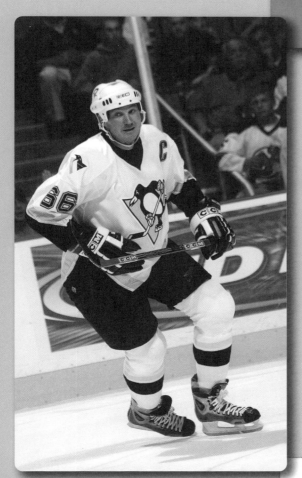

Mario Lemieux would study opposing defencemen and goaltenders to look for ways he could beat them. No wonder he was able to have his famous look of calm and supreme assurance when he stepped on the ice to pile up points and shatter records.

THIS SECTION TEACHES YOU ABOUT DOING WHAT YOU DREAMED: TO MAKE IT!

Chapter 24: prepare to succeed

"Sometimes a single contest decides everything, and sometimes the slightest circumstance decides the contest."

NAPOLEON, HISTORY'S GREATEST GENERAL

prepare to succeed

SCOUTS' PREVIEW
In this chapter . . .
- The Make-It-or-Break-It point
- The two parts of proper preparation
- Executing when it counts
- How to handle receiving your results

MASTERING ALL THE THINGS YOU LEARNED EARLIER IN THIS BOOK HELPS GET YOU TO A POINT WHERE YOU HAVE WHAT YOU NEED TO MAKE IT, AND HAVE SECURED THE OPPORTUNITY. THIS IS YOUR CHANCE.

Making It or Breaking It

For different players and their careers, the chance to make it can take different forms. It could be a set of tryouts, a training camp, or a trial call-up to a higher team. It could be a big tournament, a crucial series of games, or even a single game where a coach or manager is watching and choosing players to make their team.

These are all tests in a sense: You will be called upon to show your game to people watching and evaluating your performance. The process will occur over a short span of time. And after that, a verdict will be rendered by those making the evaluations: you either made it or you didn't.

Clearly, this is a very important step. It is your chance to use all the knowledge you've gained and abilities you've developed, including reading this book and applying its lessons, to finally make it. It is your chance to hit the jackpot on the large investment of time, money, and emotion you've poured into hockey. Of course, as we've said earlier, if you don't make it, much of what you've learned was not for naught; a lot can be used to great benefit in many other fields. But your dream was to make it in hockey, so the point at which you have the opportunity to make it or break it is obviously crucial.

Imagine an aspiring actor who has graduated from drama school, apprenticed with a famous teacher, and even had parts in some small films. He has mastered everything it takes to be a great actor. But what he hasn't got yet is a role in a major film. Finally he gets his break: He is invited to an important audition. The audition is all that stands between him and becoming the movie star he dreamed of. But others will be auditioning for the part too. He will have to outperform them in the audition to win the role. Now, although the actor is skilled, and trained, and experienced, he has obviously never been to this audition before. So what could help him accomplish his goal?

Well, he could do some research on the audition. He could find out where the audition will take place, and what lines he will be expected to read, or scenes he will be expected to perform. He could talk to people who know the casting directors and find out what they hope to see out of those auditioning. Second, he could rehearse. If he sets up a similar setting to where the audition will take place, and practices his lines and scenes there, this would help. These steps would drastically improve his odds of performing well in the audition, and thus winning the part.

So what do the above actions have in common? They were all done *before* the audition. In other words, the advantage came from *being prepared*.

The Secret to Passing Tests

Preparation is the key to successful tests. For any test you may face, whether in hockey, other sports, or outside sports, preparation can help you pass. And when it comes to your grand Make-or-Break-It test in hockey, preparation will be paramount.

In this chapter, you will learn principles and tips about good preparation. You will be able to draw upon these in facing your own life's tests. In hockey, the precise conditions of each person's Make-It-or-Break-It test may not be identical, but the various tests used to decide who makes it share much in common. So, based on the experience of players that have been through them, this chapter can help give you specific insights and suggestions for preparing to make it in your ultimate hockey test.

Preparation Step 1—Research

In the story above, researching the audition setting, the lines and scenes, and the casting directors' expectations were helpful preparation for a successful audition. Research is an essential part of good preparation. Below are some key categories of information you may want to consider researching for your hockey test. There are always limits to what you can find out, and not every piece of information will be vital. So don't feel the need to compile exhaustive answers to every possible question below. However, find out information that is important and that you can act upon, as this can help you a great deal in preparing to succeed in your test:

1. **THE "WHAT":** This category of research includes basic facts of what the test will consist of, plus any further details of what's involved that you will want to know to help you prepare. Examples of items to look into could include:

- What will the test consist of? Games, scrimmages, practices, off-ice testing? For any of these that apply, what will the details be? Are there any special rules in effect? For any practices, what drill competitions may be included? If there is off-ice testing, what exactly will be tested, and in what way?
- What will the schedule be? Will test sessions be in the mornings, afternoons or at night? How long will they be? How much rest will you have in between?
- What will the venue or location be? What is it like?
- What equipment will you need or be using? Are you used to it? Will there be refreshment drinks and foods there, or should you bring some Gatorade and Power Bars in case you need them?
- What sort of challenges will you face as part of the official agenda or aside from the official agenda? For example, is it likely that competing while tired will be a major factor you will need to prepare for? Will you likely need to prepare to face down attempts to intimidate you and throw you off your game?

The more you know about what's involved, the better prepared you can be for dealing with it.

2. **THE "WHO":** This category pertains to the people who will be involved in the test. Examples of items to look into could include:

- Who will your contact person be if you have a question arise during the test?
- Who will the other players be? How many players will be there in total? For competitions, who will the opposition be? What can you find out about their strengths and weaknesses in order to be able to respond to their strengths and exploit their weaknesses?
- Which players will be your primary competition? Who might be gunning for the same role or spot as you?
- Who will be running the sessions? How do they typically run things?
- Who are the persons that will be evaluating the players and deciding who makes it? What is there you should know about them? What are they like? What do they like?

- Who else will be involved—parents, trainers, referees, fans, media? Is there anything to consider about them that could aid your preparation?

The more you know about who will be involved, the better prepared you can be to utilize this information to advantage in succeeding in your test.

3. **THE "HOW":** This category pertains to how you will be evaluated as part of the test. You want to understand how it will be decided who makes it and who doesn't. Examples of items to look into could include:

- What will be the duties, roles, and responsibilities of each person involved in the evaluation process (coaches, scouts, managers, etc.)?
- What spots or roles might the team be looking to fill? What attributes might they be looking for in potential players they would consider? What might they feel they need to add to their team?
- What method will the evaluators be using to make their determinations? What factors will they be judging the players on?
- What will be the process for factoring in the judgments of each evaluator, and arriving at final decisions?

The better you understand how the evaluation process will work, the better you can prepare to do well by it, and have your best shot at making it.

So what are some ways to find out the above suggested information? There are a number of sources you might be able to learn valuable facts from, including:

- carefully reviewing any informational documents that have been provided, that are available upon request, or that have been posted publicly online or elsewhere;
- analyzing schedules, personnel lists, and descriptions of the test program;
- talking to test organizers, coordinators, and evaluators, or other people with whom they may have shared information about the test;
- talking to other people who may have knowledge about the test such as your existing or previous coach, your player agent (if you have one), or media persons;
- talking to other players slated to attend, and their families, to see what they know; and
- talking to past players who went through the test program for the same team or set of evaluators, especially ones that were successful, to get their insights;

- keeping an eye out for any public comments team officials make about what they feel their team needs, what they are looking for, and what their expectations are;
- considering past decisions made by this team or set of evaluators, and looking for any patterns that can help you prepare;
- attending and observing prior tests conducted by this team, or similar tests, as a spectator, before the time comes where you will be a test participant;
- watching the team play prior to the test, in order to assess what the management of the team seems to like, and any team weaknesses you feel you could help with; and
- watching your competition play, in order to identify the strengths and weaknesses of their game, and potential key rivals.

---

the inside story

When I went to my first NHL Training Camp with Pittsburgh, my younger brother Steve came to watch so that he could see what's involved, what to expect, and be prepared for his own NHL Camp with Colorado once he graduated. This research was very valuable for him. Then our youngest brother, Dominic, went to watch Steve's Training Camp in Colorado, again gaining even more valuable knowledge and insight that would allow him to prepare for his NHL Camp with the NY Rangers when he graduated.

Part of your research will also be figuring out how you can use elements of the information you've gathered. Some of the information you find will be of no consequence. Much of it will be important, but will require no action on your part aside from having made yourself aware of it, and keeping it in mind. But other pieces of information will prompt you to want to take some action or do some planning to deal with them. For example, suppose you find out there will be no refreshments on site. In that case, you will want to go get some Gatorade and Power Bars in advance, to have and bring for during the test. Suppose you find out that the goalie you will be up against is very strong overall, but is a bit weak with their catching glove. You may want to spend some time in advance perfecting your shot to the glove-side top-shelf. Suppose you find out that this team's philosophy places a lot of importance on speed. You may want to try to think in advance of a way you can really make an impression with your speed, such as chasing the puck full-speed on icings, even when you likely can't get there first. These are just a few small examples of how you can make use of information you've found to enhance your level of preparedness to succeed. Figuring out what to do with such pieces of information sometimes takes creativity and strategic thinking on your part. Don't be afraid to consult trusted advisors, experts, and friends about it.

Besides what is specific to your test, there are certain elements you know will be part of any hockey test, which you should prepare for as well. You know your hockey abilities will be judged, so you've got to make sure your game is in order. Leading up to the test, review all the different components of your game which you've learned about in this book, and start gearing them up and getting them tuned up for the test. As you get close to the test, your Psych Training will be key, as it allows you to maximize whatever abilities you have at a given point and perform your best. Lastly, no matter how well you prepare, it's impossible to have "complete information" about any test and you can't anticipate every development that may happen. So part of your preparation must be to expect the unexpected so you're not rattled by it when it happens. Take the perspective that whatever you're able to anticipate and prepare for is simply a bonus that can enhance your chances of success. For the rest, you should simply plan to stay flexible, adaptable, composed, and ready to respond in whatever way befits the situation.

Preparation Step 2—Rehearsal

As in the story of the actor, the second part of preparation is rehearsal. Rehearsal is a walk-through of what you want to happen in the real test, conducted in advance and in a simulated and controlled environment. There are two kinds of rehearsal you can use to prepare for your test:

MENTAL REHEARSAL: Mental rehearsal is just a specific kind of visualization, which you learned about in Chapters 1 and 18. Before you start the visualization, lay out everything you expect will happen or might happen during the test in order, from arriving at the test to receiving the final verdict. Then visualize these things happening, and yourself successfully handling each of them, one after another. Like any visualization, your mental rehearsal has more benefit if you repeat it. For your test, repeat your mental rehearsal on a regular basis in the weeks leading up to the test.

PHYSICAL REHEARSAL: Physical rehearsal is just a certain kind of simulation, which you learned about in Chapter 19. In this kind of simulation, you want each element as close as possible to the real thing, where it makes sense, and to the extent possible. This is limited, however, by the fact that you want a controlled environment designed to minimize the risk of injury and allow progressive training of what you will need to do in the test. Also, if the test is multi-faceted, you may need to simulate different elements separately as part of your physical rehearsal. So for example, if the test includes a game, you may want to simulate this with scrimmages, played with no body contact, to decrease the risk of injury. Or if the test includes a complex off-ice exercise, you may want to rehearse it with a slow-speed walk through, and gradually increase the speed as you repeat it and get the hang of it. Like all simulations, physical rehearsal helps you more as you repeat it and train yourself to improve at each element that will be in the test.

Together, research and rehearsal are how you prepare. And preparing is what enables you to succeed. What is left is only to *do it*. This part, which takes place during the test, is called *execution*. Execution means carrying out what you have programmed yourself to do.

Executing When It Counts

Good execution is not as easy as it sounds. Human feelings can interfere, and human error can occur. The environment in which you will be trying to execute is complex, changing, and unpredictable. To help your chances of successful execution, try the following:

- When you have completed your preparation, you have completed your preparation. Let go of further attempts to prepare. If you are still thinking about preparing after the test has started, you aren't concentrating on the test, which you must in order to successfully perform. It's often better to be worse prepared but decisive in execution than to be better prepared but hesitant in execution.

- A key benefit of preparation is a feeling of confidence that you are ready. Confidence helps performance. So don't be anxious about whether your preparation was good, as this just undermines the confidence you want. Similarly, don't question your ability to succeed. All the time you spent building your game is exactly what was required for you to be able to succeed. So don't be your own opponent by questioning yourself. Be on your own team by believing in your ability to succeed.

- Don't stress yourself or psych yourself out by dwelling on the importance of the test. At its heart, the test will just be about hockey. By the time of the test, you will have played hockey countless times before, and have been successful at it for many years. Allow your instincts, skills, and training for the sport to naturally come out and help you succeed again.

- Serve notice that you aren't just there to enjoy the ride; you are there to make it. If anyone asks you what your goal is, say your full intention is to make it. Don't say you *expect* to make it, as this may come across as arrogant and rub people the wrong way. Say you *intend* to make it, as this implies a competitive spirit and determination that teams like, and that can help strengthen your own resolve. You will encounter resistance in your attempt to make it, so applying a healthy kind of pressure to yourself *to* make it can help counteract it.

- If you make a mistake or fail in some aspect of the test, don't give up. It can happen to anyone. The issue may not be as big a deal as you think. The evaluators may be distracted by something else, and not see it. Maybe your rivals will slip up too, or maybe you will do something spectacular to make up for the error. Remember, "It ain't over till it's over." Also, scouts know that everyone makes mistakes, and are often most interested in how people react to them: Does the player give up, or try their best to bounce back? Make sure you do the latter.

  > **heads up!**
  > Don't get distracted. Aside from any strategies you come up with through your preparation, be sure to play to your strengths as a player.

- If things are persistently not going well, or something throws you off your game, don't panic. When you have a break in the action, try to assess whether you need to respond by changing your game plan, or simply refocus harder on your original one. If you do change game plans, don't lose faith in your likelihood of succeeding. Remember—the potential for adversity, the unexpected, and the need to adapt were all part of your preparation for success.

- Sometimes, an adverse circumstance may occur. Don't compound the difficulty by being preoccupied with it. Put it out of your mind, and focus only on what you can control. This gives you your best chance in that circumstance.

- If there is an opportunity to get feedback on your performance from a trusted expert or friend at intervals during the test, take advantage of this. You may have a handle on how you're playing, but remember that you won't be able to see yourself from the vantage point of another person, as the evaluators do. You may gain useful insight. Sometimes, it can also be beneficial to get feedback directly from the evaluators. If you do, make sure the way you ask does not project any lack of confidence. You can also often get some idea of what they're thinking just by observing everything going on. Whatever you're able to learn, incorporate in a positive way into your game plan.

How to Handle Receiving Your Results

When the test is finally over, you will receive your verdict of whether you have made it or not.

If you do make it, be sure to savour the triumph. You will have put *so much* into that moment, and have accomplished what you set out to do. Congratulate yourself! Find an appropriate way to celebrate.

If you don't make it, don't sulk or feel defeated. Many factors go into the decisions of who makes it and who doesn't. Try to get a better understanding of them, and learn what key lessons there are to learn from your experience. That way, in whatever test you face next, inside or outside of hockey, your chances of success will be greater.

Also bear in mind that while certain key moments, tests, tryouts, and opportunities can play a pivotal role in a hockey career, outcomes are not necessarily final or forever. There is a famous saying in hockey: "You are only as good as your last game." To those watching, your most recent play is the best indication of your future play. You never "own" a spot. You just have today's inside track to filling that spot tomorrow. So don't think that after making it, your work is over.

Likewise, if you didn't make it, you may well have another chance in the future. You should never count on getting a second chance, but it would be equally wrong to assume that you won't. Don't burn any bridges. Move on and play well, and you may yet get promoted or get invited to a new test of some kind. Whether a test is going on or not, remember that where hockey is being played, people are watching. And people talk. And new decisions are always being made.

the inside story

Many of the above principles and tips you can use in any test or tryout, not just in your ultimate one. The more significant the test, the more you should prepare.

EXPERTS' RECAP

Remember . . .

· There are key tests which can make or break a career.
· The secret to passing tests is preparation.
· Good preparation involves two parts—research and rehearsal.
· Once you are prepared, execute with confidence.
· Appreciate all your successes, and learn from any failures.

8

MAX IT!
reaching your full potential

One of the greatest goalies of all-time, Dominik Hasek didn't become a starter until age 28. He was 32 when he won his first MVP trophy, 33 when he won Olympic Gold for the Czech Republic, 37 when he won his first Stanley Cup, and 43 when he won his second.

THIS SECTION TEACHES YOU ABOUT TAKING UP THE CHALLENGE OF PURSUING YOUR FULL POTENTIAL.

"The real contest is always between what you've done and what you're capable of doing."

GEOFF GABERINO, OLYMPIC GOLD MEDALIST SWIMMER

the secrets to sticking around

CHAPTER 25

> **SCOUTS' PREVIEW**
> In this chapter . . .
> · The reasons why many players fail to stick after making it
> · Striving to make it farther

EVEN AFTER A PLAYER HAS MADE IT, THEY WILL STILL AND ALWAYS BE MAKING IT.

How could that be?

Well, even after a test is over and decisions have been announced of who made it and who didn't, a team's evaluators will always continue to assess how those decisions are panning out. They will monitor games that follow to make sure they made right the decisions, and to revise any possible mistakes. Every player who made it must continually show they are worthy of that honour.

Why Many Players Fail to Stick After Making It

If a player rests on their laurels after making it, or performs poorly for any other reason, they're asking for trouble. Often, a team is free at any time to reverse its decision and cut or demote the player. Even if their commitment to the player is guaranteed for a certain term, the player could still be benched, sat out of games, or placed on inactive "reserve." A lack of success with that team could affect other teams' interest as well.

At high levels, teams are competing intensely to win. They may have other teams above them in the standings they are trying to catch, and teams below them in the standings they are trying to fend off. And it is the job of sports coaches and managers to always keep looking for an edge, a way to make their team better.

> **heads up!** The saying "Don't rest on your laurels" is actually a sports expression. Champion Olympic athletes in ancient Greece received laurels, not medals, as their prize. So the expression began as a warning to complacent athletes. It still applies today.

Meanwhile, an equally intense competition is continuing among individual players. Sports are such a popular field that there are numerous players at lower levels burning with the desire to advance. Some could be tearing up the level just below, trying to angle for a promotion. And if they are promoted as a temporarily injury fill-in, they can play well and make a case for the team to keep them. If the team does decide to keep them, they will have to dispense with another player in order to make room on the roster. And so even a player who has made it and played well for a long period of time, but has had a recent stretch of poor games, may find themselves the one on the way out.

Hockey players should never forget that there are a limited number of spots available at high levels, lots of capable players eager to fill them, and little patience per player from teams under intense competitive pressure. Each player who makes it should therefore strive to continually play better than all the others constantly vying to take their place. In other words, they are still and always making it.

Unfortunately, some players feel that they've made it in a permanent, unchangeable sense. They relax, take it easy, and become complacent in parts of their game or in their whole approach. Soon, their game suffers, their performance sputters and they lose their spot.

Also, as players reach high levels, they often acquire prestige, celebrity, and admirers so that everywhere they go, they get the message that they are great and special. Some players mistake the message as signifying that *as a person* they are special and above others, rather than that only their past *performance* was. As a result, they may believe that success and adulation are automatically theirs, and stop doing the hard work that earned it for them in past performances. Their play therefore declines. Likewise, if a high-level player gets distracted or seduced by the perks that often come with making it (rich pro salaries, generous gifts from sponsors, various opportunities presented by fans and admirers), they can lose the strong motivation and sense of purpose that originally made them successful.

Some players, instead of striving to continually "re-make it," mistakenly strive to "just stay." But this isn't what they did to get there. It may sound reasonable, but it seldom works. That's because "striving to just stay" really means "striving not to lose the spot you have." Trying not to lose something is a negative focus, not the beneficial Positive Thinking you learned in Chapter 18. When you focus on trying to avert a negative thing happening, you often encourage that very negative thing to happen.

Another problem with the approach of trying to just stay is that it implies a satisfaction with where you currently are. That satisfaction is the opposite of the ambition that is a component of making it. It also runs against the competitive spirit of sports. You want to appreciate and be grateful for where you are, but not be satisfied, or you will lose the competitive desire and aggression you need to best your opponents.

Striving to Make It Farther

You must continually strive to re-earn the spot you first achieved, to deserve it with your performance every shift of every game. This is what it means to be continually making it after you've made it. But more than that—you must keep striving to improve, to be better, to move up, to *Make It Farther*.

Day by day, your opponents gradually know your game better, and will learn your tricks. Year by year, the quality of new players coming up gets better through advances in player development methods plus more intense competition from people determined to make it. You have to keep getting better just to keep up. In competitive sports, by trying to maintain your position, you fall back, whereas by trying to advance, you maintain your position.

And luckily, the process of doing so isn't a whole new process you need to learn. Striving to Make It Farther is exactly the same process, involving exactly the same things, as striving to make it. It *is* striving to make it—only, one step higher, or one step farther.

Striving to Make It Farther could mean:

* moving up to a higher league;
* becoming one of the top players in your current league;
* making the league All-Star team;
* becoming the top player on your team;
* becoming a team leader or captain;
* getting more ice time on a consistent basis;
* becoming one of the players your coach relies upon most in important situations; or
* winning the Most Improved Award for your team for the current season.

For the purposes of this chapter—sticking where you have made it—it doesn't matter what it is. All that is required is to have a target in mind of where you want to take your game beyond where it is now. With this forward-looking focus, you will not slip backward. Failing to understand what it takes to stick at a level after making it is a major reason that the average professional hockey career is shorter than one might expect. By applying the lessons of this chapter, you can help make yours as long as you can.

> **EXPERTS' RECAP**
> Remember . . .
> · Even after making it, you must continually re-earn your position.
> · Players that sit back, become smug, or are satisfied where they are have difficulty staying.
> · The secret to sticking around is Striving to Make It Farther.

maximizing yourself

SCOUTS' PREVIEW
In this chapter . . .
· Maxing It—the real game
· How Maxing It mirrors making it
· Using milestones to mark and measure
  your progress

IN THE LAST CHAPTER, YOU LEARNED HOW STRIVING TO MAKE IT FARTHER HELPS YOU MAINTAIN YOUR CURRENT STANDING. HOWEVER, STRIVING TO MAKE IT FARTHER IS IMPORTANT FOR ANOTHER REASON AS WELL.

A player who has made it and is fighting hard to stick around can be tempted to settle for that accomplishment itself. And indeed, it is a true achievement. Many of their peers will not have gotten as far. At the same time, though, what about the player's dream? They should think back to it, and ask themselves whether it has been fully realized. If not, they still haven't had a chance to experience the feelings of exhilaration and triumph that can come only from reaching a long-held dream. Settling for what they have could cheat them of the chance to achieve their dream, which is what has the most meaning for them.

ask the AUTHOR-ity

But aren't there risks in going for more?
There are risks and costs in striving for more, and not just settling for what you have: The risk of failing, the risk of losing what you have, the emotional cost of battling for more, the cost in time and effort of pushing for more. But as President John F. Kennedy once said, "There are risks and costs to action. But they are far less than the long-range risks of comfortable inaction." As you learned in the last chapter, the risk of losing what you have is far greater by doing nothing than it is in striving for more in the right way, which you will learn in this chapter. Also, your career is a limited-time opportunity to reach the highest level you can, realize the utmost accomplishments you can, gain the greatest prizes you can—and then it's over. This is especially true of sports careers which end so young, and often before the athlete expects. What about the risk of settling for what you've done, and thereby accomplishing less than you could have? No one wants to look back with regret at feats they might have achieved and dreams they might have seized but didn't, because they contented themselves with what they had. All we really have is some time—time that can be spent or wasted. Douglas MacArthur, the famous American general and architect of post-WWII modern Japan once said, "There is no security in life, there is only opportunity."

Maxing It: The Ultimate Aim

But what if you do reach your dream? Then what? If you reach your dream, it is time to imagine what higher level you may be capable of and that would have great meaning to you. It is time for a new or revised dream. And then you strive to make it farther and ultimately reach that new dream. Repeatedly striving to make it farther and farther still, is what we call *Maxing It.*

Maxing It in hockey means maximizing the amount of your potential that you realize. And that—not making it—is the real contest for any athlete. Realizing your full potential is your ultimate aim. It is how you attain fulfillment. Fulfillment is life's fullest and most enduring kind of happiness. All life is characterized by growth, and besides maturing into adults, developing our various potential abilities is what fulfills our purpose as living beings. Striving to become the best we can be as people and to do the best we can at everything we do is a guiding principle that many great athletes and others ascribe to for how life should be lived. You have devoted a huge part of your life to your sport. So, naturally, realizing as much of your potential as you can in that activity means more to your overall fulfillment than your average activity.

How to Max It

The first requirement for Maxing It is maintaining a humble and receptive mind. For players who have already made it to a high level, and the advisors who have helped them do so, this can be a challenge. Having success, while seeing so many others fail, can easily lead to a know-it-all attitude. This attitude shuts a person's ears to helpful advice from others. That includes experts who can help a player improve further, and sometimes even people who helped the player get to where they are. Also, if success and the admiration of others have led them to develop a big ego, that arrogance will close their eyes to their own areas of opportunity for improvement. When eyes and ears are closed, the possibility of development is shut out. Development stalls, and the player can't maximize their potential. Unfortunately, I have observed many elite youth players and Junior players with this attitude, even though they are still many challenging steps away from realizing their pro ambitions. They are sadly unaware that the statistics make them much more likely to end up in recreational hockey than in the pros, if they don't maximize their development. The top athletic performers in the world don't make that mistake. They know, even at their level, they still have room for improvement, new things they can learn, and others who can help them do so.

Before even reaching thirty years old, golf superstar Tiger Woods had already won eight majors, five consecutive PGA Player-of-the-Year trophies, five consecutive Vardon Trophies (best scoring average), and broken countless records. Many considered him the top athlete in the world, in any sport. Yet, he decided to break down the swing that had brought him all that success, and build a new one, because he wasn't satisfied! He fired his coach, and hired a new one.

"I felt like I could get better," Woods said. "People thought it was asinine for me to change my swing after I won the Masters by 12 shots. . . . Why would you want to change that? Well, I thought I could become better. If I play my best, I'm pretty tough to beat. I'd like to play my best more frequently, and that's the whole idea. That's why you make changes. I thought I could become more consistent and play at a higher level more often. . . . I've always taken risks to try to become a better golfer, and that's one of the things that has gotten me this far." Everyone doubted his decision; some even doubted his sanity as he went through a long drought without winning a big tournament. But once he had finished the work, Woods rebounded, winning six Majors in the next four years and three more MVP trophies, against improved opposition. Even his critics admitted he had been right, and that he was better than before.

The next part of Maxing It requires you to consider your dream. If you've reached your dream, it's time to create a new one. Even if you haven't reached it, sometimes it can make sense to revise it. In your journey up to this point, you will have learned much about yourself and your sport. What strengths and assets do you have for your sport, and what are some areas of natural weakness or limitation? These are not to constrain the magnitude of your dream, but to help give it shape by creating a picture of what the level of success you aspire to would look like in your case. Also ask yourself whether anything has changed over your journey in terms of what sort of achievements would be most meaningful to you. At the end of this process, you settle once more on a dream. Your new dream should have all the same characteristics and benefits you learned in Section 1. Your new dream will serve as your ultimate destination in your quest to Max It.

From your dream, you should once again create goals. For example, the target you picked in Chapter 25 to Make It Farther to could be your goal. When you reach one goal, you set another. Successive goals take you farther and farther toward realizing your new dream.

Using Milestones to Mark and Measure Your Progress

Also bear in mind that reaching a goal at this level is typically a slow and step-wise process. There are exceptions. Sometimes a player is called upon to temporarily fill a big hole in a line-up caused by a regular player's absence, and the fill-in becomes an overnight star after demonstrating exceptional play. However, normally, a progression of intermediate steps is required to get there. Sometimes it helps to mark out these steps into specific *milestones* you recognize on the way to your goal. Milestones are a way of charting your direction and marking your progress toward your goals, similar to how you learned to use intermediate goals (i.e., one-year and three-year goals on the way to your five-year goal) in Chapter 1. Intermediate goals make good sense when you are young and reaching goals is mostly a matter of developing over time. But at this level, progress is less about how much you've developed at certain points in time than it is about reaching targeted outcomes through strategic actions. This makes milestones a better way of marking your course and progress at this level. Below are examples of how they work.

Let's say Connie reached her dream of making it, and her new dream is to become one of her league's superstar forwards. Her goal might be: to become the top centre on her team. Her sequence of milestones toward that might be:

1. Securing her spot on the team.
2. Being a solid fourth-line player.
3. Being a solid third-line player.
4. Being a solid second-line player.
5. Being a solid first-line player.

the inside story

While players at high levels often play certain roles, those roles can still change. Contrary to what some people think, it isn't in a player's DNA whether they are a first-line player or a fourth-line player. In fact, it is often the case that players have to get their foot in the door with a more limited role, and then try to work their way up to a more starring role. For example, Darcy Tucker started out as a fourth-line energy player. But he gradually worked his way up line-by-line, finally becoming a first-line power forward for Toronto, where he got to play alongside Mats Sundin, and was a pivotal player and fan favourite for several years on a successful Maple Leafs team.

Connie will then have achieved her goal, and should set a new goal. Her next goal might be to become the top centre in her division or a top-twenty scorer in the league. She might set new milestones for this goal. And so on, as she strives to advance toward her dream of becoming a superstar forward.

Let's say Bill reached his dream of making it, and his new dream is to become a Hall-of-Fame defenceman. His goal might be to become his team's "horse." His sequence of milestones toward that might be:

1. Securing his spot on the team.
2. Getting on the penalty kill and key defensive situations.
3. Getting on the power play and key offensive situations.
4. Being called on to play the first and last minutes of periods.
5. Being called on to play the most minutes on the team.

Bill will then have achieved his goal, and should set a new goal. His next goal might be to record the top +/– in his division or to make the league All-Star Team, as he strives to progress toward becoming a Hall-of-Fame-calibre defenceman.

The next step of Maxing It is creating a plan for reaching milestones and goals. Your plan might include new initiatives in some or all of the areas covered in the sections of this book: character, foundations, skills, training, strategies, and preparation.

As you learned in Chapter 23, your plan should include certain components:

- **OPERATIONS**—Skills and game-related abilities you will need to reach the goal.
- **MARKETING**—Identifying what teams are looking for at each milestone toward your goal, and what you need to provide them in order to reach these milestones and eventually the goal.
- **SALES**—Securing the opportunities you need to achieve the milestones and eventually the goal.
- **MANAGEMENT**—Making smart decisions such as when to take the risks inherent in progressing, and when not to; how to pursue future goals while also taking care of present expectations (upon which reaching future goals depends).

SPORTS MASTER.TV

To see an example of such a plan for a given player, visit my website.

At this high level, a few things will be different: Your game will already be developed and have a certain form. So your plan will want to maximize your strengths and address any limiting weaknesses. Coaches, managers, and others may already have a conception of you as a player, and what you offer. Mentally, you must be aware of their conception and expectations without limiting yourself from doing more, when it makes sense, in order to progress.

Your plan must also be realistic. Factor in the circumstances of your current situation, and of situations you must go through to reach your milestone or goal. Evaluate resources available to you, and limitations upon you. Consider timing issues: Sometimes you are not able to work on all parts of your plan at the same time, due to outside factors or time limitations. In that case, what should you do now, and what should you leave for later?

When you add in all the factors outside your control, it is often the case that progress can be uneven, with temporary steps back between leaps forward. Don't lose heart. Stick to your plan and persevere. But also monitor your progress closely. At times, you may need to review and revise your goal, milestones, or plan.

If you are fortunate enough to reach this new and second dream, the process again repeats. Enjoy it! And then set another new dream. And so on. When do you stop setting and striving for new ones? Never! Why halt a process that is still bringing fun, passion, and fulfillment to your life? As long as you are moving forward, you know the limit of your potential still lies ahead of you. In fact, William James, the father of modern psychology, once said, "Compared with what we ought to be, we are only half awake. The human individual usually lives far within [their] limits." In other words, the chances are that no matter what you've achieved, you can achieve more. Doing so over and over is Maxing it.

> **jock talk**
> " The ultimate goal is to realize your full potential—to be the best hockey player, and the best person, you can be. "
> —STEVE MOORE, COLORADO AVALANCHE

EXPERTS' RECAP

Remember . . .

· The real game is Maxing It.
· Maxing It is Striving to Make It Farther and farther—striving to reach your potential.
· Use milestones to help guide your progress along with your goals.

9

WHAT NEXT?
preparing for when the game is over

Hall-of-Famer Pat Lafontaine's career ended when he was forced to retire due to post-concussion syndrome. But Lafontaine saw a way to channel his passion into other positive pursuits. You can read more about Lafontaine on page 299.

THIS SECTION TEACHES YOU HOW TO THINK BEYOND HOCKEY, AND HOW TO PREPARE FOR WHEN THE GAME IS OVER.

"From the end spring new beginnings."
PLINY THE ELDER, ANCIENT ROMAN HISTORIAN

keeping your quest in perspective

SCOUTS' PREVIEW

In this chapter . . .

· Pursuing your dream with all your heart
· Keeping your quest in balance with all your mind
· Factors that can affect careers
· The right perspective
· What to do with disappointments

IT AIN'T EASY TURNING DREAMS INTO REALITY; IF IT WERE, THEY WOULDN'T BE DREAMS.

To realize a dream, you've got to pursue it with *all your heart.* But to be smart about how you live your life, you've got to try to keep that quest in balance with *all your mind.*

That might sound like a contradiction, but it's not. There is a subtle difference between those two commandments, a subtle difference with stark significance in your quest.

Pursuing Your Dream and Keeping Your Quest in Balance

Pursuing your dream with all your heart includes being dedicated and determined. With much required and lots of rivals, a wholehearted effort is critical if you hope to make it in hockey.

Keeping your quest in balance with all your mind means realizing that while your dream has great meaning for you, it does not define you. Pursuit of your dream is only part of your life. Success or failure in hockey doesn't decide your worth as a person. It includes being aware that although you might make your absolute best effort, you don't control every factor affecting whether you make it, so you can't *guarantee* the outcome you want.

Pursuing your dream with this combined approach allows you to maximize your chances of making it without compromising everything in the event that you don't.

Factors that Can Affect Careers

There are many factors that can affect the outcome of careers. Each person is born with an innate set of talents, and much of this book is devoted to developing and maximizing those aptitudes. However, sometimes one person's set of talents may prove a limiting factor in terms of how far they advance in hockey, while the same set of talents gives them exceptional advantages in some other field.

heads up! Don't think you have to be a "natural" to succeed in hockey. Plenty of people have enough talent to make it, if they do what it takes, as you've learned about in this book.

At each higher level, there are also fewer spots available. With lots of competition, it's simply a fact that not everyone can make it. In fact, at certain points some people will look at their odds, compare them to their odds in some other pursuit, and voluntarily switch paths. Others will continue in hockey.

Another factor that can influence a player's career is health considerations. Injuries occur on and off the ice and an illness or medical condition may arise that would make it unsafe or unwise for a person to keep pursuing their hockey dream. In other cases, conflict with parents, coaches, or rivals can occasionally get carried to an extreme and cause a player to lose their enjoyment of the sport and decide to quit.

Also, whether or not a player makes it is partly up to other people. A player can demonstrate all the abilities required, but ultimately, making it depends on a team deciding to select the player for their squad. As you read in Chapter 21, sometimes politics or corruption interfere in the decisions made, including the right players advancing. Sometimes families will move to locations where it is no longer possible to play hockey or to pursue it at a level where a player has a reasonable chance to make it. Likewise, a family's financial situation, time restrictions, or other commitments could potentially affect a child's ability to continue playing or pursue adequate hockey development. Or it could happen that more pressing concerns force a player from the game—the need to care for or cope with an illness or death in the family, for example.

These possibilities shouldn't bring any sense of discouragement, resignation, or despair. Indeed, many of these scenarios are very remote possibilities. And the most important factor by far is your ability to learn, apply, and master what it takes, as we have helped describe in this book. But the point is, such things are *possible*. There can never be guarantees about outcomes when outcomes involve things beyond our personal control. It is wise to hope for the best, but prepare for the worst. Your hope, intention, and efforts are all devoted to making it. But being aware that there is no guarantee, it is important to prepare for any outcome.

The Right Perspective

One way you should prepare for it is from a psych standpoint, by pursuing your dream with proper mental *perspective*. This begins with maintaining a lifestyle that includes a healthy balance of activities outside your sport, as you learned in Chapter 6. These activities ensure you have a full and rich life completely aside from hockey. A balanced person is a fundamentally stronger person who can survive and thrive despite even the hugest potential disappointments.

Perspective can also come from the character you learned about in Section 2. Instead of hockey success, which partly relies on other people and circumstances, you have your character which relies only on your actions through which to measure your self-worth. That way, while outside factors beyond your control may threaten your hockey career, they won't threaten your identity as a person.

Perspective also includes accepting that you cannot dictate outcomes. You can dictate trying your hardest and doing your best. But at the same time, you must appreciate the other factors that can influence outcomes if you wish to have a perspective that is realistic and mature.

additional help

Inspired by the many children he visited in hospitals during his career, and by the benefit to their well-being he was told by medical professionals his visits were having, Pat Lafontaine devoted himself to helping them full-time when he retired. He has won numerous awards from humanitarian organizations as well as the Patriot Award from the United States Congressional Medal of Honor Society for his charity work. After retiring, Lafontaine wrote a book called *Companions in Courage*. And his Companions in Courage Foundation builds interactive game rooms in children's hospitals throughout North America. You can visit them online at www.cic16.org.

Perspective can also come from feeling good about the fact that many of the skills, abilities, strategies, and experiences that you learned in this book are not only important to making it in hockey but can be applied to good use in other fields and areas of your life. In the next chapter, you will see how even if you don't make it, the time and effort you invested in hockey can still pay off outside of hockey. So don't think that if you fail to reach your desired destination, all your efforts will have been wasted. Many retired athletes say that their achievements and awards were not the true prizes of their career; the process of striving that you have learned about in this book is what they valued as the true prize.

Developing perspective in all these ways does not diminish your determination. In fact, it strengthens your ability to pursue your dream by giving you firm grounding in reality.

Be sure to enjoy each success, each positive relationship developed through hockey, as well as the journey itself. As I found out in having my career suddenly ended by injury, you never know which of these steps could unexpectedly be the last. Some players enjoy keeping a scrapbook, souvenirs, photos, and other mementos. There is also your hockey diary, in which you can record your personal notes and sentiments. In the future, when looking back and recognizing your accomplishments, you will likely be glad you kept these items and documented these experiences.

Keep your own custom hockey diary, and refer back to it, on our website, free, at www. sportsmaster.tv.

What to Do with Disappointment

Now, let's suppose that for whatever reason, a player's career does come to an end without making it. What do they do then?

First, this will be the most important time to have hockey in perspective, as detailed above. As profoundly disappointed as they will be, the player can also recognize the fact that everyone's playing days must end sometime, whether they make it or not. This can make "the end" part a little bit easier to accept. It will still be tremendously difficult, but at least they might get a head start on moving in the direction they decide to take in their life after hockey.

Some people believe that whatever happens was meant to happen, which helps them cope with disappointment. In my life, I've always found it hard to know whether that was true. But one thing I certainly believe is that there are always positive things to take out of any negative experience. Not making it could be an opportunity to learn a lesson and apply it to a future cause, or impart that lesson to someone else. Seeing a positive in something very negative is not always easy or obvious. But an open and creative mind will find positive possibilities when it looks. We might not be sure that what happens is always for the best, but we can always be sure to make the best of what happens.

the inside story

While playing Junior hockey in Windsor, Ontario, Paul Maurice suffered an eye injury that put his hockey career in serious jeopardy. The team's owner, Peter Karmanos, now the owner of the Carolina Hurricanes, knew that Maurice would have trouble making it after the injury, and offered Maurice a position as a coach. It must have been difficult for him to give up on his lifelong dream of being a pro player, but Maurice knew the wise thing to do was to accept the coaching position. He went on to a successful coaching career in the OHL, and reached the NHL after all, at just twenty-eight years old—as a coach. Maurice has since coached more than ten seasons in the NHL, and has been to a Stanley Cup Final and another Final Four.

Many people find that when one door closes in life, another opens. And sometimes that new door leads to amazing new things that could never have been anticipated. Lots of people have pursued a dream, and as circumstances unfolded, ended up achieving a different and even more meaningful dream. This includes famously successful people whose dreams once were to become hockey players.

the inside story

A promotional copy of my first book was sent to Alex Trebek, the Canadian host of the knowledge-testing television game show *Jeopardy!* A short while later, a letter came back from Trebek thanking us for the book and for thinking of him. At the bottom of the letter, below his name he had crossed out the title "Host/*Jeopardy!*" and hand-written a different title: "former amateur hockey player!"

When dealing with disappointing events like the end of a dream, it's also wise to seek support from loved ones. Sometimes it can also help to seek assistance from professional counsellors or psychologists as well as support from others who've been through similar experiences.

Lastly, "Mom's advice" to immediately get involved in other things, rather than sitting around stewing about what's been lost, is simple but often very good advice. Even small or mundane things that occupy body and mind can help a great deal.

When you know you can handle the worst, you can rest assured in striving for the best.

PRO-file

Scotty Bowman

Scotty Bowman dreamed of becoming an NHL player. However, a head injury suffered while playing minor league hockey ended his playing career. So Bowman moved into coaching, and became the most successful coach in history. He became Head Coach of the St. Louis Blues at just thirty-four, and took the expansion team to the Stanley Cup Finals in each of their first three years of existence. Bowman's 1,244 wins is by far the most by a coach in the NHL. He won nine Stanley Cups as a coach spanning four decades, a record. And he won them with three different franchises (Montreal, Pittsburgh, and Detroit), the only coach in any of North America's four major sports to accomplish that feat. Since retiring as a coach, Bowman has worked as a consultant with Detroit and Chicago. When I was playing in the minor leagues in Augusta, Georgia, Bowman was in town on

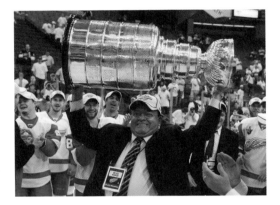

vacation, but he loved hockey so much that he would stop by to watch us practice! And when our coach, former NHL defenceman David Wilkie, asked him for advice, he gave it freely and was generous with his time on every occasion.

EXPERTS' RECAP

Remember . . .

· Pursue your dream with all your heart, but keep your quest in balance with all your mind.

· Many factors can affect your career outcome, including ones outside your control.

· Maintain perspective by enjoying each success you have, and appreciating how what you are learning for hockey can also help you in many other areas of life.

· Resolve to find and seize a positive opportunity within even the most disappointing events.

the wisdom of a fallback plan

CHAPTER 28

SCOUTS' PREVIEW

In this chapter . . .
- What a fallback plan is, and why it's wise to create one
- What you want in a fallback plan
- The four factors for creating a solid fallback plan

IF YOUR HOCKEY CAREER SHOULD COME TO AN END BEFORE YOU INTEND, WHAT WILL YOU DO? HOW WILL YOU EARN A LIVING?

The situation faced by every aspiring young player is this: You can never be guaranteed of making it in hockey, yet you don't want to give up on it, because it's your dream. You have every right and every reason to do everything you reasonably can to make it. But to be smart about how you pursue your dream, you should also simultaneously plan and prepare from a practical standpoint for what you will do if you don't make it. Since your passion and first preference is hockey, the backup option is called a *fallback plan*: If your hockey career doesn't work out, you can fall back on this other career.

Having a Fallback Plan: A Wise Idea

Unfortunately, many aspiring hockey players don't create a fallback plan. In some cases, it's because they overestimate their odds of making it and ignore the possibility of anything going wrong. But for most players, it's probably just because there's nothing they love quite like hockey, so they don't know what else they might like to do. And so they think, "If I don't make it, I'll find something else to do then." But waiting until then costs valuable time and experience, and can restrict the choices left available.

As an example, let's suppose a teen prodigy named Hotshot dreams of making it in the NHL. Drafted high into Major Junior, and already a celebrity in the town he is from, he is sure he will someday make it in the NHL. So he lets his schoolwork lapse as he focuses all his efforts on his Junior hockey career and spends most of his spare time having fun with his teammates. The years of his Junior career pass, and Hotshot has been a pretty good player for his Junior team, but there were lots of other good players in the league too, and he simply didn't outpace them enough to catch interest from professional teams. He reaches Junior hockey's age limit, and his hockey career is over. As he is trying to figure out what to do next, Hotshot is watching his favourite TV show when it occurs to him that the forensics the show's about are something he finds fascinating. He would love to become a forensic scientist. But because he neglected school during his junior career, Hotshot doesn't have a high school diploma and the series of science course credits which he needs to be admitted into the forensic science program. Almost twenty-two, and needing income to support himself, Hotshot feels he can't go back and essentially start high school over again. Instead, he is forced to take the best job he can get, so he takes a job offer from a friend that doesn't have a very bright future and is in a field he really doesn't like.

Unfortunately, stories with endings similar to Hotshot's are much too common. Players who don't develop a fallback plan can pay a heavy price, including:

- difficulty making a living, and even greater strains when trying to raise a family;
- lives spent doing jobs they don't like, or that don't make good use of their talents;
- years lost taking first steps toward a career in a new field, which should have been done earlier as part of a fallback plan; and
- other negative circumstances, plus "collateral" effects from any of the above negative situations, including increased exposure to some of Chapter 7's pitfalls.

The wise way to pursue a dream is to pursue it in tandem with a fallback plan. That doesn't mean you have to pursue the dream any less than 100 per cent. It just means pursuing the dream without a bottomless void beneath you if for any reason it doesn't work out. Indeed, if you are fully committed to your dream, a fallback plan can help you pursue the dream even more effectively by decreasing the negative pressure and psych effects on your hockey performance that would be present if hockey is your "all or nothing."

In fact, having a fallback plan from the get-go makes even more sense, because whether your career is cut somewhere short or runs the entire course you dreamed of, it must end sometime. And for an athlete, that will be while you are still relatively young, with most of your life ahead of you. When those playing days are over, you will need something to occupy and fulfill you. You will need something in which to channel the drive you previously put toward hockey. And you might need a way to earn income too. So you might as well start early and let those plans double as your fallback plan.

The goal of a fallback plan is to provide an attractive, realistic, and reliable career option for you, in the event that you are not able to sustain your preferred career of hockey. In order to be realistic and reliable as a backup, your choice for a fallback career shouldn't be another career with stiff odds, like your dream of a high-level sports career. For this reason, while you learned in Chapter 1 that you may in some cases be able to pursue things like making it in another sport or being a rock star or movie star as a second dream, these are not suitable choices to serve as a fallback career. You want your fallback career to be something more readily attainable. Beyond that, what makes an appropriate choice depends on your talents, interests, and personal preference. As you read on, you will find tips to help you make a good choice.

Like your initiative to make it in hockey, the sooner you start the process of developing a fallback plan, the better. In the early stages, this might mean nothing more than paying attention to your experience of various activities you do to fulfill the balance outlined in Chapter 6. These activities should expose you to a wide variety of experiences related to different potential career fields. Over time, they will allow you to learn about yourself, what you like doing, what you find interesting, what you are good at, and what provides meaning for you. These should all provide good hints as to which fields may be suitable for you.

These activities also give you a little bit of expertise, credentials, and some personal connections that could potentially be useful as you further develop your fallback plan, and especially if and when you need to employ it. For example, suppose one of these activities for keeping you well-rounded is a nature camp you attend for a few weeks each summer. Being in an isolated natural setting where you constantly must work together with other campers can help you create strong and lasting bonds of friendship. These personal connections could prove extremely handy later in life, if your hockey career hits a snag, and one of those friends can open a door for you in the field you chose as your fallback. Also, attending the camp year after year will cause you to build up expertise, and at a certain age, the camp may invite you to join their staff. This job experience can help you get other jobs which overlap with one of your camp job's areas of expertise. Now let's say your fall-back career is to be a phys-ed teacher. The resume credentials you build up from these jobs could someday help you get into teachers' college and land a job at the school of your choice. Or suppose your fallback career is to be a sports coach. The credibility you gained from those job experiences could help you break into sports coaching and move up to the position you want.

The Four Factors for Building a Solid Fallback Plan

As in the examples above, certain parts of your balanced set of activities are of special significance to developing your fallback plan. As you get progressively older and closer to the age where you will need to earn a living, pay more attention to making sure you *choose* and carry out activities within your balanced set that cover these. Essential to constructing a strong and solid fallback plan are the *Four Factors* below:

1. **EDUCATION:** Most careers have educational requirements or expectations. Stay in school, and take your academics as seriously as your athletics. Even if you think school just isn't for you, doing as well as you can in school can only help you. But education doesn't just mean school alone. As you get older and start to hone in on some potential fallback careers, find out what you will need to learn in order to practice them. All of that—whether it is academic, vocational, practical learning, or a combination—is education, and can be crucial to a fallback career.

2. **SECONDARY INTEREST/PASSION:** When you are young, it is good to have a very broad set of experiences, in order to discover which activities suit you, and may point the way to a potential fallback career. But as you get progressively older, it can help to narrow these down somewhat, so that you can spend quality time on areas that seem particularly promising. Typically, you eventually want to focus even more on one realistic and reliable non-hockey career-related interest, which will be your "second passion," after hockey. If hockey is your "major," you can think of this second passion as your "minor." Your fallback career will come from this, so do everything you need to prepare for this as a career, in case it is needed.

3. **WORK EXPERIENCE:** For almost any career, prior work experience is a must. Younger years can be a time to try different kinds of work, and see which types seem best suited to you. As you get older, your work experiences

should be more tailored. As you progressively narrow down your potential fallback career choices, you should choose work experiences related to those you are considering. For a hockey player, summer jobs or internships are a good time to get work experience. During the season, volunteer work or flexible part-time jobs may also be possible.

---

the inside story

Several members of my College team took summer internships on Wall Street, as the financial industry was one that came to recruit on campus, and one that appreciated the commitment and teamwork of hockey players.

After their College careers, several of these players who didn't end up having pro hockey opportunities were able to use the summer work experience they'd had to land highly desired permanent jobs in the field of their internship.

---

4. **SOCIAL NETWORKING:** At its heart, social networking just means making friends and developing those friendships. While you are young, don't restrict your friendships to people from any one activity or within any one network. Make friends in hockey, school, and other activities. You can learn a lot from friends about many different fields in which they've had experiences but you haven't. Don't restrict friendships to people your age, either. Adults (teachers, coaches, parents of friends, etc.) have years of career experience, which make them an especially good source of information and advice. All of this will give you a broad base which you will be able to build on when you get older and start to head in a particular direction for your fallback career. At that point, you might need to prioritize your time, and ensure you devote a sufficient amount to friendships you have within your fallback career network. You never know when you might need to resort to your fallback career, and might need a helping hand to open a door into it for you. A person is more likely to do this for someone they know is a true friend.

Within your balance of activities, taking care of these four factors allows you to "cover all the bases" of what is likely to be required to transition successfully and quickly into a fallback career of your choice, if you need to.

This brings us to the issue of that choice—what will your fallback career be? In Chapter 30 you will learn about some of the many options. But making this decision requires much more research and careful consideration. You can find in-depth information for most career options through books from your local library or online resources. Talking with school guidance counsellors or career advisors can help you learn what's involved and required for various choices, and which might be a good fit for you. Also consult the people who care about you most and know you best because they may see aspects of you that you've overlooked, which may point to additional good options. Then make a decision, and pursue it in the ways described above.

Many fields are keen to recruit former athletes because of the drive, teamwork, and other attributes they developed pursuing sports. In virtually any field you choose, you will find practitioners near the top who are not only huge sports fans, but were once youngsters with athletic career aspirations themselves. For any of a number of reasons, including a conscious decision to switch paths, or factors that had nothing to do with their abilities or efforts, they didn't realize their sports career dreams. Yet what they learned in pursuing sports, they applied to good use outside sports. And they were wise enough to have a fallback plan, and found success with their fallback career. If you need to, you can too.

> **EXPERTS' RECAP**
> Remember . . .
> · A fallback career is for in case factors outside your control thwart your hockey career.
> · Your fallback career choice is a personal one, but it should be realistic and reliable.
> · Develop your fallback career through education, work experience, a secondary interest, and social networking at the same time you are pursuing hockey.

what you make out of where you make it

CHAPTER 29

SCOUTS' PREVIEW
In this chapter . . .
· What success brings
· Evaluating opportunities
· Additional tips for making the most out of where you make it

WHENEVER A PERSON HAS A DREAM, THEY HAVE A PASSION FOR WHAT THEIR DREAM IS ABOUT. IT COULD BE DANCING, IT COULD BE SINGING, IT COULD BE WRITING, IT COULD BE TEACHING—IT COULD BE ANYTHING. BUT IN YOUR CASE, IT'S YOUR SPORT. THERE IS SIMPLY NO OTHER ACTIVITY YOU WOULD RATHER DO.

And when people chase dreams, it's because they're inspired to realize an ambition tied to their dream. As an athlete, your ambition is to make a career in your sport. You long for the pride and the glory of achieving greatness in it. You love the fulfillment you get from pursuing your potential in it.

You chose your dream because of what's *in* it. But where your dream takes you can also bring you opportunities to derive benefits *out* of it.

What Success Brings

You have read that much of what this book suggests for making it in hockey can also help you outside of hockey. Those benefits come from your *process* for pursuing making it, and can start to apply even when you are quite young. But the benefits discussed in this chapter are different. As you get older, there will be a chance for you to derive benefits from whatever *success* you have achieved in making it. Doing so depends on you dealing with the effects of success in the right way. Otherwise, you might miss out on these benefits, or even experience detriments. The issue here is what you make out of where you make it.

An important fact of life, well put by the famous ancient Chinese strategist Sun-Tzu, is this: "Opportunities multiply as they are seized." When you seize the opportunity to make it somewhere, new opportunities will open up. One of those is a chance to make it still higher in your sport, as you learned in Section 8. But since "opportunities multiply," there must be others too. Success opens doors. Since sports are valued so highly in our society and receive so much attention, success in them brings an especially large number of opportunities as well as unique ones. The trick to making the most of your sport success is making the right choices in response to this array of opportunities.

Evaluating Opportunities

The right response starts with the right attitude. Part of the right attitude consists of being *open* to opportunities. A person who is open to opportunities is alert to their presence and willing to consider possibilities that seem good.

An open attitude involves appreciating the potential benefit of opportunities beyond your sport, rather than dismissing them all as pointless nuisances. This requires you to have a broad view of life, in which experiences outside your sport can have value, rather than your sport being the only thing that matters. It also requires having a long-term outlook on life in which you recognize that your sport career can't last forever, and that developing outside opportunities now will pay off later when your playing days are over.

The right attitude toward opportunities also includes being *guarded*, which means "doing your homework" on them. It means not rushing into them without first checking out what's involved, and spending a bit of time assessing their merit. It involves asking yourself questions such as: Does this opportunity look like one that will lead me to something good or something bad? Is it consistent with my values? Are the others involved character people? What are the potential risks besides the potential benefits? Would it hurt my quest to Max It in my sport? Would it take too much time and focus away from what I need to succeed in my sport? Answering these questions, including any research that is worthwhile doing, will allow you to distinguish opportunities, and pursue the beneficial ones while rejecting the detrimental ones.

It's impossible to predict all the opportunities that success might create. Good judgment, guided by the attitude above, is particularly essential for opportunities that haven't been predicted, because it's all you have to rely on in those cases.

Other opportunities are common enough products of athletic success that we can describe them. Below you will find a list of some of them, including what's involved, and what to consider in deciding how to respond. As you attain success at progressively higher levels, more kinds of opportunities present themselves. Our list below is arranged according to the levels at which you may first encounter each type of opportunity.

Older Ages within Youth Hockey

JOB OPPORTUNITIES: Even at this level, making it shows possession of certain hockey abilities, as well as the more general ability to meet objectives and to succeed over time. People familiar with your possession of these abilities may see a way you can help them by doing a job for them. A good job can help give you the work experience you learned the importance of in Chapter 28, teach you lessons you can apply in various aspects of your life, and provide you a bit of spending money. Not all job opportunities are good, however. Sometimes, certain people try to exploit younger people by having them do difficult or valuable labour without providing them valuable work experience or the proper compensation warranted. If you get a job offer, show gratitude, but don't give an immediate answer. Find out what you can about the job from the person directly, as well as from others whom you trust and who may know something about it. Assess what impact the job may have on your hockey career, fallback career, and character. Talk about it with your closest advisors. Then you can announce your decision.

NETWORKING OPPORTUNITIES: Another thing you learned the importance of in the last chapter was networking. The group size of a hockey team is just the right size for developing a number of positive friendships—with teammates, their parents, coaches, and managers. As you learned in Chapter 7, just make sure to choose your closest friends wisely. At higher levels, there can be additional networking opportunities with team management, player agents, fans, program supporters, and media. People will admire your accomplishments, and may enjoy the opportunity to be closer to them through a relationship with you. Even when they are not friendship relationships, there can sometimes still be mutual benefits to relationships between acquaintances. Just make sure the relationship includes mutual respect, and is healthy and reciprocal. If you find either party just using the other, then such relationships are not healthy or sustainable. In general, start off by being courteous but maintaining your privacy and a safe distance until you know a person better. Over time, by observing the way they deal with you, as well as others, you can learn more about the kind of person they are. Then you will be in better position to decide what more of a relationship, if any, you want to develop with them.

OPPORTUNITIES TO EXERT AN INFLUENCE: Whether a person likes it or not, by achieving success they become a role model, and gain power to influence other people. It's important to use this opportunity to have a positive influence, not a negative one. It starts with simply setting a good example in your own personal conduct, which others will observe and emulate. You can also find ways to "give back" the appreciation others give you, by taking action to make a positive difference in the lives of others or in your community. Charity work, visiting the sick, or participating in community programs are a few such examples. You can use your influence to aid any good initiative that has meaning for you in terms of your values. Taking such action will allow you to feel more connected to others, and feel good about the positive impact you are having on others and on the future. Don't make the mistake of setting a bad example, or of responding to others' appreciation by developing a selfish sense of entitlement. Heroes are not heroes for the awards they get, but for what they give of themselves.

OPPORTUNITIES TO "BROADEN HORIZONS": Being part of a hockey team allows you the opportunity to get to know many people from different backgrounds and with different personalities. This can help broaden your view of the world, and make you a wiser person. If your team travels to tournaments in different regions and far-off places, you may have this opportunity on an even grander scale. If you reach higher levels, such travel is constant. At the same time, you want to stay grounded. Getting blown over by every new person you meet with a novel and engaging personality, or every exciting and unfamiliar culture you encounter, will hurt your progress. Strike a balance between beneficial opportunities to "broaden your horizons" and the virtue of staying centred with knowing who you are, who the people are that truly care about you, and what direction you have chosen for your life.

On the Road to the Pros

EDUCATIONAL OPPORTUNITIES: If you've made it to the Road to the Pros, you may have an opportunity to get a formal education, paid for through your sport, as you learned in Chapter 22. That education can be crucial to your fallback plan. The college experience can be a tremendous opportunity for rewarding experiences and personal growth. Many graduates look back on their college years as the fondest of their life, as well as the period when they matured most.

FREE TIME: If you are playing hockey at a high level where you are not in school, you may find you have more free time than when you were younger. If you have such free time, it's important to use it for positive things, such as working on your fallback plan, hobbies, or personal development. Otherwise, free time can become a negative opportunity. Struggling to "kill time" can lead to counterproductive habits including video-game addictions, over-sleeping, or worse pitfalls.

ENDORSEMENT OPPORTUNITIES: Starting in this phase you may have fame or credibility that people might like to use to market their products through your endorsement of them. This can be a positive financial opportunity, and a chance to learn a little about business. But before you put your name or word behind something, make sure you check it out and truly do believe in it. You are attaching your reputation to it, and your reputation is important because it always precedes you. It is precious and valuable, and not worth damaging for a fistful of dollars.

FREE STUFF: Starting in this phase, often players are offered free stuff, some related to hockey, some not. Is the free stuff prohibited by league or team rules, or actual laws? Is it potentially detrimental to you, such as banned performance-enhancers, or recreational drugs? If so, just say no, of course. Are strings attached, making you bound to whoever gave you something, or publicly associating them with you? If so, you will need to consider these factors.

At the Professional or Other Top Levels

MONEY: Getting paid to play is what makes a player a pro. It might seem like "easy money" to get paid to do something you love. But don't squander that money, because hockey is your profession, just like any other one. And you never know how long your career will last. Saving money can provide important financial security for your future and that of the family you may someday have depending on you. Wherever there is money, there can also be conflicts between people. Don't let your key relationships get hurt by financial disputes.

FINANCIAL OPPORTUNITIES: Players who reach a level that brings them fame and money can expect to be approached by people with business or financial propositions. At that point, investing wisely becomes as important as saving.

If people offer to manage your finances, make sure you research them and their track record. Only ever start off by placing a relatively small amount. The same holds for business ventures you are approached about. In both cases, staying involved and keeping an eye is essential to protecting your investment. Learning how to manage your finances will be useful throughout the rest of your life, and can aid in developing post-hockey career opportunities.

Additional Tips

A few general principles apply to making the most out of the opportunities you get from where you make it:

- Maintain a support network of people you trust to consult about non-hockey opportunities, similar to the one you learned to create for hockey in Chapter 23.
- Don't just wait for opportunities to come to you. If you see a positive opportunity that may be available, be proactive in pursuing it.
- If you reach a level where you are a public figure, you will need to set up a system by which people and things are filtered and checked out before they get to you personally.
- Earn a good reputation and the admiration of others in how you conduct yourself on and off the ice, and more support and opportunities will naturally come to you.

The idea of making the most out of where you make it is to translate the benefits of success in hockey into other kinds of benefits that can enhance the quality of your life. This is especially important in that it allows you to *diversify* (outside hockey) the kinds of positives you have in store, to draw or fall back upon when you need them. Hockey recognition might be what drives you, but as a human being, you have other needs, and you never know when a broadened base and extra security will come in handy.

> **EXPERTS' RECAP**
> Remember . . .
> · Success brings all kinds of opportunities—especially success in sports.
> · Keep an "open but guarded" attitude to use in judging these opportunities.
> · Try to make the most out of where you make it, and translate whatever sports success you have into positives you can spread across other areas of your life.

post-career plans

SCOUTS' PREVIEW
In this chapter . . .
· Why it's important to think ahead to when the game is over
· A new mission
· Other areas of post-career life to plan for

NO MATTER HOW FAR YOU MAKE IT AND HOW LONG YOU STAY THERE, AT SOME POINT YOUR CAREER AS A HOCKEY PLAYER MUST END.

Thinking Ahead to When the Game Is Over

Unless prevented by some health issue, you will still be able to keep playing organized hockey in recreational leagues or in alumni "old-timer" programs. You'll still have a chance to play informal pick-up hockey at your local arena and shinny hockey on your local river, pond, or lake. You'll still be able to use all you've learned about the game in coaching, or teaching children. But never again will playing hockey be your career. It won't be the main mission that drives your hopes and actions, as it did when your dream was still in front of you.

At that point, your career as a hockey player may be finished, but your life will not. Not even close! In most fields, the typical retirement age is sixty-five or older. But athletic careers are very different. Few players play past the end of their thirties (with odd exceptions such as Gordie Howe who retired from professional hockey at the age of fifty-two!). So in all likelihood, the vast majority of your life will still be ahead of you when you retire. To borrow a phrase from the famous British statesman Winston Churchill, "Now this is not the end. It is not even the beginning of the end. But it is, perhaps, the end of the beginning." The end of your playing career is just the end of the beginning. Your whole time as an athlete is only the first phase of the rest of your life.

So what will you do when it's over? In Chapter 28, you learned to prepare for in case you don't make it, in the form of a fallback career. However, what about the case where you do make it? What you need then is a Post-Career Mission for when you've finished playing.

For all the reasons above, it's wise for aspiring athletes to think ahead to when their playing days are over and what they might do then.

Here is an exercise to help you get an idea of what Post-Hockey Mission might interest you:

- Visualize that you have made it, just as you did in Chapter 1, just as you have dreamed. Now imagine time moving forward until you reach the point of having finished playing. Do this while continuing to visualize, complete with imagined details, sights, sounds, smells. With the thoughts and feelings you might have at that time currently present in your mind, *now* ask yourself what you might like to do next.

Repeat this exercise every now and then, not always imagining things ending exactly the same way. This "fast-forward" exercise can help force your mind to think now the way it needs to serve your needs then, in the future.

For many people, of course, their choice of fallback career might be the same choice they'd have for a Post-Hockey Mission. Yet for others, particularly if they don't need to earn money from their Post-Hockey Mission, it

---

ask the AUTHOR-ity

But if I make it, what does it matter what I do after? Why do I need to think about it?
There are a whole host of reasons why it's important to think about it.

For players who make it, hockey will have been a consuming mission for them as far back as they can remember. So if they haven't thought about what they might do when they stop playing, all they see is a giant and frightening void. As a result, they may try to hang on and keep playing when they can no longer do so in a way that is safe, responsible, enjoyable, and that makes them proud. Whenever they are forced to retire it may not be on their terms, leaving them bitter at how things ended.

Such former players then enter the void they'd been trying to avoid. With no mission to replace what they had in the form of their sport, they can find themselves inactive, or spinning their wheels without going anywhere. This can leave them feeling frustrated, confused, anxious, or depressed. And that in turn can hurt their general health, or make them more vulnerable to relationship conflicts or some of the pitfalls from Chapter 7. At a minimum, players who didn't think ahead lose precious time trying to figure out what to do, which they could have thought about long before and could now already be doing.

But why do they need to do anything, especially players who've saved enough money to live off of?
Similar to how you read in Chapter 27 that it's crucial in the most negative of circumstances to find a positive, it's vital anytime you experience a major loss to create something new yet appropriate to make up for what you've lost. This is the case with athletes who had so much bound up in a sport that they can no longer play as a career. They need something that can soak up the time, attention, and energy that before were devoted to hockey. In fact, having a purpose and passion are key to the health and happiness of any person. Drifting or just existing is not living life to its fullest.

may not. Some critical thinking is another tool that can help you identify a post-hockey mission that will suit you. Here are some factors to consider:

- Do you anticipate the mission needing to provide income for you or not? Do you want a mission that is income-earning, charity-related, or neither? What interests you most between businesses, public service, and other institutions?
- What will your personal and practical needs from your post-hockey mission be, and what might the needs be of loved ones who could be dependent on you?
- What are your natural strengths and weaknesses? What assets and resources do you have at your disposal, and what limitations?
- Over time, what has the balance of activities from Chapter 6 taught you about your interests, abilities, and skills?
- What do your character values tell you about different choices?
- What sort of opportunities might your social networks help make available?
- What sort of time commitment, lifestyle, and location might you want?
- What other life commitments might you have, and how will those affect things?

All of these factors can affect your choice of Post-Hockey Mission. And each person's answers to the above questions will be different. This is what makes it a personal choice.

In terms of Post-Hockey Mission options, there are many and they are impossible to list. Below is a sample list of some common possible choices.

career	aspects of making it that can help you
firefighter	courage, teamwork
pilot	focus, secrets of successful training
doctor	keeping up your education, tips to avoid getting sick
lawyer	strategies and planning, dealing with conflict
foreman	the right equipment, constructiveness!
broadcaster/reporter	observation and imitation, psych training
business manager	the business-like approach, responsibility
salesperson	social skills, goal-setting
school teacher	instruction and explanation, time-management

>

career	aspects of making it that can help you
youth hockey coach	hockey skills, fun and spirit
athletic therapist	safety skills, fitness training
charity volunteer	consideration, spotting pitfalls

You will notice above that each of the potential missions had specific items you learned from pursuing making it in hockey that you could utilize toward them. Of course, each also has other requirements. Indeed, once you have identified what you might like to do when hockey is over, it helps if you can plan in advance. As you learned earlier in this book, having a plan and being prepared give you the best chance of attaining a positive outcome from a situation. And this includes achieving your aims for your Post-Hockey Mission and the other elements of your life after hockey.

Other Areas of Post-Hockey Life

Speaking of these other elements, here are some you will want to think about and plan how you will take care of when your hockey career is over. These apply not only to players who make it, but to all players for after their careers end.

HEALTH: As people get older, they must pay more care and attention to their health, and make choices that nurture it. Athletes are often used to good health being "automatic" as part of their foundation for playing and performing. So paying attention to it when they have finished playing may require extra focus at first. Here are some health matters to give thought to for when hockey is over:

- a plan for maintaining physical fitness for when you no longer have a training and performance regimen that provides it as part of your sport.
- appropriate changes in food consumption to compensate for reduced physical exertion levels when your career is over.
- a plan for having regular medical care and attention, without the regular check-ups needed for clearance to play sports.
- a person close to you who can help you re-learn how to pay attention to pain and other signs of potential health issues, that you may have more often learned to ignore while playing hockey.

FINANCES: Beyond earnings from hockey, fallback careers, or Post-Hockey Missions, some other financial matters everyone should learn about, including athletes for when they finish playing, include:

- budgeting;
- basic accounting; and
- financial planning.

RELATIONSHIPS: When hockey ends, there is often more time for family and intimate relationships. At the same time, there is less opportunity for the bonding-type relationships players had with teammates. Here are some relationship issues to plan to manage for when hockey is over:

- how your intimate and family relationships will change through being around more.
- how you can maintain key hockey friendships when hockey no longer brings you together and keeps you in touch.
- a plan for developing non-hockey friendships.

HOBBIES: When your hockey career is over, particularly if you don't continue playing at all, you may want a new hobby to provide your life with some of what you previously got from hockey. Your balance of activities from Chapter 6 should point to some possibilities. But there may be other activities you haven't had time to really pursue, but could once hockey is over. Be open-minded about options, and expect to go through some trial-and-error. It may even take multiple activities to replace different aspects of what hockey gave you (fun, passion, competition, creative expression, physical activity, etc.).

PERSONAL DEVELOPMENT: Sports careers are about striving. They are not only journeys of athletic development, but of personal or spiritual development in learning about yourself and expanding your limits as a human being. When hockey ends, that other journey shouldn't. You will want to plan new ways to continue growing. This could be through your hobbies, relationships, and new mission. It could also be through special personal development initiatives, such as:

- reading books, taking courses, or attending seminars related to personal development;
- seeking guidance from counsellors (life coaches, psychologists, religious advisors, etc.); and
- travelling to experience new cultures, ways of life, and regions of nature.

SUPPORTING GOOD CAUSES OR "GIVING BACK": When players who make it finish playing, they often have a desire to "give back" in return for the wonderful experience they've had. In Chapter 29, you learned some ways of doing this. Even players who don't make it will have more time and energy when hockey is over to devote to good causes that they believe in. Here are some ideas to consider for whenever that time might come:

- How can you share what you learned with others, in order to help them?
- Are there communities you feel gratitude or attachment toward, that you would like to help by getting more involved in?
- Is there a certain charity you'd like to volunteer for?
- Do your values signal any positive causes that might provide added meaning to your life if you gave your attention and support to them?

PRO-file

Ken Dryden

Ken Dryden is a Hall-of-Fame goaltender. In just eight NHL seasons, he won six Stanley Cups, and was in goal as Canada won the Summit Series in 1972. Out of 397 career games, Dryden lost only 57, and meanwhile recorded 46 shutouts! Dryden knew that he couldn't and wouldn't play hockey forever. A pioneer for hockey players taking the College route to pro hockey, Dryden delayed turning pro in order to get an Ivy League education at Cornell prior to joining the Montreal Canadiens. During his pro career, he pursued a law degree that would enable him to become a lawyer when his hockey career ended. He also kept a diary of his experiences and thoughts while playing, enabling him to write a book after retiring called *The Game*, which was critically acclaimed and a bestseller. Never devoid of a mission, Dryden has served as author or co-author of four more books since, including one on education. He was president and GM of the Toronto Maple Leafs, who made two final four appearances while he was with the club. He then decided to leave hockey to enter politics, was elected to Canada's Parliament, and became a government Cabinet Minister.

EXPERTS' RECAP

Remember . . .

· You can't play hockey forever, so you should think ahead to what you will do after.

· Planning a Post-Hockey Mission is important, to replace your completed hockey mission.

· You may also want to give advance thought to plans for your health, finances, relationships, and personal matters for when hockey is over.

conclusion: final thoughts

OVER THE COURSE OF THIS BOOK, YOU HAVE LEARNED A GREAT DEAL: YOU'VE READ ABOUT HOW TO MAXIMIZE YOUR CHANCES OF MAKING IT. YOU'VE DISCOVERED HOW TO PURSUE MAKING IT THE RIGHT WAY. AND YOU'VE FOUND MUCH THAT YOU CAN APPLY IN OTHER AREAS OF YOUR LIFE.

Keep this book as an important reference as you pursue your quest. You may find great value in returning to it again and again to refresh your memory about key concepts, pick out new things, further develop an area of your game, or search for solutions to problems you encounter. You can think of it as your own personal coach or mentor. In addition, you can learn much more on topics from this book and other topics, as well as find interactive tools to help you apply lessons learned here to your own career on my website www.sportsmaster.tv.

I would also suggest that it may be beneficial to have other people close to you read the book as well: family, friends, teammates, coaches, teachers, trusted advisors, etc. While our website may provide clarification, further information, or assistance you need related to *hockey*, having people around you read the book allows you to discuss issues raised in the book with them, to see how these issues might best apply to *you*. It can be valuable to have someone familiar with both the book material and with you to talk with, and explore ways in which you can work together to apply what you've learned to maximum benefit.

As you pursue your quest, remember that a great journey travels over peaks and valleys along its way. Mistakes are sometimes necessary for you to improve, and failures are often where you must start before you can succeed. The key is to learn lessons from these experiences. As the famous author C.S. Lewis once said, "Failures are finger posts on the road to achievement." If you take the directions they give you, you will ultimately move in the right direction.

You believe in the glory of your dream. But I hope you've also come to believe in the value of pursuing your dream—including whether you make it or not. Chasing a dream should bring fun, fulfillment, and meaning to your life. Pursuing sports will help you learn about yourself, life, and success. Striving will teach you how to do your best, improve, face challenges, overcome obstacles, reach goals, and enjoy your accomplishments. Working with teammates and others will help you appreciate what it means to be part of something larger than yourself. And competing will train you to vie with opposition and endure for the sake of a purpose you are committed to.

Most of all, I hope you've come to believe in your potential to realize your personal dream, however difficult it may seem. If I told you that a young man from a place of little renown could set out and conquer almost the entire known world by the age of thirty-two, would you believe me? Probably not. But it happened, and the person who did it, Alexander the Great, had this to say: "There is nothing impossible for who will try." Making it may be difficult, but it is far from impossible. Believe in yourself that you *can* do it, and give it everything you've got.

I wish you joy on your journey, and luck in realizing your dream of someday *making it*.

glossary

Bag Skate: A series of extremely tiring skating drills used for conditioning purposes or by a coach to punish their team (i.e., the players skate until they are "bagged").

Carioca: An exercise often used as part of a warm-up which consists of "running sideways" with your lead foot hopping laterally, and your hind foot alternating between hopping laterally in front of the lead leg and hopping laterally behind the lead leg.

Deke: A deceptive move designed to fake an opponent or draw them out of position in order to faciliate skating by them, or in the case of a deke on a goalie, to facilitate shooting the puck by them and into the net.

Drill: An exercise used to practice a specific skill repeatedly (i.e., to "drill it in").

Butterfly: A common goaltending posture in which the goalie is on their knees with their lower legs fanned out sideways to block the bottom portion of the net.

Butterfly Slide: A lateral movement in which a goalie makes a T-push and then immediately drops into the butterfly position while sliding sideways, typically to face a shot on the far side of the net.

Give-and-go: A passing combination in which, to avoid an approaching checker, a player passes the puck to a nearby teammate, skates by the defender, and then receives a pass right back from the teammate.

Half-Butterfly: Similar to a butterfly, except the goalie is on one knee, with the other leg upright facing the potential shot.

Half-butterfly Slide: Same as a butterfly slide, only that after the T-push, the goalie assumes the half-butterfly position.

Handmanning the Puck: Passing the puck to a teammate farther ahead up the ice.

Jill: Protective equipment for women's private parts.

Jock: A protective cup for men's private parts.

One-timer: A type of slapshot executed on a moving pass, rather than stopping the puck first and then shooting.

Peripheral Vision: What you are able to see outside (i.e., on the "periphery") of what you are actually focusing your eyes on (e.g., if you are carrying the puck with your head up and eyes focused on watching the players in front of you, you should still be able to see the puck on your stick with your peripheral vision).

Plyometrics: Training exercises designed to improve acceleration and explosiveness, by slowly loading muscles and then rapidly flexing them. Common examples include: jumps, hops, lunges, thrusts, etc.

Sani-sport Machine: A device used to cleanse equipment by killing the bacteria in it.

Saucer: Also called a "sauce-pass," it is a raised pass designed to float over an obstacle in between the passer and the recipient (e.g., a defender's stick) and land flat on the ice before reaching the recipient.

Save Execution: The actual process of a goaltender making a save.

Save Preparation: The various actions taken by a goalie to get ready to make a save.

Save Recovery: Various actions taken by a goalie after making a save in order to get back into position to make a potential subsequent save.

Shuffle: Small, lateral sideways steps used by defenders or goalies in order to move small distances and to remain in position while continuously facing the play, ready to react.

Spinorama: A 360-degree spin used to deke a defender.

Squeeze-by: A physical move that can be used by a puck carrier when a defender is trying to squish them against the boards in order to slip and push themselves by the defender, along the boards.

Sub Skills: Specialized skills that are part of a larger skill (e.g., shooting "off the rush" is a sub skill of shooting).

T-push: A lateral push-stride in which the back (pushing) foot is turned sideways, and the front (gliding) foot is facing forward, forming a "T."

endnotes

1 The record was the fastest five goals by a team in NHL history.
2 Source: MSNBC, March 12, 2004.
3 Source: *Toronto Sun*, December 3, 2003
4 Source: *Sporting News*, April 7, 2003.
5 Nine of these experiences originated from playing affiliations as follows: Mark Moore (Pittsburgh Penguins, Anaheim Ducks, Columbus Blue Jackets, Phoenix Coyotes), Steve Moore (Colorado Avalanche), Dominic Moore (New York Rangers, Minnesota Wild, Toronto Maple Leafs, Buffalo Sabres). The tenth comes from an elite prospect summer training program Mark Moore and Steve Moore attended in Finland prior to turning pro, where the Fitness Training component was directed by the Dallas Stars.
6 Technically, in the United States, the USHL is considered Tier I. However, it does not have the rules and properties mentioned in this book as belonging to Tier I hockey (Major Junior) as the CHL does. Rather, the USHL has the same rules and properties mentioned in this book as belonging to Tier II leagues (including retention of amateur status that allows a player to be eligible to subsequently play NCAA College hockey). Therefore, to avoid confusion, wherever this book talks about Tier II hockey, this may be considered to apply to and include the USHL.
7 Source: USHL.
8 Source: Government of Canada, Census 2006.
9 Source: United States Government Federal Statistics, 2006.
10 Source: USHL.

photo credits

The publisher has made every effort to obtain permission for images used in this book.

16: Michael Valenti; 17: Robert DeMarco; 29: CSRO; 30: Getty / 81343444; 35: CP Images / 824884; 43: Getty / 53122298; 46: CP Images / 899915; 59: Getty / 56125432; 68: Getty / 52562218; 72: Reproduced with the permission of Public Works and Government Services Canada, 2006; 88-94: Courtesy of Bauer; 91: mouth guard images, Getty / 84480336 and 10067958; 94: Getty / 84993122; 97: Hockey Hall of Fame; 106-137: Robert DeMarco; 138: Sudarshan Maharaj; 139-144: Robert DeMarco; 148-162 (diagrams): John Lightfoot; 164-167: Robert DeMarco; 184: Jim DeMarco; 190 (top): Getty / 1492488; 190 (bottom): Getty / 81344786; 191: Getty / 84240639; 192: Getty / 57216779; 193: Getty / 84314193; 194: Getty / 86189081; 195: Getty / 90113804; 197: Getty / 91655034; 200: Getty / 224320; 244: CP / 991707; 261: Getty / 53129876; 271: Getty / 85824721; 275: Getty / 55889038; 286: Getty / 80695830; 296: Getty / 84420495; 302: Getty / 81437290; 320: Getty / 81862938.

acknowledgements

I must start by acknowledging the fact that to write this book was actually not my idea! If you enjoyed this book or have found it helpful, part of your thanks should go to the parents of children who have attended Ivy Hockey Academy, to other hockey parents and officials who have attended conferences at which I've made presentations, as well as to Mike, Chris, and Jackie, without whose encouragement this project would never have even been started.

As much time and care as were devoted to this by the author, completing a project of this scope also requires the assistance and efforts of a great many others. Above all, I would like to thank Jordan, Jackie, and Linda, without whom this book would not exist. I would also like to thank my family (for their suggestions), W.R. (for her patience), and Tim (for his advice). I am grateful to Jennifer Botterill, Sean McCann, Nicole Corriero, Angela Ruggiero, Dr. Anthony Galea, Dr. Jim DeMarco, Sudarshan Maharaj, Doug Stacey, Dan Bellissimo, Pavel Valenti, Anthony Fisher, Wes Huether, and Darryl Hughes for their involvement in the book. This was a complex project, with many photos and diagrams and other design work, and for that I extend my appreciation to Sonya, Robert, and Michael as well as Rob Tunney and the staff at St. Mike's. Finally, I must acknowledge the efforts of all the staff at Key Porter Books, including those whose work is essential but whose names not even an author, let alone a reader, ever knows....